LONDON: HUMPHREY MILFORD
OXFORD UNIVERSITY PRESS

Inscribed to my
long-suffering colleagues
at Dumbarton Oaks,
who have listened to
me "sing."

Howard Mumford Jones

IDEAS IN AMERICA

Ideas in America

BY

HOWARD MUMFORD JONES

DEAN OF THE GRADUATE SCHOOL OF ARTS AND SCIENCES
HARVARD UNIVERSITY

14807

CAMBRIDGE, MASSACHUSETTS
HARVARD UNIVERSITY PRESS
1944

PRINTED IN THE UNITED STATES OF AMERICA

To

PAUL HERMAN BUCK

PREFACE

ACCORDING to Thoreau the youth begins by assembling materials with which to erect a bridge to the moon, and ends by building a shed in the back yard. In American university life the scholar (unless he is that un-Emersonian type, a library recluse) has an analogous history. Too many demands are made upon him. There is, I know, a theory floated by sentimental critics that scholars on college faculties have too little sympathy for undergraduates and too little interest in teaching them. All I can say is, after a somewhat varied university life, that I have never seen a single institution of this sort. Indeed, the charge must strike the judicious as a rather astonishing *non sequitur*. Scholarship is, or ought to be, evidence of a living and curious mind interested in truth. To argue that the pursuit of truth by the scholar somehow stultifies his pedagogy seems to say that if he knew less, he would teach more. The history of learning scarcely substantiates the theory.

However this may be, I was rash enough almost twenty years ago in a book called *America and French Culture* to say that I hoped some day to follow that volume by a sequel in which I should trace the reception of French literature in the United States. I have been trying to get at that sequel ever since. What I blithely assumed in 1927 was that it would be simple enough to assess our reception of French *belles lettres* in terms of an intellectual, moral, and aesthetic valuation by those strange readers, the Americans. The difficulty was—and is—that we do not yet know enough about the history of ideas, or of morals, or of taste in the United States to make any such assessment viable. Our first task is still to comprehend the baffling process by which a transplanted European culture has been changed on this continent into the unique American thing.

These essays and addresses are but the scattered fragments of that other work, dreamed of long ago. That they have almost nothing to do with French literature in the United States is patent. The reason I have just given. I have been unable to proceed to that mythical second volume because we still lack a comprehensive and illuminating history of ideas, of morals, and of taste in the United States. The items in this collection are contributions to such a history; I wish they were better.

In writing them I did not follow any plan. They have been done on an *ad hoc* basis. But now that I have sunk to be an administrator of sorts, I do not see any prospect of rounding out the history of which these inchoate fragments might be parts; yet I have enough vanity to hope that, collected in one place, these pieces may be of help. The *ad hoc* element in their making explains a few repetitions. If I seem to single out Parrington's volumes for running criticism in the first three essays, it is merely because no other work of similar magnitude has appeared in the field of American literature, intellectually conceived. My comments are therefore my tribute to a great, solitary and imperfect work.

The triple division of this book is one both of matter and of style. The history of the battle to win proper respect for scholarship in the field of American literature has been such that not erudition, but persuasion has been needed, and the pieces under the first heading are therefore all addresses. Obviously, we are not going to get a sound history of ideas in this country until we are prepared to say it is important that we have one.

The middle section—a group of essays in the history of ideas and their influence—is, I fear, more "scholarly" than "popular." Furthermore, they live in that debatable land between history proper and the history of literature. I hope the general reader will at least find the text clear and persuasive, and the scholar will find the supporting evidence convincing.

The last section treats of more recent phases of our literature, and is again general and hortatory. I hope the information is correct; if it is, the essays are scholarly enough. But I think Archibald MacLeish is right to regret the split between the scholar and the writer in this country; and the essays and addresses under this head have at least the modest merit of attempting to be the expression of the man of letters.

I suppose the central doctrine in these papers is that a mature interpretation of our own intellectual and cultural history ought to be one of the important concerns (to use a good Quaker term) of American scholarship. But it does not therefore follow that this should be the sole concern. I have no more enthusiasm for the movement towards "required" American history than I have for the attitude which regards American literature as unworthy the highest scholarship. The second of these states of mind is waning; unfortunately, under the stress of war, the first is gaining ground. A sound interest in the American mind is no reason for closing that mind against the rest of human culture.

Grateful thanks are due to *American Literature,* The Colonial Society of Massachusetts, The American Philosophical Society, *The Huntington Library Bulletin, The Southwest Review, The Atlantic Monthly,* and *The Harvard Alumni Bulletin* for permitting me to reprint essays and addresses originally published by them. The paper entitled "The Drift to Liberalism in the American Eighteenth Century" was originally printed in the volume of the Harvard Tercentenary Publications entitled *Factors Determining Human Behavior.*

Harvard University   HOWARD MUMFORD JONES

CONTENTS

PART I

The Need for Literary History

PART II

Studies in the History of Ideas in America

PART III

The Responsibilities of Contemporary American Literature

IDEAS IN AMERICA

I

AMERICAN SCHOLARSHIP AND AMERICAN LITERATURE *

WRITING in 1924, Professor F. L. Pattee issued a call for a mature historian of American literature. He possessed, he said, over a hundred histories of the subject, all of them built on the same bad model; and he proceeded to enumerate the qualifications of a proper historian of the subject. How has Professor Pattee's appeal been answered by the scholarship of the country?

Ignoring textbooks, I shall glance briefly at some leading volumes discussing American literary history published in the last decade. The most important is the late Professor Parrington's *Main Currents in American Thought* (1927–1930) in three volumes, unhappily never completed, an influential study, but not a history of American literature. "I have undertaken," he said, "to give some account of the genesis and development in American letters of certain germinal ideas,"[1] and the work is really a history of political, economic, and social ideas. Like Macaulay, Mr. Parrington was enthusiastic for the good cause —in this case, Jeffersonian democracy; and he gave us a history of ideas written from that point of view. Mr. Lewis Mumford published *The Golden Day* (1926), a smaller study, admirable in its kind, the limitations of which are obvious from the fact that it was delivered as a lecture series in Switzerland. We have also had Mr. Charles Angoff's *A Literary History of the American People* (1931), still incomplete, a pro-

* An address to the English Section of the Modern Language Association of America, December, 1935.

duction so bad that Professor Pattee indignantly repudiated it as possessing "no originality . . . little perspective, no sense of proportion . . . scant stylistic excellence . . . haste and slap-dashery."[2] Dr. Canby's *Classic Americans from Irving to Whitman* (1931) is, alas! but a torso; planned as a history, it treats thoroughly only seven authors. Mr. Ludwig Lewisohn has published *Expression in America* (1932), an exposition of American literature in Freudian terms designed to support a peculiar theory of artistic creation. The book is valuable for its *obiter dicta,* but when one reads that Howells "was acutely and negatively sex-conscious,"[3] Mr. Lewisohn's failure to grasp the nature of literary history is clear. Mr. V. F. Calverton has written *The Liberation of American Literature* (1932), designed to prove that our literary history is the story of the repression by an unillumined upper class of the rest of society; and Mr. Granville Hicks has published *The Great Tradition* (1933) to show that literature improves in proportion as it approaches the proletarian point of view.

The *ad captandum* character of most of these volumes needs no comment. Literary history is not properly a vast political pamphlet nor an attack on conventional aesthetics nor an exercise in Freudian psychology nor a demonstration of Marxian dialectic. We need a literary history on the level of Lanson, Elton, or Fitzmaurice Kelly. Professor Pattee, it is true, has published a scholarly survey of part of the field, but there is in fact no history of American literature worthy the name in a country which supports so vast and active a body of organized scholars as the Modern Language Association of America. Why is the native literature excessively ignored by American scholars?

It will be replied that American literature is not ignored. Why do not scholars in the American field supply the lack? What have they been doing in the past quarter-century? The answer is that scholars in the American field have been doing all they can under the handicaps which conditions in our

English departments now impose upon them. There has been a quiet revolution in the field. Most of the standard biographies, written in the nineteenth century, need revision in the light of new evidence, and American scholars are at work in this direction. The bibliographical aids are being brought up to date. The cultural history of the country is being explored, and the relations of our literature to foreign literatures and cultures are being studied. A juster appreciation of American literary history has widened the earlier conception of the subject, so that large areas, formerly out of bounds, are being investigated, such as the literature of the Middle Western frontier, the American ballad, and the like. American speech is being scrutinized. Failing to find in the learned journals that hospitality to which papers on the national literature have a just claim, scholars in American literature have founded their own journal. If an understanding of American literature by American students lags behind the appreciation of their several national literatures by British, French, German, or other students, scholars in the American field cannot be charged with negligence. They are struggling with a well-nigh insoluble problem—a problem created by the attitude of professors of English literature and expressed in the policies of English departments and of organized scholarship in this country.

Let us analyze the personnel of a typical university department of English, with a staff of fifteen or sixteen. Five or six of these will devote most of their time to composition. One, at least, of the remaining ten, will be a "philologist" in the sense that his principal work lies in Old and Middle English. This leaves eight. The field of one of these is Shakespeare; of another, the Renaissance; of a third, Milton and the seventeenth century; of a fourth, the classical period; of a fifth, the romantic poets; of a sixth, the nineteenth century; of a seventh, the English novel or perhaps the drama. The remaining man is assigned to American literature. In other words, one-fifteenth

3

of the department is at work in the literature of his own country.

I do not premise any hostility on the part of the English department to American literature. But what is the professor of American literature expected to do? The field of the linguistic specialist is clear. The Renaissance man devotes himself to literature from *Tottell's Miscellany* to, let us say, Bacon, or the seventy-five years from 1557 to 1626; and if we add twenty-five years, he will still take in only a century, and he will leave the Elizabethan drama to the Shakespeare specialist. The seventeenth-century man specializes in Milton and his age; that is, he ranges from Bacon to the Restoration or beyond—three-quarters of a century. The classical authority goes from 1660 to 1780 or thereabouts—a little more than a century. The romantic man spends his time on the half century from 1780 to 1832. The Victorian specialist ranges from the death of Scott to 1900 or 1914—some seventy or eighty years. The specialist in fiction or drama confines himself to a single genre. But the American literature man is expected to deal with everything from 1607 to 1935, that is to say, with the history and literature of over three hundred years, and in these three centuries he is supposed to speak authoritatively of poetry, the drama, the essay, fiction, biography, and history, not to speak of such complex problems as the intellectual make-up of Puritanism, the debate over Revolutionary principles, the conflict between Hamilton and Jefferson, transcendentalism, the issues of the Civil War, and the meaning of evolution and pragmatism. Not only that, but he is supposed to make constant illuminating reference to British literature. The task is three or four times as heavy as that of any other member of the department, but it seems to occur to nobody but himself that it is so; and when, as inevitable result, large portions of the subject receive superficial treatment, the professor of British literature is likely to murmur something about the lack of depth and richness in American literary scholarship.

4

Surveying the treatment of the subject since 1900 in twenty-five leading colleges and universities, I find that in most of these there has been only the most elementary treatment of the subject, and I know of only two or three in which the distribution of emphasis is something like what it should be. The national literature not only receives much less proportionate attention than British literature—a fact which is perhaps justified by its relative youth—but it actually receives less attention than any of the periods of British literature, a fact for which there is no justification whatsoever.

In this country education in English literature is education in British literature. Not only the undergraduates, but our doctors of philosophy are primarily specialists in the literature of a foreign land. We require them to familiarize themselves with the literary history of Great Britain; we require them to know Chaucer and Shakespeare, Milton and Swift, Wordsworth and Browning, but when it is a question of familiarizing them with the line of geniuses which begins with Franklin and extends to Whitman and beyond, we display only a tepid interest. The large majority of our professors of English have only a superficial acquaintance with American literature, and only the vaguest notion of what scholarship under immense difficulties has accomplished in this field. Many of the learned display an affable condescension to the field. They expect their students to know how the Elizabethan theater was organized, but do not expect them to know how the American theater operates. They expect them to get up the party quarrels of the Whigs and the Tories in order to understand Addison, Swift, and Steele, but do not require them to understand the Jacksonian political revolution, though it would seem that bickerings among the Venetian oligarchy of Great Britain are of less moment to American citizens than the fortunes of political democracy. Our students read British fiction from Richardson to Galsworthy; they are permitted to ignore the rich and interesting history of the American novel, the importance of

5

which German students of the United States cordially recognize. I do not deny that many departments now "permit" dissertations in the American field, but I am describing the average interest of our doctors and professors of English in the literature of their own country.

This is an extraordinary state of affairs, and it is only because we are used to it that we do not see how extraordinary it is. Defenders of the existing order present several arguments. British literature is as much a part of the American inheritance as it is a part of the British inheritance. The United States came late to literary maturity, and has not developed a Shakespeare, a Milton, or a Wordsworth. The variety of themes treated in the national letters is meager compared with the variety of themes in British literature, the history of which is longer and richer, and British literature therefore deserves preferential treatment.

I do not wish to cut off American students from British literature, and if any department were to embark upon so insane a program, I should at once protest. The superior richness of British literature is undeniable; and it is true that ten centuries of literary history require more time and space for their study than do three. The difficulty lies, however, in the reduction of these arguments to practice, and the actual situation is that the zeal of specialists in British literature leads them not to claim a lawful preponderance only, but to reduce American letters to a minor and insignificant place which they do not deserve. They take the point of view that American literary history is an appendix to British literary history, a tail on the British lion. They will not see that to American students British literary history is the background of the scene—a rich and varied background, a background which cannot be ignored, but still a background; and they seldom admit that American literary achievement has a right to be considered in and for itself. Were American literature as poor and thin as specialists in other fields profess to consider

6

it, it would still be true that a knowledge of the national literature is as necessary a part of the equipment of the American scholar as a knowledge of his national literature is a necessary part of the equipment of the French or German or British or Italian or Spanish scholar. It is only in the United States that professors of literature are permitted to be scandalously ignorant of their own national achievement.

Let us turn to the implications of the statement that the United States came late to literary maturity. It is true that this country has not developed a Shakespeare or a Milton, but it does not follow that American literary history can be either minimized or ignored. If the United States has not developed a Shakespeare or a Milton, Great Britain has not developed a Whitman or a Mark Twain; and I lay special emphasis upon the fact that the bead-roll of American "classic" writers—Franklin, Bryant, Irving, Cooper, Emerson, Hawthorne, Longfellow, Whittier, Poe, Holmes, Thoreau, Lowell, Melville, Whitman, Twain, Howells, Lanier, William James, Henry James—is an impressive one; and that, if some period of British literature had hitherto been totally unknown to us, and if we discovered that period and found it to contain this galaxy of genius, we should exclaim and wonder at its excellence, and declare that alongside of the Elizabethan age and the Victorian period, we should want to set an age so wonderful in its power and so rich in its talents. The constant tendency among specialists in British literature to depreciate the Americans is a mark of ignorance.

Few have remarked the danger of this attitude. The following quotation from Walter Millis's *The Road to War* may come to many as an unpleasant surprise. Discussing the ways by which this country was drawn into the World War, he says:

The educated leaders of the New Freedom were steeped in British literature more deeply than the old-fashioned politicians. As a student of domestic government, President Wilson throughout

7

his life had been profoundly influenced by English ideas and political institutions; while our rare experts in the elegant fields of foreign policy had modeled themselves for a generation upon the giants of British liberal imperialism . . . the statesmen—Roosevelt and Lodge, John Hay, Taft, Leonard Wood—had rejoiced to create an empire almost as glorious and perhaps even more righteous than that of Great Britain.[4]

I turn to the biography of the American ambassador to Great Britain during the Wilson régime, Mr. Walter Hines Page. Mr. Page, it will be recalled, softened or ignored the many violations of American rights by the British, failed to present American protests in the manner of a representative of an injured country, bombarded the President and the Secretary of State with letters that are sheer propaganda, and finally helped to sweep this country into the orbit of British politics. He was a student at Randolph-Macon College. In *The Training of an American,* with no consciousness of the irony of his title, Mr. Burton J. Hendrick tells us that "Page chiefly owed his love of English literature" to Professor T. R. Price; that Price taught him "to love not only the English language and English literature; above all he taught him to love England itself. Years afterwards, when this particular pupil became Ambassador to Great Britain, his admiration for England informed all his speeches, his letters and his interpretations of great events." Price "day after day filled his plastic mind with the greatness of England's writers, thinkers and statesmen. England became to Page his 'mother' land. English literature to him meant writing produced in England. For American authors he had a lack of sympathy that, viewed in the larger outlook of today, was a limitation."[5]

What has been the attitude of this association towards American literature? When it was organized in 1883, Tyler's history of American literature in the Colonial period, already five years old, might, one thinks, have indicated to American scholarship a fruitful cultural field, but the association ignored

8

the challenge. Tyler was driven into history, helped to organize the American Historical Association, and published his second great work as a professor of American history. In 1873 he pointed out the desirability of an Early American Text Society.[6] The need is still great; but neither the photostatic reproductions nor the publications in volume form of this association contain to this day [1935] a single American item.[7] In 1887, A. H. Smyth, the distinguished editor of Franklin, told the association that "it is certainly discreditable to us that we have done so little toward a faithful and affectionate study of what is purely native and national in our American writings." Discussing his paper, Professor Bright of Johns Hopkins remarked, "I insist upon the importance of American literature for the purposes of advanced work,"[8] but in fifty volumes of *PMLA* this is the sole record of any interest in the national literature by the national association of scholars. When Professor Manly delivered the presidential address which led to the setting up of the present research groups, he said that the association had room for "all those who study literature in any large and sincere and intelligent way," but he did not mention American literature, and the report of the committee which set up the first research groups, though it outlined forty-one such groups under five heads, completely ignored American literature.[9] In fifty years the association has had forty-three presidents; with the exception of Lowell, no one of these has been a distinguished scholar in the American field, and Lowell was chosen, not for his distinction as a scholar in the American field, but because he had written essays on British authors. The association has listened to thirty-nine presidential addresses in half a century, but, though these addresses have touched upon almost every other modern literature, not one has discussed American letters. The number of scholars distinguished for work in American literature among the executive committees of this association is so small as to be negligible. The same is true of the editorial committees. I have taken the

9

trouble to go through the entire body of *PMLA* from 1884 to 1934; in fifty years we have published 1,405 articles and studies, and of these only forty-five [10] have had anything to do with American letters, and only twenty-nine of the forty-five have dealt directly with American literature as such. The only special recognition of American literature by the association is that the present research group in that field is allowed to have two meetings instead of one. If scholarship in American litera-ture has gone forward, it has not been because of the Modern Language Association of America.

I have no hostility to any form of literary study. I am neither chauvinist nor fascist. But the purpose of scholarship is to en-rich the cultural life of a nation, and it would seem that an association of scholars should give central place to the literary traditions of the nation, and not relegate that study to an appendix in the volume of their labors. I do not propose a con-stitutional change in this association. I do call for a searching of heart among English departments and among the members of this group. In a period of intense social strain the country needs the steadying effect of a vital cultural tradition; it needs, in Van Wyck Brooks's phrase, a "usable past." This is not sup-plied by the books I first described. In a general sense scholar-ship, whatever its field, supplies that past; but scholarship makes a very bad job of it so long as scholarship neglects or minimizes the importance of American literary tradition to the life of the nation. We cannot substitute for an American past a British literary past. I do not say that British literature should be ignored; I do say that American literature should have a central place in the thinking of American scholars. My at-tention has been called to a passage in Lowell which goes directly to the mark: "It is idle to say we are Englishmen, and that English history is ours too. It is precisely in this that we are *not* Englishmen, inasmuch as we only possess their history through our minds, and not by life-long association with a spot and an idea we call England." [11] Change "history" to "literature" and we reach the point. The continuing tendency of this association to ignore, patronize, or minimize the national literature is a weakness of the first order. I firmly believe that unless this organization sees the need of associating itself vitally with the cultural history of our common country, it will come in time to count for less and less in the intellectual life of the United States. Shall we leave the field to the social scientists, or shall we accept the challenge which the situation gives us?

2

DESIDERATA IN COLONIAL LITERARY HISTORY *

MEMBERS of this audience will doubtless recall that when Mark Twain first met General Grant, whom he greatly admired, he could think of nothing to say. Finally he blurted out: "General, I am embarrassed. Are you?" *I* am embarrassed, whether you are or not. Out in the mid-west, from whence I come, the Colonial Society of Massachusetts has an almost legendary aspect; and I am tempted to imitate Daniel Webster and address you as "Venerable men!" Nor is the legend without foundation. There are the solid and substantial volumes of your *Publications,* in which you have followed the example of Samuel Willard, of whom Cotton Mather said that "by his *Printed Works* [he] has erected himself a *Monument,* that will Endure when the Famed MAUSOLEUM'S of the *World* shall moulder down, and be buryed in their own Ruines." I need scarcely comment upon the famous names among your members—for example, that of the historian of witchcraft in Old and New England; that of the biographer of Increase Mather, whose book has revolutionized the whole concept of colonial biography; and that of the historian of Harvard, of whom I shall boldly say that his volumes have instructed the learned world in the use of academic annals as a key to intellectual history. The president of Harvard is also a member; and to those living in outer darkness on the other side of the Connecticut line, the president of Harvard is an awful figure, somewhere above that brief, transitory shadow,

* An address before the Colonial Society of Massachusetts, November, 1936.

the president of the United States, and not very far below that of Zeus, the father of gods and men. In view of the long line of really distinguished speakers you have had, I can on this occasion only ask you to obey the injunction which Paul laid on the Corinthians when he said: "We then that are strong ought to bear the infirmities of the weak and not please ourselves." As for me, though I am far from feeling my calling and election sure, I can at least argue that my speaking to you was foreordained and, like a good Calvinist, rejoice in my own damnation.

My subject has to do with desiderata in colonial literary history; and I begin by remarking that our first need—perhaps, indeed, our only one— is that there should be a comprehensive history of American colonial literature. Apparently we are not the men our fathers were. When Professor Moses Coit Tyler died at Ithaca in 1900, there passed away not only the last and greatest of the founding fathers of scholarship in American letters, but also, if one is to judge by some of the volumes purporting to be histories of colonial literature which have since appeared, the last person capable of undertaking so tremendous a task. So remarkable was Tyler's work that it remains today in some respects unsurpassed, and in all respects unrivalled. This fact is the more astonishing when one comprehends the difficulties under which he completed his monumental studies. The first two volumes, *A History of American Literature, 1607-1765,* were written at the University of Michigan where Tyler was at the time a member of the English department, and were published by the firm of G. P. Putnam's Sons in 1878. The University of Michigan, at that time only forty years old, was not the institution which it has since become. There was no William L. Clements Library of American historical material to which the scholar might turn, and the university's general library, though adequate for the modest demands which the collegiate instruction of the day made upon it, contained little of first importance for his purposes.

13

Moreover, the American Historical Association had not then been formed—Tyler was to join in founding it in 1884—and the publications of that organization were of course not available. The inter-library loan system had not yet been dreamed of; and the happy thought of duplicating the library cards of the great American collections and depositing these duplicates in the libraries of other institutions was still far in the future.

Under difficulties which would have frightened a weaker man away from his task, Tyler went to work, resolved to deal only with source material and—a characteristic in which it is to be wished that more literary historians would imitate him—resolved also to read all the works which he discussed. The university purchased some materials, and the librarian borrowed more; the publisher hunted up books in the East for the author, who built a fire-proof study to receive these precious documents; Tyler bought as his slender resources permitted him, and devoted his vacations to collections like those of the American Antiquarian Society and the various libraries in Boston and Cambridge. He had, moreover, been profoundly impressed by Buckle's theory of history, and by the literary criticism of Sainte-Beuve; and had determined to make a careful study of the personality and environment of his various authors, a principle which further increased his trouble by requiring him to inform himself adequately of the biographies and characters of men concerning whom material was usually scattered, and sometimes scanty. It is to the credit of American criticism in the eighties that Tyler's work, when produced, was at once hailed as an intellectual achievement of a high order. Indeed, some reviewers were so astonished at the prodigious industry represented by these two impressive volumes that they doubted whether there was enough American literature in the period which Tyler had investigated to furnish the basis of a work so thorough and so profound!

The writing of *The Literary History of the American Revolution, 1763-1783,* was done at Cornell, where Tyler had been called by Andrew D. White to a chair in American history. In some ways his task was made easier, though the Cornell library was not what we should now call adequate. But other duties intervened, the mass of material proved greater than he had anticipated, and the second two volumes, though thorough and good, neither completed the task which he had originally set himself nor possessed quite the authority of the first two. Taken together, however, Tyler's four volumes still remain standard.

Why, then, it may be asked, is there need for a new history of American colonial literature?

Although Tyler was possessed of critical as well as historical skill, so that, in his first two volumes especially, he sorted out better work from mediocre and laid down the lines along which colonial literature has, in a sense, been studied ever since, other discoveries have been made in the half century since his various volumes appeared. Especially is there a gap between the second volume of *The Literary History of the American Revolution* and, shall we say, the appearance of Bryant's "Thanatopsis" in 1817, from which many historians are inclined to date the beginnings of a truly national American letters. Hence, if for no other reason, it would still be desirable to fill out the picture to that year, or to some other significant date, in order that the full sweep of our literary development before the nineteenth century could be understood. Naturally also, there are some errors in Tyler—though it is miraculous, considering the difficulties under which he wrote, how few these are—and some judgments which time has modified or perhaps reversed. More important, however, is an understanding of the presuppositions on which Tyler wrote.

For while it was Tyler's purpose to illustrate the interests of the American people as expressed in or determined by their literary production, he belonged to a generation of historians who were primarily concerned with political history in the usual sense; and furthermore, to a school of history which tended to interpret the colonial and revolutionary periods as being marked by a steady and inevitable growth of political and religious liberalism. A greater man than the writers of some text-book histories, he was quite fair to the other side—indeed, in Tyler's history the literary productions of the American Tories received for the first time full and sympathetic treatment—but he was nevertheless committed to an evolutionary hypothesis, to a doctrine of genetic growth along lines of force, the outcome of which had been determined by a general historical tendency towards liberalism and democracy. He therefore marshalled his thinkers and writers in an order which these presuppositions determined, and showed less curiosity about other phases of human endeavor. He worked fully and ably in the light of the information which he had, and fortunately for us, this information was broad and fine. None the less, it was determined by the historical assumptions of his age. The world of the seventeenth century was in the main closed to him except in its religious and political aspects; and though in the eighteenth century he did not neglect the poets or the casual essayists, the main line of his argument is with the political writers.

It is probable that every age must reshape the past in its own image; but certainly there is need for a re-examination and revaluation not only of the writers with whom Tyler so ably dealt, but also of the vast bodies of printed matter which he scarcely touched upon, or touched upon not at all. It is true that one or two attempts at such a survey have been made. . . . The three-volume study by Professor Parrington, *Main Currents in American Thought,* was unfortunately left unfinished at his death; but the first volume of this study, *The Colonial Mind,* is complete in itself. Mr. Parrington's approach was certainly fresh, and he delivered himself of many stimulating judgments. No part of this book seems to me so good as the really extraordinary study of the ante-bellum South in the second volume of his work—a study which brings to light important thinkers that the victorious North has cruelly forgotten. There are in *The Colonial Mind* many excellent passages. There are, unfortunately, also many passages which are not excellent—passages which are vitiated either by Mr. Parrington's inability to get at the original materials (he was professor in the University of Washington in Seattle) or by his refusal, when he did get at them, to follow the wise dictum of Emerson that every scripture should be read in the light of the spirit which brought it forth. If Tyler was committed to a theory of world-process in history, Parrington was enthusiastically enlisted upon the side of Jeffersonian liberalism. And, like Macaulay, he found that the problem of history was really very simple: there is a bad cause, and there is a good cause, and the business of the historian is to spotlight the hero and underline the villainies of the other side. Temperamentally opposed to Calvinism, it was impossible for him to live sympathetically the life of a seventeenth-century Calvinist. He makes a hero of John Wise, and casts the Mathers in the rôle of spirits who deny; and the same simple dichotomy appears throughout his volumes, varied, it is true, by his honest endeavors to see virtue in the conservatives. If Tyler's presuppositions were essentially those of political democracy, Parrington's were those of economic liberalism; and, I think without really meaning to, he pushed the doctrine of economic determinism so far that it damaged his intellectual judgments. Since Parrington, we have had no attempt at a complete survey.

In the meantime, modern scholarship—literary, political, religious, economic—has wrought so thorough a transformation in our understanding of both the seventeenth and eighteenth centuries as to make obsolescent, though it can never make obsolete, many of Tyler's chapters. As I am more familiar with what has been done in the eighteenth century than with what has been done in the seventeenth, I can perhaps best illustrate what I mean from the later period. When Tyler published his first volumes, scholarly interpretation of the eighteenth century in England was just beginning. Men like Sir Leslie Stephen, Austin Dobson, Edmund Gosse, and others were bringing out volumes in the main biographical and critical—that is to say, their task was to establish correct lives for the great eighteenth-century authors, together with adequate texts, and to evaluate these texts in the light of their critical assumptions. It is a commonplace that the romantic and post-romantic generations in England and the United States had experienced an over-violent reaction away from the age of Pope and Johnson and from the literary canons of Augustanism. One of the tasks of the rising generation of critics and scholars in the seventies and eighties was to secure a sympathetic reading for the eighteenth-century men; and it was their valuable achievement to reinform their readers of the literary virtues of the age of reason. Some, indeed, were able to do more; Sir Leslie Stephen, for example, produced his great study of English deism. But the great bulk of the material concerning eighteenth-century literature which Tyler might read was of this critico-biographical order. It was, in the Latin sense of the word, apologetic; and the tasks of clearing the ground and re-establishing the importance of eighteenth-century thought and literature necessarily prevented scholars from making detailed studies of the content of that thought. Moreover, no one can get outside his time. The judgments made upon Pope or Swift or Sterne or Goldsmith were judgments colored by Victorian points of view; and, unhappily, the prestige of a book like Thackeray's *English Humourists of the Eighteenth Century*—that curious compound of literary charm and Victorian snobbery—colored the whole view of the eighteenth-century world.

It is the pleasing illusion of modern scholarship that it understands the eighteenth century—and, for that matter, the seventeenth also—much better than did the Victorians. We have passed out from under the penumbra of Victorian morality, whether for better or worse, just as we have passed out from under the weight of Victorian literary criticism. Great masses of new biographical data have permitted a recasting of the lives of many eighteenth-century thinkers. We now see virtues in the prose and verse of the Augustan age which the Victorians, including Tyler, did not see.

The interest of this newer scholarship has not been confined to polite letters, but has broadened itself to include the general field of intellectual history. Such a book as the late Professor Kay's edition of Mandeville's *Fable of the Bees* not only gives us an authoritative text of an important work, but traces the history of the ideas which Mandeville presents. And such a study as Professor R. S. Crane's recent article on the genealogy of the figure who is the hero of Mackenzie's once notable, though now forgotten, novel, *The Man of Feeling,* enables us to trace the filiation of ideas which culminate in this sentimental masterpiece. The work of Professor A. O. Lovejoy of Johns Hopkins has been especially influential in the recasting of eighteenth-century scholarship, and literary scholars in this aspect of British life have universally gone to school to the Baltimore philosopher. As it would be tedious to discuss all the important concepts which have been shaped as keys to that famous century, I shall content myself with merely enumerating a few of them. The rich complex of ideas associated with primitivism; the idea of a chain of being; the acceptance of the Newtonian view of the universe, and the working out of the implications and analogies of that concept in the literary, the theological, and even the political spheres; the concept of the imagination and its relation to eighteenth-century notions of reason; the rich and elusive doctrines of deism; anti-intellectualism and its paradoxical twin, intellectual equalitarianism—such are some of the central ideas which the literary historian of the eighteenth century now has at his command for a fuller understanding of the thought and literature of the time.

Meanwhile a similar revolution has been wrought in the

seventeenth-century field, with which I shall not trouble you further than to say that one of its results has been to minimize the break which earlier literary historians had assumed to be true of the period of the Restoration as against the earlier portion of the seventeenth century. The implications of the theory that seventeenth-century thought is more of a *continuum* than previous historians had supposed are obviously of considerable consequence for an understanding of colonial literature, particularly that of New England, in the period in question.

Now it can be said, I think, that the transit of civilization from the Old World to the New in the case of the American colonies is one of the most remarkable instances of intellectual transplantation that the world has ever known. One must go back to the colonizing of the ancient Greeks to find its parallel. I do not recall any other colonizing venture in the history of mankind since the Greeks—certainly none in the western world—in which the adventurers, once they were physically established, so quickly and so conscientiously set themselves the task of creating in the wilderness a mature intellectual life. Necessarily this was done under colonial conditions; necessarily few great geniuses appeared, and almost no books of the first order of merit were written. But anyone who sits down to read in orderly fashion the products of the colonial pen must be impressed, I think, with the extraordinary intellectual energy which these sermons, these pamphlets, these controversial volumes display. And if historians of American letters have not in every case been prepared to admit the existence of this relatively high intellectual level among the colonial minds, it has been because of two errors: either they have been looking for something they could not in the nature of the case expect to find, or they have been carrying back into the colonial centuries the standards and predilections of their own day. To search among colonial writers for poetry or prose in the shape of *belles-lettres* is to search for something which the colonial centuries do not yield. Yet, even with the great example of Tyler before them to teach them better, literary historians, confusing the absence of imaginative works of high order with the supposed absence of intellectual energy, have supposed that the colonial period had little to offer them. As for the fallacy of expecting seventeenth- and eighteenth-century authors to write as if they were living under the consulship of Roosevelt, it is too gross to require comment, except that it is a fallacy which is ever and again being committed by literary commentators.

The problem of the literary historian of the colonial period is then, as I see it, to evaluate this transit of intellectual interests from the Old World to the New in the light of modern scholarship, and to observe and report the slow change which took place in some of these dominant ideas, their reinforcement or death, as the intellectual life of the New World conformed itself to American demands. Before the task can be completed, we shall doubtless need many more special studies of the type represented by Professor Perry Miller's valuable book on orthodoxy in Massachusetts or by Professor Hornberger's researches into the colonial interest in scientific thought. Yet it is not too soon to begin thinking about the general pattern into which these special studies can be fitted. We need synthesis as well as analysis, especially if the analysis is to be properly directed and not to remain, as too many of our literary studies remain, random excursions into the wilderness.

Many of the materials are at hand, and require only analysis and interpretation. In the preservation and publication of these materials it is a commonplace that New England, and particularly Massachusetts, is well in advance of the rest of the old colonial area. This has arisen partly from the fact that the intellectual life of New England was, in all probability, richer than that of the rest of the colonial world; partly from the fact that New England early displayed an antiquarian interest; and partly from the continuing enthusiasm of societies such as yours. At the same time, it is, I think, fair to say that the excellent zeal of New England historians has inevitably thrown the picture out of balance; and the historian of colonial thought and literature, when he arrives, will have to guard himself against placing New England too much in the center of the picture.

To avoid this error, much work remains still to be done in discovering and organizing the evidence concerning the intellectual life of the middle and southern colonies. Particularly is the intellectual and literary history of colonial Virginia deserving of more attention than it has received. The Virginians have dispayed commendable zeal in recording and discussing their history in the seventeenth century. But, fresh from going through the Virginia historical magazines, I am compelled to report that this zeal does not carry through with the same thoroughness into the eighteenth century. Lest I seem ungracious, let me hasten to add that what I have in mind is the lack of any such studies of eighteenth-century Virginia life as the late Professor Bruce provided for the seventeenth century. Moreover, with reference to both the seventeenth and the eighteenth centuries in Virginia, it is curious how little we really know about the intellectual interests of a colony which was, with Massachusetts, the leader of the American Revolution, not only in men, but in ideas. For lack of proper background studies, men like Patrick Henry, Thomas Jefferson, Washington, Mason, Madison, George Wythe, and the rest of that great and influential group have a curious air of arising out of the void. It is almost impossible to understand, in the present state of our knowledge, why they should have taken the philosophical positions that they did; and not until we have explored more thoroughly than we have yet done the climate of opinion in eighteenth-century Virginia may we hope to have a better understanding of this powerful group of writers and political leaders. Much of the material is available and has only to be interpreted: we have, for example, a rather rich list of the books in Virginia libraries, resulting from the printing of hundreds of Virginia wills; we have a good deal of data about the curriculum of William and Mary College, which remains to be interpreted as Professor Morison has interpreted the data he has accumulated about the early years of Harvard; and we have a good deal of correspondence. We have also Mr. Swem's extraordinary two-volume work, the *Virginia Historical Index,* the most exhaustive work of its kind yet prepared, I suppose, and an invaluable tool of analysis to the historian.

Not all the thirteen colonies are so fortunate as Massachusetts in being able to confine genealogy to a separate magazine. And one of the quirks of human nature over which the literary historian is inclined to sigh is the rage for genealogy which results in a good many pages of the various state historical magazines being devoted to information which, however interesting to the families involved, is of but little value for other purposes. Some odd things also show up in the Swem *Index,* indicative perhaps of the relative importance of such matters in colonial Virginia, or else, as I am inclined to think, indicative of the interests of those who have concerned themselves with the colonial history of that state. Seven columns of the index are devoted to books, but there are almost as many columns devoted to cattle. Eleven columns are devoted to horses—many of the entries referring to various horses by name —and a total of fourteen columns is devoted to arms, ammunition, and arsenals! Cattle, horses, and guns are obviously of importance to the life of a colony, but the literary scholar may be pardoned for wishing that historians of a state which was distinguished in the eighteenth century for philosophic leadership would pay a little more attention to intellectual history and a little less to blooded horses!

The historian of colonial American literature will, then, be required to possess a sound knowledge of the results of recent scholarship in the English and Continental fields, no less than in the American. He will have to do a good deal of individual exploring. And he will also, in my judgment, have to display some degree of courage in the way of synthesis and of independent critical judgment. He must be prepared to deal sympathetically at great length with a body of material which does not have the appeal of *belles-lettres*—that is to say, he will have to be more of an intellectual, and less of a literary, historian than the latter term commonly allows for. That he will discover any new or neglected genius, or that he will turn up any work of first importance is doubtful. Yet among writing of the second order—that is to say, writing that is clear and talented—some surprising finds still await the patient investigator. Many colonial sermons are possessed of considerable eloquence, and most of them are written with a lucidity and intellectual rigor far beyond the attainments of sermon-writers of later times. The political literature of the American Revolution still awaits a historian who will have the courage to pronounce upon its very great merits in that department of letters.

There are other books and pamphlets which display a rather remarkable degree of literary merit—that is to say, stylistic and rhetorical excellence. While reading in the Huntington Library some years ago, I stumbled upon a pamphlet which may be well known to others, but which was new to me, and which has certainly not received the praise which its racy style and ingenious speculation deserve. Under the unpromising title of *An Essay on the Invention, or Art of making very good, if not the best Iron, from black Sea Sand,* Jared Eliot published at New York in 1762 an account of his experiments, together with various bits of philosophy about science and religion, which seems to me to possess considerable literary merit. I shall quote from it as an example of the unorganized realms of interest which still await the literary explorer. Eliot explains that he is very much interested in the social implications of new invention, but that "by Reason of my Situation in the Country, Want of proper Instruments to lend Assistance in searching into the Secrets of Nature, and State of Bodies, have been able to make but a slow Progress in that which I have so much at Heart"; and goes on (p. 4) to discuss with delightful frankness his experiments in trying to make iron out of the black sand on seabeaches, which appears and disappears at various seasons of the year.

I once thought these Sands were brought up by the Waves of the Sea, and then by the Agitation of the Sea in Storms, and by the great Hurry of Waters, were carried back again to the Sea; but am now fully convinced that this Conjecture was unphilosophical, and not founded on true Principles . . . I am now certain, that the black Particles of these Sands are Iron, well washed from all Impurity, and that they are derived from the upland Earth adjacent, as also from other distant Lands. . . .

This somewhat novel theory he defends most ingeniously, arguing (pp. 5-6):

That what has been called the Generation of Metals in Mines, and those great Beds of Ore called Mountain or Rock Iron, as also Bog Mine Ore, both are no other than a Collection of these Iron Particles, conveyed by Water to such Places as are fit, in their Formation, as in a Bed to receive them; where we find them in such great Masses, and in such a State of Cohesion, that we are obliged to break it up with Crow Bars, Sledges, Wedges, and Gun Powder. There is good Reason to conclude, that this great Collection of Sand Ore would long before now have been formed into Masses as we find it in Bog Mines, and in Mines of Rock Iron, were it not that these Iron Particles are so frequently put in Motion by the Agitation of the Sea, in its Flux and Reflux, that there is not Time to form a Cohesion; this Motion of the Iron Particles is what keeps them so pure and free from all fabulous and other heterogeneous Mixtures. . . .

He had, of course, to explain why particles of iron thus floated in the water, but regarding this phenomenon he argues that since "Iron may be plated so thin as to swim in Water, and . . . these Particles of Iron are much less than Plates made by Hand," the theory is not improbable. He continues (pp. 7-8):

As these Particles of Iron were on the Surface of the Sand, so they must have floated on the Top of the Water by which they were conveyed; if these Particles of Iron were much larger, the Velocity and rapid Motion of the Water might thrust them forward, as we see Gravel and even Stones tumbled forward by the Force of Water.

There is not time to quote Eliot's curious probings into the circularity of matter, but he is, in my experience, the first person to prove the Resurrection from a theory of metals! Here is the passage (p. 12 note):

It is well known that Mercury or Quicksilver is a mere Proteus, can by Art be so ordered, as to appear in a great Variety of Forms, of divers Colours, Consistence, and Operation; as that of Salves, Ointments, Pills and Powders; yet can be reduced back to its primitive State—Yea, of itself it inclines to its original State or Condition, for in the Grave Dust of those who in Life had been salivated, it has been found returned back to Quicksilver with all its true Qualities, tho' it has been exhibited in a very different Form.—So Iron after it has passed through several Stages, and subsisted under various Forms, and having assumed different Types, Colours and Figures, may return each Particle to its original and primitive State: As we may conclude both from Analogy and Experience that this is the Case—From these Facts we may infer, that the Doctrine of the Resurrection is neither inconsistent with, or contrary to the true Principles of Philosophy, as founded on Observation and Experience.

The question whence Eliot derived these philosophical ideas would plunge us back into the intellectual history of Europe and illustrates the need for a mastery of that background in judging American thought. But leaving to the learned the problem of the genesis of his ideas, I make the point that this is very lucid writing, the style easy and familiar, the sense quickly attained. It is as good as the remarkably lucid prose in which Franklin framed his reports on his experiments; and, however fantastic Eliot's theories may be, there is never the slightest doubt as to what he means. My judgment is that there is much more of this easy, lucid prose in colonial America than our literary historians have supposed; and that to call attention to the merits of such writing would be part of the task of the literary historian.

But above all we need a history of colonial letters to comprehend the roots of the American tradition. A colored barber in Austin, Texas, was proud of having shaved every governor of the state and every president of the university living in Austin while his barber shop had been operating. One day he told Robert Vinson, then head of the university: "Mistah Vinson, ef I wuz daid, you'd be sorry and send flowers, wouldn't you, suh?" Mr. Vinson said that was true. "Well," said Jim, "I'd much rather have the money while I'se alive." Mr. Vinson saw the point. So did Jim's other friends, and a sum was raised large enough, not only to send Jim's boy to a Negro college, but to send Jim on a trip. He chose Plymouth as his destination; and some days after his departure, Mr. Vinson was delighted to receive a gaudy postcard of Plymouth Rock, with the message: "Dear Mr. Vinson: this is where our ancestors landed!" Plymouth Rock and Jamestown, Massachusetts Bay and New Amsterdam—these are symbolically where our ancestors landed. And if we are to trace the history of the ideas which have formed the United States, if we are to understand the ideas on which the republic operates, we must, I think, give more careful attention to the intellectual history of the colonial period and to the literature in which that history is embodied than some of our literary critics and some of our literary scholars are at present willing to admit.

3

AMERICAN LITERATURE AS AN INSTRUMENT
FOR CULTURAL ANALYSIS *

THE late John Matthews Manly once remarked that no-body knew enough to teach one course for one semester; and it is also true that nobody knows enough to discuss American literature as an instrument for cultural analysis. For this appalling subject I have only myself to blame. But if I proposed to your committee so difficult a theme, it is because the topic is fundamental for an understanding of American life. In our imperfect state of knowledge, my remarks can be only suggestive and hypothetical, but in the present grave hour even a suggestive and hypothetical approach to studying a significant expression of national ideas and ideals is better than indifference. It is also curiously true that the interpretation of American literary history has fallen more and more into the hands of writers of the left; and though left-wing interpretation is not *per se* fallacious, the failure of objective scholarship to deal effectively with the problem deprives us of the opportunity of knowing whether *any* preconceived system of interpretation is right or wrong.

This failure of scholarship arises from a number of causes, of which I shall enumerate four. In the first place, the mature study of American literature either by scholars or by critics of a particular school of thought or of no school, is a comparatively recent thing, and we are as yet without competent knowledge of our literary origins and development. In the

* An address before the Program in American Culture and Institutions of the University of Michigan, July, 1940.

second place, we are still in the conjectural stage concerning the relations between literary art and society, particularly in the United States; and yet conjecture has been so incessant that I know no part of cultural history more subject to extreme interpretation or improbable hypothesis. In the third place, there is no agreement about terms; and until the grammar of a subject is well established, confusion necessarily continues. And in the fourth place, there is no aspect of the problem, whether it be the nature of literary history or the relation of society and literature or the meanings of terms, which is not the occasion of bitter controversy.

I shall make certain assumptions and employ certain terms; and I shall try to be as consistent in my assumptions and definitions as I can. I shall not attempt to define "literature," but I shall assume that there is such a thing as American literary history, without thereby committing myself to any school of historians, though I shall feel free to indicate how some kinds of literary history help or hinder the student of American culture. I shall occasionally refer to something called intellectual history, by which I understand the breaking down of historical and literary documents into unitary ideas and the tracing in time and place of the historical fortunes of these ideas as they take on varying shades of meaning and emotion. Professor Lovejoy's *Great Chain of Being* is of course a brilliant example of intellectual history. I shall also speak of the education or development of sensibility, by which I refer to the changing degrees of emotional loyalty which an audience yields to myth and symbol, pattern and type, aesthetic novelty and familiar convention, particularly in the arts, including literature. For example, a hundred years ago fictional heroines commonly fainted more than once during the development of a novel; now they do not faint at all. A hundred years ago the slightest hint of unchastity degraded a woman from the rank of heroine; today novelists equip their leading ladies with an illicit love-affair almost as a matter of course. The shift in the emotional response of readers to the changing concept of female virtue is part of the history of sensibility. Again, intellectual history and the history of sensibility depend, if they are to be studied, upon a semantic approach to crucial words. In certain branches of literary and philosophical history we are already familiar with the historical fortunes of words like "nature," "progress," and "machine." But in American literary history we are not yet aware of the shift in emotional response to such words as "horrid," "pure," "desert," or "vast." We are, I think, still less familiar with the shifting responses, both intellectual and emotional, which at various times in our history have been evoked by terms like "Federal Union," "trade and commerce," "republic," "democracy," or "New World." Finally, that elusive word, "culture," I shall leave in an agreeable ambiguity, though I am impressed by the point of view set forth by Dr. Heinz Werner in his remarkable book, *Comparative Psychology of Mental Development*. He says:

A genuine continuity, an intrinsic significance, can be arrived at only by avoiding any definition of the cultural form as the sum of the cultural elements. There must be a uniform cultural gestalt from which the concrete objective expressions of the culture draw their meaning. The unity of any such generic, all-embracing pattern is intelligible only as a psychological unity. . . . *The mentality of an ethnic group becomes audible in its folk songs, one might say, just as it becomes objectively visible in its arts and crafts.*

Substitute "literature" for "folk songs" and "nation" for "ethnic group," and we have in this passage, in contrast to theories of economic determinism, Freudian psychology, or Marxist literary history, the only concept of national culture which a literary historian can hope successfully to use.

How has literature been employed as an historical instrument hitherto? By one school of historians dominant until recently, it has not been regarded as evidence but as decoration. Thus, although the American frontier evoked a rich variety of literary responses, Turner's celebrated essay scarcely touches literature and is content to cite statistical, political, economic and social material. Thus a writer like McMaster, though he lists the authors of a given decade, just as he lists its scientists, painters and reformers, seldom passed beyond enumeration. Even in our own day a book like the Beards' *America in Mid-Passage* prints an enormous list of authors and titles and comments on currents of thought and opinion in some of these works; but the historians are mostly interested in this material as a mirror of social and economic trends. Life, however, is more than the sum of its economic trends; and to define literature as the reflection of sociology is to destroy its peculiar value to the historian.

What I may call this refusal of literature as literature, what I may call the reduction of literary evidence to a minor and decorative role in history followed upon the concept of "scientific" history. Under this dispensation, when the real work of the historian was over; when, in other words, he had analyzed political trends, international pressures, the statistics of trade, the development of commerce, the triumph of the bourgeoisie and the rebellion of labor, then he might turn to literature and the other arts, thus to indicate that he was not necessarily opposed to culture. Culture was not a part of history, but only an adjunct to historical writing, a mysterious affair involving value judgments which the historian declined to pass. "Scientific" history did not wish to employ value judgments, but only such pure forms of evidence as statistics and state papers. Literature was unfortunately rendered suspect by the presence of value judgments in the material itself and in the passing of such judgments upon the material by an even more mysterious process known as aesthetic criticism. The historian therefore, at this juncture, modestly stepped aside, summoning the literary scholar into the rostrum, from whose pronouncements the historian borrowed such paragraphs as he might need to fill lacunae in his own book. The literary scholar, it is important to note, was required to appear in the ambivalent role of aesthetic critic and objective historian. The historian proper might legitimately say that Shelley published such and such works and that his politics were radical, but were his poems great works of art? The historian threw up the question as insoluble on his own terms. To associate Shelley with architecture (then exhibiting a Hellenic revival), to ask how far Shelley's vaporous women satisfied the feminism of the age, to inquire whether Shelley's martyr-heroes were in contradiction to, or affirmation of, actual political ideals, to discover any connection between *Prometheus Unbound* and the astronomical, physical, chemical and zoological speculations of his time, to look into the relation between Shelley's lyrics and the state of sensibility in Regency England—these problems were out of bounds for the scientific historian. Until recently they have also been out of bounds for the literary historian, but that they are problems proper to intellectual history, the development of sensibility and the study of culture as the mentality of a nation is, I trust, evident.

The refusal of literary evidence has not always been characteristic of history. In the vast interval which separates prehistory from the time when state papers and statistics began to be regularly published, literature preserved a considerable portion of what we know about the past. The rise and decay of classical Greece, the history of Rome as city state, republic and empire, the so-called Dark Ages, the development of ancient China, Japan, and India—if, for these parts of world history, literature does not furnish all the data, it furnishes so much of the data that, without literature, the historian would be crippled. How large a part of Dill's invaluable *Roman Society in the Last Century* depends upon a careful sifting of pertinent Latin poetry and prose! How many misconceptions of Anglo-Saxon England have arisen from the failure to sift Old English literature and to see that literature, then the amusement and instruction of a minority, was highly conventionalized and scarcely an image of the world! How scanty would be our knowledge of Teutonic origins if Jordanes had not written his *De rebus Geticis,* that "hasty pamphlet by a half-educated Gothic monk!" How much of Voltaire, of Gibbon, of Macaulay would disappear if all their citations from literature were to vanish; and, even among our contemporaries, what would historians like Halévy do without *belles-lettres* to aid them!

But the word "literature" is ambiguous, and is never more ambiguously used than by literary historians. This ambiguity adds to the historical confusion. Much material included in formal histories of literature, for example, is "literary" only by an unexampled intellectual generosity. I question if even the most skillful dialectician could frame a definition of literature which would include the Strasbourg oaths and the *Divine Comedy,* the Anglo-Saxon Chronicle and the novels of Thomas Wolfe. Literary historians are eager to mount up the river of time to its earliest springs, and like explorers traversing barren lands, they are apt to leave a good deal of baggage behind. What is too often left behind is the writer's critical sense. When I read in textbooks that "the literature of the modern European languages really begins" with Beowulf, or that that confused poem "forms no unworthy opening to the splendor and richness of the literature which the English language was to contain," or that "law and freedom and devotion to liberty ring out in the old [English] writings as they still do in English literature," I can only admire this holy simplicity. As M. Legouis has said, "However it may be with the English language, there is no other literature which has lived and developed in as much ignorance of its indigenous past as English literature." The confusion of what is and what is not literary in the early periods; the difficulty of ascertaining whether ancient written fragments of antiquarian interest exhibit aesthetic or critical qualities of equivalent importance —this confusion and this difficulty express the collector's natural instinct to translate scarcity into value. The resulting ambiguity gives us that kind of literary historian who solemnly discusses the Anglo-Saxon chronicle because it is old and unique, and silently ignores the letters of Abigail Adams, the *Memoirs* of General Grant, and the prose style of Thorstein Veblen because these are modern.

Compared with almost any European literature of importance, American literature at first glance seems to offer an ideal opportunity for simple exercises in intellectual history. There is nothing in its development corresponding to the Anglo-Saxon and Middle English periods. At no time does the student need to master a special language like Old French or Old High German. Its development has taken place since the Renaissance. The first printed work in English to mention America dates from about 1511; the *Divers Voyages* of Hakluyt, the earliest influential volume to turn Tudor minds to the New World, dates from 1582; and the first printed work by Captain John Smith, with whom American literature conventionally begins, dates from 1608. At the outer limit we have to treat only a little more than four centuries; at the inner, only a little more than three. American literary history, moreover, is continuous; it displays no break due to invasion, subjugation by a foreign tongue, or slavish imitation of remote models. Its history is free from such eccentricities as Gongorism or metaphysical conceits. Its general frame of reference is the history of English literature, and for the most part the familiar European classics are its background. Its documents are easily available. Moreover, the first two centuries are confined to colonial and provincial literature; only for a century and a half have we had a national letters. Surely the literary history of the United States offers a simple, easy, and natural laboratory for the employment of literary history as an instrument for cultural analysis.

But this appearance of simplicity is in truth wholly specious, a fact which has not prevented some exceedingly naive judgments or hindered the manufacture of some of the most amazing theories of the relation of literature to society in all scholarship. And the radical fallacy common to all these theories is something like this: American literature was first a colonial literature, then a provincial literature, and only recently a literature of major importance. To be colonial is to be parochial, and to be parochial is to be simple. Hence, in the opinion of many writers, American literature in the colonial period is without real pertinence to the cultural history of a vast industrial nation.

The term "colonial" is, however, deceptive. On one level it connotes a simpler organization of society, a simpler manner of warfare, a simpler, scantier and more homogeneous population, a simpler manifestation of the arts and learning than is true of the complex industrial present. Colonial necessity thus frequently simplified European custom and institution, an example being the abandonment in Nova Scotia and North Carolina of a system of nobility based on feudal land tenure. And when, as was true, many of the arts and crafts were simplified and coarsened in being transplanted from the Old World to the New, the implication is natural that literature was also simplified. Perhaps it was, but the implication sometimes takes shape in such an argument as this: the writings of the Mathers are inferior to the writings of Milton as art; therefore the minds of the Mathers were more childish than Milton's mind. This is of course an unproved and unprovable hypothesis, but it is the kind of hypothesis which, I trust unconsciously, leads many writers to view the colonial period as something vaguely like the early centuries of literature in Great Britain. Only the other day a 400-page volume on the history of American literary thought summarily dismissed the colonial centuries in fifteen pages.

The specious simplification rests upon a second fallacy, which I can only describe by saying that it reverses the error I have tried to illustrate from the instance of the Anglo-Saxon chronicle. Certain literary historians, I said, raise that document from the level of antiquarianism, where it is exceedingly useful, to the level of literature, where it does not belong. American literary historians have moved in an opposite direction. They have depressed the monuments of our extraordinary colonial period from the level of literature, where they belong, to the level of antiquarianism. In the wrong sense of the word they have thrown an atmosphere of mediaevalism about the seventeenth century. The assumption that an immense distance separates us from the old colony days, the days of the Pilgrims, makes Miles Standish "quaint," accuses *The Simple Cobbler of Agawam* of crabbed English, and sets Increase Mather to work at black-letter folios as if he were Roger Chillingworth in *The Scarlet Letter*. Even the colonial eighteenth century seems more distant from us than the European eighteenth century. This feeling of a vast gulf between us and John Cotton springs in part from the amazing imaginative triumph of Hawthorne, Whittier and Longfellow in creating for the colonial period a feeling of picturesque antiquity necessary to their romantic theory of literature, and it is testimony to the power of their genius that they have bemused almost everybody since. When the rich and formidable literature of our first two centuries is, save for a few figures like Franklin, swept aside as uninteresting or unimportant, it is of course easy to dispose of the colonial period in fifteen pages.

It ought to be unnecessary to labor the point that Bradford and Winthrop, Ward and Sewall, Roger Williams and Increase Mather were contemporaries of Bacon and Descartes, Dryden and Molière. It ought to be unnecessary to say that Cotton Mather was a contemporary of Pope, and William Byrd of Jonathan Swift. What is more important is to underline the profounder truth that, though colonial life may have been simple, colonial literature was not therefore simple. The colonial settler had to begin all over again; but the colonial writer did not have to begin all over again. The settled ways of an English farm had to be abandoned on the frontier, but the settled ways of an English style did not have to be abandoned on the frontier. Far from being simplified, colonial literature presents the inquirer with a complex problem of points of reference.

Thus the rich library of travel literature which constitutes the first chapter in American literary development rests in an even richer matrix of philosophical, theological, political, legal, and ethical speculation. The whole concept of colony-making had to be re-invented in Renaissance England; and colonialism thereafter touched upon delicate questions of international relations, upon the rudimentary but not unskillful economic thought of Tudor and Jacobean England, upon the population problem, upon the nature and sanction of imperialism, theories of government, the relation of colony to crown and parliament, the ethical sanctions of trade, and theories of the providence of God as displayed in history. In the seventeenth century, to assume that the Puritanism of Milton is the same thing as the Puritanism of Massachusetts is as wrongheaded as to assume that eighteenth-century American Whiggism was synonymous with English Whiggism. Nevertheless it is only under the impact of studies like Miller's *The New England Mind* that scholars have ceased to look at American Calvinism through the spectacles of Oliver Wendell Holmes. A theory of providence, a theory of history, a theory of the relation of natural philosophy to God, a theory of the relation of church and state and of the individual to both, a theory of style—these seventeenth-century interests do not add up to that literary simplicity which too many discussions of colonial literature assume. I shall not pause to point out the immense advances in our knowledge of European intellectual history in the eighteenth century; I shall only sadly acknowledge that advances in our knowledge of American intellectual history for the same period are as yet slight.

The relative neglect of an analytical study of the colonial

37

period as intellectual history has permitted easy dogmas about the relation of American literature and American social history to spring up like weeds. Having for the most part no greater help than the books by Tyler and the first volume of Parrington, political and social historians have failed to see the implications of a situation unique in literary history, at least in modern times; namely, the importation of a mature literature expressing complex values and intricate systems of thought into a society which, in order to survive, had to dissolve and reform itself in a new world. Here it is that economic determinism as a "cause" of literary development goes wildly astray. No amount of faithful study devoted to land tenure, class conflicts, colonial administration, the effects of mercantilism, smuggling or international rivalry will "explain" colonial American literature. We need to complement the work of social historians by the work of historians of ideas and of sensibility. Fortunately the foundations for this new study are being laid by scholars such as Murdock and Miller at Harvard, Hornberger at Texas, Wright at the Huntington Library, Miss Baldwin at Duke, Howard at Northwestern, and others.

When we pass to the larger problem of American letters as a whole or of American letters in the national period, we move into a realm of confusion. There is no agreement on even elementary principles of intellectual order. There are many attempts at analysis, but their premises conflict, their methodology is naive, their aims are cloudy, their bias more notable than their scholarship. In addition, the failure of Victorian specialists to explore the intellectual history of the British nineteenth century has added to the cloudiness of American literary history.

One scarcely knows how to categorize the books which have appeared. There is a group of left-wing critics and historians, of whom Calverton, Hicks, and Bernard Smith are representative. There is a group to whom politico-economic ideas are dominant, and of these the late Professor Parrington and the living Professor Gabriel are characteristic. There is a group of old-line academic historians like Boynton. And there is a group, ranging from Van Wyck Brooks to Ludwig Lewisohn, who proceed from psychological assumptions about the nature of the creative process, or from sociological assumptions about the nature of American development, or from *a priori* assumptions about the needs of contemporary art.

Twenty-two years elapsed between the date when Moses Coit Tyler proposed to his publisher a history of American literature and the date of the final volumes, and over thirty years of reading in source material went into preparing his two great works. In comparison, many recent books on American literature are superficial and jejune. Parrington and Gabriel are of course competent professional scholars, and Mr. Van Wyck Brooks, by confining himself to New England, has produced something like a study from sources, albeit if his book were re-titled *The Flowering of Beacon Hill and Concord,* the phrase would not be too inaccurate. Other studies are unfortunately products of a casual attitude toward scholarly objectivity and of that amateur spirit which, though it occasionally turns up interesting ideas, is so impatient to get results that it rarely includes all the relevant facts.

So far as the Marxist historians are concerned, it must be granted that they have achieved a kind of intellectual order, but it is difficult to assume that it is a trustworthy intellectual order, since the Marxian historian is committed to a preconceived theory of world-history. He is therefore more interested in seeking confirmation for an *a priori* argument than he is in deriving appropriate interpretations from the full and careful consideration of data. His errors are the errors of Marxian literary criticism, cogently pointed out by Mr. Henry Hazlitt at the University of Michigan in 1935 when he delivered his Hopwood address, "Literature versus Opinion," and except to reaffirm my belief that Mr. Hazlitt clearly and elegantly indicated the deficiencies of the theory, I shall not say anything more about it.

Even less pertinent to our purposes is such a book as Mr. Lewisohn's *Expression in America*. Marxism as an historiographical formula is at least self-consistent; Freudianism cannot be. Mr. Lewisohn, Mr. Waldo Frank, and others insist that the creative process is irrational, and that its desirable capriciousness has been hitherto wrongfully controlled by various social and moral checks which they vaguely identify with Puritanism. Now one may admit that the creative imagination is not logical without thereby proving that literary history can be safely made capricious, but the capriciousness of Freudian literary history is so notable as to render it invalid as scholarship.

We are nearer the center in the classic volumes of Parrington, the only twentieth-century historian to comprehend the fundamental importance of the colonial period for modern America. The merits and defects of *Main Currents in American Thought* have been hotly debated, most recently in a spirited exchange between Mr. Bernard Smith and Professor Morris R. Cohen in issues of the *Journal of the History of Ideas*. It is agreed that Parrington also represents a kind of intellectual order; and it is admitted by both Mr. Smith and Professor Cohen that Parrington failed to describe large portions of the history of ideas and the history of literature. Mr. Smith argues that as Parrington never intended to write literary history, it does not matter how he treats literature; and Professor Cohen argues that since he announced a study of main currents in thought, to have omitted such main currents as science and legal theory renders the work imperfect. As for Parrington's literary history, is it notorious that he dismissed Poe, who was a genius, in a little more than two pages, and devoted ten pages to Hugh Swinton Legare, a writer so obscure that most of us have never read him. From this it is argued that Parrington was insensible to the aesthetic appeal of literature.

I suggest, however, that giving more space to Poe and less to Legare will not guarantee better literary history, and that including observations on science and law will not give us a better instrument for cultural analysis.

Parrington's failure to treat Poe adequately did not arise from aesthetic insensibility. We have no reason to suppose that Parrington failed to respond to poetry and prose. The difficulty lies in too narrow a concept of the history of ideas. When Parrington wrote: "The problem of Poe, fascinating as it is, lies quite outside the main current of American thought, and . . . may be left with the psychologist and the belletrist with whom it belongs" he revealed as by lightning the inadequacies of economic determinism as history. Note the appalling assumption that *belles-lettres* lie outside the currents of thought. Note the dismissal of the whole question of art into the hands of those queer fellows, the psychologist and the "belletrist," whoever he may be.

Now Poe was not, as Parrington seemed to think, merely an "aesthete and a craftsman" who "made a stir in the world." He was not merely a disappointed artist or merely a disgruntled and deracinated Southerner. He was, so to speak, a complete product of the publishing world of his time and of American taste and sensibility in the same epoch. The seventy-odd stories he wrote had been anticipated in almost all their aspects by British and American magazine fiction; and what Poe was principally trying to do was, like O. Henry and Ring Lardner, to master a market. His originality consisted in doing better than anybody else what everybody else was trying to do. His famous critical theories are to a surprising degree the rationale of successful magazine writing in his day. He had, to be sure, a difficult personality, but to think of Poe in terms of a damaged and therefore ineffectual angel, a misunderstood genius, a Satanic being, a problem for the psychologist and the belletrist only, is to give up literary history as an instrument for cultural analysis.

Literature, I submit, is not just a mirror reflecting social trends and economic predilections. It is not a faithful but amateurish replica of philosophical ideas only. These may influence it and furnish some part of its substance, but literary history is also a study of the relation of the forms of art to the development of sensibility in that portion of society which responds in a given epoch to literary appeals. The writer is neither wholly the embodiment of a primitive, irrational creative urge, nor wholly the half-conscious product of sociological and economic determinants. His appeal is of course to thought and feeling, but his emotive direction like his emotional apperception is part of the sensibility of his time, and his intellectual energy is not confined to the ideational content of what he writes but is also expended upon the conscious manipulation of form for the sake of aesthetic freshness. To assume that only social, economic, or political thought is thinking is of course naive, but to assume that the "aesthete and craftsman" stand outside something called main currents of thought is even more disastrous. Style is a way of looking at material, not something which only the belletrist can understand; structure is a way of arranging light and shade for emotive appeal which rises above a reportorial effect. Style and structure are, to be sure, vehicles for the sensibility of a given time, but they are also forms of thought as significant for cultural analysis as more conventional intellectual "trends."

Viewed in the setting of this larger universe of discourse, the study of American literary history has scarcely begun. As I have indicated, we are not even yet beyond such naive prepossessions as the notion that colonial literature is unimportant or "quaint" or the notion that the national period is to be interpreted mainly in terms of class struggle, economic determinism, political liberalism or the suppression of the libido. In many portions of the field we are not beyond the primitive stage of assembling bibliographical and biographical data. The neglect of the subject until recently by departments of

English has delayed the completion of those preliminary operations of scholarship beyond which experts in better established specialties have usually advanced. And until recently academic histories of American letters have been mainly of that categories-of-writing-cum-biography type of comment which seems to many of us so singularly futile. They suggest, as John Macy said, if not conspiracy, at least collusion.

In the first stages of any pioneer movement of scholarship one must expect a good deal of leaping at conclusions, rash generalizations, and untenable hypotheses. This is the present condition of most of the non-academic histories of American literature. Our next step must be, as I see it, one of destruction; that is, the overthrowing of these easy and glittering simplifications. Whenever I see the word "romantic" in discussions of American literature, whenever I see such a phrase as "the influence of the frontier" or the "mind of the antebellum South," suspicion overcomes my better nature and sours the milk of kindness in my breast. What is meant by the word "mind?" Whose mind, or rather whose minds, are included in the "mind of the antebellum South?" What does the word "South" mean, for there are many Souths, topographically, sociologically, racially, culturally. Does "antebellum" connote the entire history of the South before 1860, or does it refer chiefly to the period from the invention of the cotton-gin to Sumter, or more specifically still to the period from the Mexican War to the creation of the Confederacy? As for the word "frontier," when one finds over-enthusiastic partisans discovering frontier "influence" in the fiction of Henry James, one can only exclaim: "O liberty! what crimes are committed in thy name!"

We have, I think, five specific needs in American literary history. The first is to employ general terms with a higher degree of precision. The second is to establish more accurately a series of significant unitary ideas and symbols appearing in literature and to study the history of these concepts and sym-

43

bols, as Henry Nash Smith has studied the literary fortunes of the concept: "The Far West." The third is a series of careful studies of the culture of particular regions and cities in severely limited but significant areas of time, as Daniel Aaron is doing in the case of Cincinnati. And we need, in the fourth place, mature studies in the development of American sensibility—by which I do not refer to that mechanical assembling of the arts in parallel columns which too often passes for the "cultural background" of an age, but rather an examination of the responses which have been evoked by artistic pattern and aesthetic appeal. The little symposium entitled *Romanticism in America,* just published by the Baltimore Museum of Art, is a suggestive example of this type of approach, and so is Professor Gabriel's interesting chapter on American patriotic mythology. And in the fifth place we need mature and independent scholars, men who have long since abandoned the notion that American literary history is unimportant and who are prepared to break the bonds of that literal-minded German methodology which has too long enslaved the creative imagination in literary research. We need, in sum, to ask the right questions, we need the courage to break through conventional classifications and merely erudite prestige values if the study of American literary history is to aid us in achieving and maintaining a real culture at a period when the European world seems to be dissolving like the fragments of a dream.

4

ORIGINS OF THE COLONIAL IDEA *

DESPITE the vast amount of writing which concerns the settlement and growth of British colonies on the North American continent, little attention has been paid to the sources whence the idea of colonization sprang. A concept unknown to the England of Chaucer had become commonplace in the England of Shakespeare; and it is a matter of more than antiquarian interest to inquire, not into the origins of colonies, but into the origins of the idea of colonies. How did the concept of a colony arise in England? What historical or foreign precedents helped to shape it? Upon what experience did the British draw, and how did this experience color their interpretation of New World projects? The present paper seeks to investigate two or three aspects of this important problem.

I

What were the origins of the colonial idea among the English?

The terms customary in sixteenth and seventeenth century writing about over-seas settlements were "colony" and "plantation." In this sense both were novel words. Although statesmen, explorers and "adventurers" were children of the Renaissance, there is no evidence that English thinking about colonization was notably influenced by Greek or Roman theory.[1] Jamestown, to be sure, was at first a Stuart counterpart of a Greek colony in the Aristotelian sense that its inhabitants could be reached by the voice of a single herald,[2] and developed as a military garrison on lines vaguely suggesting a

* An address before the American Philosophical Society, April, 1942.

45

Roman *colonia,* but these parallels are without real signifi-cance.[3] The consequence of this negative relation to the ancient world was that a whole train of thought which might con-ceivably have influenced colonial policy did not come into being.[4]

In Middle English the word "colonie" referred, like its Mediaeval Latin counterpart, to a settlement of agricultural laborers associated with a particular portion of the earth's surface, and did not seem appropriate to settlement overseas. Even as late as 1436 Adam Moleyns (if he wrote the poem) in his *Libelle of Englyshe Polycye,* though he set forth the de-sirability of strengthening English settlements in Ireland, had no single word to designate what he wanted:

> I herde a man speke unto me full late,
> Whyche was a lorde and of ful grete astate,
> That exspenses of one yere don in Fraunce,
> Werred on men well wylled of puissuance
> Thys seyde grounde of Yrelonde to conquere . . .
> Myght wynne Yrelonde to a fynall conquest . . .[5]

In the sixteenth century one of the earliest works discussing the possibility of English settlement in the New World lacks any technical word for what the author advocates:

> O what a thynge had be than,
> Yf that they that be Englyshemen
> Myght have ben furst of all
> That there shulde have take possessyon,
> And made furst buyldynge and habytacion,
> A memory perpetuall![6]

The earliest discoverable appearance of "colony" in the sense of a settlement in a new or foreign country politically de-pendent upon the parent state, is in a Scottish document of 1548–9, its first appearance in English is in Eden's translation of Peter Martyr in 1555.[7] According to the *New English Dic-tionary* Bacon in 1622 was the first to use the verb "to colonize." Even "plantation" in the sense of "colony" appears relatively late, the first recorded instance being in Hooker's *History of Ireland* (1586).[8] The late appearance of these technical terms can only mean that, despite the activity of the Spanish, the Portuguese and the French, English thinking on colonization had to begin almost *de novo*—perhaps because foreign nations jealously guarded the secrets of their colonial endeavors.

Nevertheless, there were foreign precedents which may have influenced English thinking.[9] These were the colonies of the Hanseatic cities in the Baltic and of the Italian city states, notably Venice and Genoa, in the Levant. Although her colonies required military protection,[10] by establishing outposts in the Ægean islands, at Athens, in the Black Sea, in Egypt and elsewhere, Venice founded trading posts or *fondachi*. These were communes, or states within states. Over them the influence of the metropolis was supreme. The original grant permitting their creation was obtained by the metropolis, buildings were erected at public cost, and magistrates were appointed by the home government. These magistrates, chosen for specified times and given specific instructions, were responsible in Venice to a body somewhat like the (later) English Board of Trade. Venetian laws were carried into the *fondaco,* the trade of which was of course monopolized by the mother city. Associated with the creation and management of the colony and its trade was the joint-stock company, a fourteenth-century invention by which state action could be concealed as quasi-private enterprise.[11]

Because of the prestige which Italian commercial enterprise enjoyed in Renaissance Europe and because trade relations between England and Venice were traditionally close,[12] it is to be expected that the theory and practice of the *fondaco* should influence Tudor thinking. And in fact the parallels are instructive. Like the Italian colony the English settlement was often a trading venture managed by a joint-stock company [13] chartered by the state, which formally retained control. The governor, "admiral" and council, if there was one, were originally appointed by the crown or its representative; their terms of office were regulated from England without reference to colonial desire; and they were given specific instructions by the home authorities. English law was carried into the plantation by express provision of patent or charter; colonial trade was a monopoly of the mother country; and the plantations in their earliest phase made continual appeals for the erection of such public buildings as forts and storehouses at public expense. Indeed, the conflict between the demands of communal interest and of individual enterprise in the early years of the settlements might not have arisen, had the plantation not been thought of as a "factory." [14] From the point of view of the state the creation of an exporting *fondaco* was the important end; from the point of view of the colonist, however, the individual ownership of land and the prospect of private gain outweighed political and mercantile considerations. As in Italy, the connection of a joint-stock company with a particular city or cities was sometimes close.[15] One curious aspect of this uncritical acceptance of the "factory" idea, given the English misconception of the Indians as living in feudal states governed by a king or emperor, is the solemn treaties entered into between these potentates and representatives of the British crown. These treaties stipulate the granting of land, rights of trade and monopoly, and the like, and are analogous to the grants obtained by Venice. To be sure, King James claimed the mainland by right of prior discovery, but the juridical ambiguity did not prevent the Virginia Company from recognizing Powhatan as a reigning sovereign, nor relieve anxiety about the possible legal rights of Indians to lands that had been immemorially theirs.[16] Finally, the ambiguous status of the first colonial administrators, at once military chieftains, ambassadors, and commercial agents, results in part from the acceptance of the Italianate idea of a *fondaco,* semi-public and semi-private in nature.

II

More immediate, however, was the example of Ireland;[17] and the experiences of sixteenth-century Englishmen in their attempts to subdue the wild Irish and to strengthen imperial rule profoundly colored the whole concept of a plantation, influenced the appeal of "promotion literature," and created certain important misconceptions about the New World.

Before the accession of Henry VIII English power in Ireland had sunk to the lowest ebb in history. In rebuilding his empire Henry at first attempted conciliation as a means to draw the natives into civilized life that would benefit trade. But the Irish proved recalcitrant, a combination of conciliation with coercion seemed necessary, and only by the ruthless suppression of rebellion did Lord Grey manage to govern Ireland without undue bloodshed to 1540. After Henry's death disaffection became chronic and desolation spread. Though the English monopoly of gunpowder gave an overwhelming superiority to the royal forces,[18] it became increasingly evident that mere military forays could not hold the country. Accordingly the idea of English plantations in Ireland became prominent during the reign of Elizabeth.

Before discussing the implications of these attempts, however, one may note that Irish anarchy carried with it three important corollaries. One was that the Irish service became unpopular. It was "well known to be the most miserable war for travail, toil and famine in the world," said one observer in 1598, and in 1599 Sir John Dowdall wrote Cecil: "most part of the army . . . seem beggarly ghosts, fitter for their graves than to fight a prince's battle. The report hereof so works in mens minds that they had as lief go to the gallows as to the Irish wars."[19] Reasons for this unpopularity were many —bad pay, insufficient provisions, incompetent leadership— but one leading element was the character of Irish warfare.

That warfare was compounded of ambush and treachery. The Irish, wrote Gainsford in *The Glory of England* (1618),

will plash down whole trees over the passes, and so intricately wind them, or lay them, that they shall be a strong barricade, and then lurk in ambush amongst the standing wood, playing upon all comers as they intend to go along. On the bog they likewise presume with a naked celerity to come as near our foot and horse as is possible, and then fly off again, knowing we cannot or indeed dare not follow them. . . .[20]

The second result of Irish conflict was the desolation of the country. The island acquired the reputation of being a desert. Every one is familiar with Spenser's famous description of the starving Irish, but Spenser was not sole and singular in his observations. In 1575 Sir Henry Sydney wrote the Lords of the Council regarding Offaly and Leix, where English plantations had been attempted, that the land was

spoiled and wasted, by the race and offspring of the old native inhabitors, which grow great, and increase in number; and the English tenants decay, both in force and wealth. . . . They are daily so spoiled and burned, the charges they have been at, and their daily expenses they be at, to defend themselves, so weakeneth them, as their state is to be pitied. . . .

In 1598 Chief Justice Sir William Saxey said in a letter to Cecil that Munster had been left desolate by Irish rebels. He described

infants taken from the nurses' breasts, and the brains dashed against the walls; the heart plucked out of the body of the husband in the view of the wife, who was forced to yield the use of her apron to wipe off the blood from the murderer's fingers; [an] English gentleman at midday in town cruelly murdered, and his head cleft in divers pieces; divers sent into Youghal amongst the English, some with their throats cut, but not killed, some with their tongues cut out of their heads, others with their noses cut off. . . .

In 1599 an official minute declared that

we see by manifold experience, what madness it is for a Deputy or General to lead royal forces against naked rogues in woods and bogs, whom hounds can scarce follow, and much less men. Their ordinary food is a kind of grass. Neither clothes nor houses, generally, do they care for. With this their savage life are they able to wear out any army that seeketh to conquer them.

The writer compares the wild Irish to wolves and foxes. And in Fynes Moryson's *Itinerary* (1617) one reads of

a most horrible spectacle of three children . . . all eating and gnawing with their teeth the entrails of their dead mother . . . the common sort of the rebels were driven to unspeakable extremities.

He reports that old women caught, killed, and ate little children.[21]

Finally, it appeared that a race capable of these atrocities was little better than bestial. Said William Thomas in *The Pilgrim: A Dialogue on the Life and Actions of Henry VIII* (1552):

. . . the wild Irish, as unreasonable beasts, lived without any knowledge of God or good manners, in common of their goods, cattle, women, children and every other thing . . . nor yet any justice executed for murder, robbery, or any other like mischief; but the more force had ever the more reason. And hereof it followed that because their savage and idle life could not be satisfied with the only fruit of the natural unlaboured earth, therefore continually they invaded the fertile possessions of their Irish neighbours that inhabited the . . . English pale. . . .[22]

Surely, Sir Henry Sydney wrote the queen in 1567,

there was never people that lived in more misery than they do, nor as it should seem of worse minds, for matrimony among them is no more regarded in effect than conjunction between unreasonable beasts. Perjury, robbery, and murder counted allowable. . . . I cannot find that they make any conscience of sin, and I doubt whether they christen their children or no; for neither find I place where it should be done, nor any person able to instruct them in the rules of a Christian; or if they were taught I see no grace in them to follow it; and when they die I cannot see they make any account of the world to come.[23]

Spenser found them essentially barbarians, and returned to the ancient concept of the Scythians for his parallel:

There bee other sortes of cryes all so vsed amongst the Irishe, which savoure greatlie of *Scithian:* barbarisme, as theire Lamentacions at theire burialls, with disparefull outcryes, and ymoderate waylinges . . .

. . . since I latelie spake of theire manner of cryes in ioyninge battaile, to speake also somewhate of the manner of theire Armes and arraye in Battaile . . . And first of their armes and weapons, amongst which theire broade swordes are proper *Scithian:* . . . Also theire shorte bowes and little quivers with shorte bearded arrowes, are verie *Scythian.* . . . Moreover theire longe broade sheildes, made but of wicker roddes which are comonlie vsed amongst thee . . . Northerne Irishe. . . . Likewise theire goinge to battayle without Armour on theire bodies or heades, but trusting onelie to the thicknes of theire glibbs, the which they saye will sometymes beare of a good strooke, ys meere salvage and Scythian . . . besides theire confused kynde of march in heapes without any order or arraye, their Clashing of swordes togeather, theire fierce rvnninge vpon theire Enemies, and theire manner of feighte, resembleth altogeather that which is redd . . . to haue bene vsed of the Scythians. . . .

. . . so haue I sene some of the Irishe [drink] not their Enemies but frindes bloode, as namelie at the execution of a notable tratour. . . . I sawe an old woman . . . tooke vpp his heade whilst he was quartered and sucked vpp all the blood running there out sayinge that the earth was not worthie to drincke yt, and therewith also steeped her face and brest and tare her haire cryinge and shriking out most tirriblie.[24]

The point of passages like these for the student of American literature is that this picture of Ireland and the Irish preceded or accompanied the voyage literature having to do with the New World; that English experience with one wild race conditioned their expectation of experience with another; and that the deep popular disfavor into which Irish expeditions fell colored colonial enterprise unfavorably.

Point by point these observations on Irish life can be paralleled in writing on the American Indians. Take the matter of ambush, for example. The Jacobean reader of Hakluyt's translation of a narrative of the De Soto expedition, *Virginia richly valued* (1609), would discover that the Indians are

a people so warlike and so nimble, that they care not a whit for any footemen. For if their enemies charge them, they runne away, and if they turne their backs, they are presently upon them. . . . They never stand still, but are alwaies running and traversing from one place to another; by reason whereof neither crossebow nor arcubuse can aime at them; and before one crossebowman can make one shot, an Indian will discharge three or foure arrowes; and he seldome misseth what hee shooteth at.[25]

Or he might read of the bloody treachery at Mavila or the burning of De Soto's horses at Chicaca.

. . . for all their faire and cunning speeches, they are not overmuch to be trusted, for they be the greatest traitors of the world, as their manifold most craftie contrived and bloody treasons, here set down at large, doe evidently prove. They be also as unconstant as the wethercock, and most readie to take all occasions of advantages to doe mischiefe. They are great liars and dissemblers; for which faults oftentimes they had their deserved paiments. . . . To handle them gently . . . will be without comparison the best; but if gentle polishing will not serve, then we shall not want hammerours and rough masons enow, I meane our old soldiours trained up in the Netherlands. . . .[26]

This is a summary view of the Indian problem; it might be a discussion of the wild Irish.

If Spenser had said the Hibernians scarcely knew the purpose of clothing, John Smith pictured the Indians "couered with the skinnes of wilde beasts," wearing "large mantels of deare skins not much differing in fashion from the Irish mantels," adorning themselves with "a dead Rat tied by the tail" or with live snakes that "often times familiarly would kiss [their] lips." [27] The leggings of the New England savages reminded the author of *Mourt's Relation* of "Irish trouses," and Thomas Morton declared that the "Natives of New England are accustomed to build them houses much like the wild Irish."[28] Remembering Spenser's description of Irish "cryes in ioyning battaile," listen to its echo in John Smith:

Vpon the first flight of arrowes, they gaue such horrible shouts and screeches, as though so many infernall helhounds could not haue made them more terrible.[29]

William Morrell in his *Nova Anglia* could make the methods of Indian warfare clear only by comparing them to those of the Irish;[30] and in 1637 Roger Williams, writing to John Winthrop, could find no worse threat in Indian warfare than that, if the savages were not kindly used, they might "turne wild Irish themselues."[31] In sum, America was uncomfortably like Ireland. As Sir Humphrey Gilbert regularly put men, women and children to the sword in that unhappy island,[32] so in Virginia Sir Thomas Dale dealt mercilessly with the Indians and with those who consorted with them:

Sr Tho: Dale haveinge allmoste finished the foarte, and settled a plantacyon in that p'te dyv^{rs} of his men being idell, and not willinge to take paynes, did runne away unto the Indyans; many of them being taken againe, Sr Thomas in a moste severe manner cawsed to be executed, some he appointed to be hanged, some burned, some to be broken on wheels, others to be staked, and some to be shott to deathe, all theis extreme and crewell tortures he used, and inflicted upon them, to terrefy the reste for attempteinge the lyke, and some wch robbed the store, he cawsed them to be bowned faste unto trees, and so starved them to deathe.

Indians bringing food were treated as spies:

Some of them Sr Tho: Gates cawsed to be apprehended and executed for a terrour to the reste, to cause them to desiste from their subtell practyses.[33]

The doctrine that the only good Indian is a dead Indian first took shape in the belief that the only good Irishman is a dead Irishman.

While Ireland was being terrorized into "civilitie," discharged soldiers returning to England filled the land with ill report of Irish life, just as disgruntled sailors and settlers, returning from some ill-starred American venture, spread unfavorable reports about the New World. The two regions, as it were, played into each other's hands. There have been, wrote Thomas Hariot,

divers and variable reports, with some slanderous and shamefull speeches bruted abroad by many that returned from thence: especially of that discovery which was made by the Colony transported by Sir Richard Grinvile in the yere 1585. . . . Which reports have done not a little wrong to many that otherwise would have also favoured and adventured in the action. . . .

Such malingerers had perhaps been punished for misdemeanors in Virginia, and were persons who "had little or no care of any other thing but to pamper their bellies." [34] The misfortunes of the New World echoed the misfortunes of the Old; the situations were too much alike not to strengthen the assumption that colonial experience was everywhere of a piece; and Ireland, suffering from a "bad press," infected the image of the New World. Unable to comprehend the Brehon laws, the English simply decided that the wild Irish were savages; the English were equally unwilling or unable to understand Indian "laws." Used to savagery in the one place, they looked for and provoked it in the other. Experience led them to approach Virginia and New England with the natural prepossessions generated by Tudor conquest in Ireland.

A succession of schemes for planting Englishmen on territory wrested from the wild Irish began at least as early as 1551. [35] Anti-Irish gossip had to be offset by effective printed propaganda, the formula of which set the pattern for American "promotion literature." Thus *A Letter sent by T. B. Gentleman unto his very frende Mayster R. C. Esquire, wherin is conteined a large discourse of the peopling and inhabiting the Cuntrie called the Ardes* (1572), a pamphlet on the Sir

Thomas Smith enterprise, not only outlines the same mode of settlement that was to be tried at Jamestown, but anticipates a good many of the arguments used in promotion literature concerning the New World.[36] The climate and the fertility of the country are praised, and private possession of land is promised. "How say you now," he inquires, "have I not set forth to you another Eutopia . . .?"

And to the ende the Souldiours should be the more vigilant, I am minded to lay all the very frōtier Lande diuided by proportion . . . so that every Souldiour shal put in his share towards the sowing and manuring thereof, and receive his part of the Corne and other profite. . . . Now, if he keepe and defend [his own possessions] hee is a Gentleman, a man of liuely hode and of inheritaunce, and who hath and shall haue his ground ploughed and eared for him without his paines, for that we haue provided for, if hee lose it, he loseth his own inheritaunce, and hindreth his posteritie.

Prospective colonists were assured the land was empty and "lacketh only inhabitants, manurance, and pollicie." Three themes recurrent in American promotion literature also appear. England, says the writer, was never so full of people,

and the dissolution of Abbayes hath done two things of importance heerin. It hath doubled the number of gentlemen and marriages, whereby commeth daily more increase of people, and suche younger brothers as were wonte to be thruste into Abbayes, there to liue (an idle life), sith that is taken from them must nowe seeke some other place to liue in.

Again:

To inhabite and reforme so barbarous a nation as that is, and to bring them to the knowledge and law, were bothe a godly and commendable deede, and a sufficiĕt worke for our age. . . . Let us, therefore, vse the persuasions which Moses vsed to Israel, they will serve fitly in this place, and tell them that they shall goe to possesse a lande that floweth with milke and hony. . . .

Finally:

. . . it shall be furnished with a companie of Gentlemen and others that will liue frendly in felowships togither reioysing in the

56

frute and commoditie of their former trauaile, which (through
noble courage) for estimatiō sake, and the loue of their owne
countrey the[y] first enterprised, deseruing . . . to be crowned,
with garlands of honour and euerlasting fame.

Unemployment and over-population, the missionary motive,
and a union of profit and fame—experience soon taught the
persuasive quality of these arguments.

In 1589 another characteristic pamphlet [37] shows the deep
unpopularity of the plantation idea and the persistent desire
to make emigration attractive. Robert Payne attempted to
soften current prejudices against the wild Irish. He found the
better sort of people "very ciuill and honestly giuen," said
that most of the kerns and gallowglasses had been slain in the
Desmond rebellion, and described the remaining Irish as
harmless, idle folk like English beggars. They hated the Spaniards because of "their monsterous cruelties in the west Indians"—a note that is to recur in the American material. Ireland is of course incomparable, and he praises Irish forests,
stone and mineral wealth, wild fowl, seafood, hunting, and
agricultural plenty. "You may keep a better house in Ireland
for L.li. a yeere, then in England for CC.li. a yeere." The
author admitted there had been fraudulent men among previous "undertakers" in Ireland, who "haue enticed many honest
men ouer, promising them much but performing nothing,
no not so much as to pay their seruants, and workmen wages"
—a revealing glimpse into the unpopularity of emigration.
But of course *his* undertakers, "many good knights and gentel-
men of great worship," are worthy men. Much of his pamphlet
is directed to allaying popular fears. Any one of the six million English, he says,

is good innough for three wetherbeaten spainerds whom a fewe of
our frostie nightes will make shrinke like rotten sheepe. yet thus
much I must say for them, if almightie God for our contempt of
his holye worde hath giuen them power against vs, as hee did the
frogges against the Egiptianes, Then is there no force able to resiste
them: (without that) I see no cause why we either in England or
Ireland should feare them. . . .

The document addressed by the Privy Council to the City of London in 1609 to further the plantation of Londonderry is more business-like than Payne's but equally revealing.[38] It enumerates eleven "Land Commodities" and seven "Sea and River Commodities" in Ulster, and lists the following economic advantages:

1. The country is well watered, and supplied with fuel either of trees or turf. 2. It supplies such abundance of provisions as may not only sustain the plantation, but may furnish provisions yearly to the city of London, especially for their fleets, as beeves, pork, fish, rye, bere, peas, beans, and in some years will help the dearth of the city and country about, and the storehouses appointed for the relief of the poor. 3. It is fit for breeding of mares and for cattle, and thence may be expected store of hides, tallow, etc. 4. The soil is suited for English sheep, and if need were, wool might be had cheaply out of the west of Scotland. 5. It is fit in many parts for madder, hops, and wood [woad]. 6. It affords fells of red deer, foxes, sheep and lambs, cony, martens, squirrels, etc. 7. It grows hemp and flax better than elsewhere, and thus might furnish materials for canvass, cables, cordage, and such like requisites for shipping. Also for thread, linen cloths, and stuffs made out of linen yarn, which is finer there and more plentiful than in all the rest of the kingdom. 8. Timber, stone, lime, and slate, and building materials are to be had; and the soil is good for making bricks and tiles. The goodliest timber in the woods of Glanconkein and Killeitragh may be had, and may compare with any in his Majesty's dominions, and may be brought to the sea by Lough Eagh and the Ban. Fir masts of all sorts may be had out of Loughnaber in Scotland (not far from the North of Ireland) more easily than from Norway. 9. All materials for building of ships (except tar) is there to be had in great plenty, and in countries [regions] adjoining. 10. There is wood for pipe staves, hogshead staves, barrel staves, hoop staves, clap boards, wainscot, and dyeing ashes, glass, and ironwork; copper and iron-ore are there found abundantly. 11. The country is fit for honey and wax.

The document stressed the fact that "these coasts are ready for traffic with England and Scotland, and lie open and convenient for Spain and the Straits, and fittest and nearest to Newfoundland." With some slight change of names it might serve for a pamphlet on Virginia. The usual argument drawn from over-population was included.[39] Constituted in January, 1610/11 and chartered in 1613, this enterprise was somewhat more successful than previous ones; yet in May, 1615, George Canninge drew an unflattering picture which shows how un-alluring plantations were:

Theise mischiefes and miseries [*i.e.,* "divers robberies and some murders"] causeth us to stand continuallie upon our guard, and when we travell we take good strength with us. . . . The dangers of these troubles have hindred the settling of land much, and must be more on some other proportions [lands surveyed and allotted to settlers] than ours. There are yet divers out in rebellion in the woodes, and some tymes light uppon passengers and robb them and sometymes light into the houses and doe manie vil-lanyes. . . .[40]

A survey of 1618–9 showed only 1,974 families in the six counties of Ulster, and the historian of the plantation declares it gives "a humiliating picture of the results of the movement, after so much effort on the part of the Government during the preceding twelve years."[41] The cause of this failure, however, lay deeper than the unattractiveness of Irish life; it lay in the character of those who migrated. Said Barnaby Rich in *The Irish Hubbub* (1617):

Ireland for these many years hath been the receptacle for our English runagates, that for their misled lives in England, do come running over into Ireland. Some for murder, some for theft; some that have spent themselves in riot and excess are driven over for debt, some come running over with other men's goods, some with other men's wives, but a great number now lately, that are more hurtful than all the rest, and those be recusants.[42]

Similar complaints were to be made about the American settlements. Nevertheless, by the 1620's English plantations in Ireland, notably in Ulster, were well established, and like "King" Carter or the Byrds, well-born Englishmen—Sir Christopher Hatton is an example—possessed princely estates in the sister kingdom.[43]

The transfer of experience and ideas, expectation of behavior and emotional attitudes from the struggle to "plant" Ireland to the endeavors to colonize the New World was made easy by the fact that many of the leading proponents of American colonization, many of the "adventurers" and many of the actual leaders had had previous connections, sometimes unfortunate, with Irish affairs. Among the more famous names are those of Sir Humphrey Gilbert, Sir Walter Raleigh, Sir Francis Drake, Sir Ferdinando Gorges, the Earl of Southampton, Captain Ralph Lane, Lord De La Warr, Chief Justice Popham, Captain Christopher Carleill, and Lord George Carew—many of whom are also the authors of influential reports on the New World. Sir Humphrey Gilbert had a military career in Ireland. After his raid on Nombre de Dios Sir Francis Drake spent some time with Essex in Ireland, from which he emerged in 1575 to plan his circumnavigation of the globe. In January 1598/9 Sir Ferdinando Gorges was named sergeant-major of the army in Ireland; though he seems not to have served, he must have learned something about Irish affairs.[44] The Earl of Southampton went to Ireland in 1599 and again in 1600 on missions semi-military and semi-political.[45] In these same years Lord De La Warr not only fought under Essex but was knighted by the Irish Lord Deputy. Gorges, Southampton and De La Warr were of course members of the Council of Virginia. Lord George Carew, a member both of the Council and of the Virginia Company, fought under Sir Henry Sydney in Ireland during the seventies, held a succession of important Irish posts in the eighties, and rose to ever greater distinction in the Irish establishment at the close of the century. In 1603 he retired as Lord Justice for Ireland, though he revisited the country in 1610 to survey the Ulster settlements.[46] Bacon's report to James I entitled "Certain Considerations Touching the Plantation in Ireland"[47] praises Chief Justice

Popham for his successes in the Munster plantations. Raleigh, of course, received a grant of 12,000 acres in Ireland and settled a large number of English families in Cork and Waterford about 1594. Ralph Lane was muster master in Ireland in 1592 and submitted a project for musters in Ireland to the English authorities while he held that office.[48] Captain Christopher Carleill served in Ireland in 1584 and again in 1588.[49] Lord (formerly Captain) Chichester, another prominent Irish official, served with Carew on the committee to draw up a frame of government for Virginia.[50] And in general it can be demonstrated that a considerable number of the incorporators and "adventurers" of the original Virginia company had an active interest in Irish "plantations." [51]

In addition to such obvious matters as the inability or unwillingness of the English to comprehend the culture of an alien race,[52] the doctrine that a plantation had to be in its original a military establishment,[53] or the excuse that native sloth made invasion and settlement necessary,[54] perhaps the most important idea developed in the Irish experiments and thence transferred to the New World was the notion that the subjugation of a colony implied a system of feudal tenure. Having in mind the experience of over a century, Bacon proposed that the king should be the *"primus motor"* of Irish settlement; that the title Earl of Ulster be added to that of the Prince of Wales; and that an Irish nobility be created, basing itself on Irish land. He also sketched out a council in residence (in Ireland) and a council at London for the governing of the plantations. He likewise argued that there was no necessity for undertakers to execute their duties in person, their kinsfolk, servants and tenants sufficing, and said that settlement must take the form of towns.[55]

In the light of these experiences and this theory it was natural that American plantations should be creations of the crown; that the institution of a quasi-feudal system of landtenure should follow; that the lords proprietor should stand in relation to colonists as a count palatine in relation to his followers; and that the New World should be expected to support a new nobility. Endless amusement has been excited by John Locke's constitutions for Carolina, but this attempt to create a feudal nobility in the South is not so ridiculous as it seems. The parallel case of Nova Scotia shows how deeply the Irish example was felt. In 1621 Sir William Alexander received a royal patent for all the land between New England and Newfoundland; and on the express analogy of the Ulster settlement of 1609 (which carried into practical effect Bacon's proposal of an Irish nobility), Alexander was authorized to set up the scheme of the Knight Baronets of Nova Scotia. For the sum of 3000 "merks" (150 pounds sterling) any person approved by Sir William and the king might receive a patent of nobility on the Nova Scotia establishment and 6000 acres of land. On this land it was then his duty to establish settlers.[56] As a matter of history 113 such baronets were created, though most of them, through the payment of fines, were released from the necessity of providing settlers. Wars with France and exchange of New World possessions between France and Great Britain stopped the operation of the scheme, but in making propaganda for his colony Sir William and his associate, Sir Robert Gordon of Lochinvar, addressed themselves mainly to the upper classes.[57] Before one decides that so aristocratic a program sprang from the pedantry of James I, let him remember that it was in some such fashion, amid a thousand discouragements, that Ulster was subdued.[58]

IV

The example of the Italian (and Hanseatic) city states in founding trading posts abroad, and English experience with Irish plantations were formative in the development of the colonial idea. One other, if more familiar, consideration must, for the sake of completeness, be also urged, the idea implicit in a statement of J. A. Williamson:

62

A statesman of Charles II's reign, if asked to appraise the various colonies in the order of their value to the nation, would probably have placed Barbados first, followed by Newfoundland, Jamaica, and the Leeward Islands; after them Virginia and Maryland; then the Middle Colonies and the Carolinas; and last of all, New England.[59]

The question of the relative importance, political and economic, of the mainland colonies to the mother country is a matter of some consequence in estimating the elements which make up the colonial idea.

From the point of view of American literary history, documents having to do with mainland colonies in the future United States are naturally of primary significance, and for that reason our literary histories customarily begin with Captain John Smith. American historians have also naturally arranged documents having to do with colonies in an order convenient for the understanding of American development, just as they have frequently interpreted these documents from a cis-Atlantic point of view. Provided the omissions of such an approach are clearly understood, no harm is done, but, the omissions not being understood, a false order of importance may be imposed upon history, from which misleading conclusions may be drawn regarding the transit of civilization from the Old World to the New. Thus an older group of historians wrote as if an irresistible impulse towards political and religious freedom transferred to Jamestown or to Plymouth the better parts of an English tradition thwarted by "tyranny" at home. A more recent school has interpreted American colonization as a direct function of economic pressures in Great Britain itself. There is truth in both these points of view, but the importance of colonial beginnings to American history is one thing, and the status of American colonies in their beginnings in comparison with the status of other British ventures, colonial and otherwise, is something else.

It is therefore not impertinent to observe that the Elizabethan freebooters and Jacobean merchants to whom American settlement is due had no notion of creating the future United States. The primary aim of almost all the maritime activity of England in the later sixteenth and earlier seventeenth century was the checking of Spain, and in the beginning the thought of settlement was subordinate to the thought of trade and of cutting off the trade of the enemy. English delay in founding colonies was not due solely to English sloth, English provincialism, or English ignorance. It must be remembered that the years from 1540 to 1570 were, in the words of one historian, "the winter of the sixteenth century," a period of depression which, following upon the prosperity of the preceding half century, seemed all the more disastrous.[60] England looked forth on a world dominated by Spain and Portugal, upon a New World in which various well-meant French schemes to challenge the supremacy of the Iberian powers had singularly failed.[61] Neither Edward VI nor Mary spent money to create a navy which might successfully challenge that of Spain, even if these sovereigns had desired to; and consequently, when, after Mary's death, the disgruntled Spaniards discovered that England was not to become part of their empire, the most immediate weapon upon which patriotic Englishmen could seize was the weapon of trade. As early as 1551 trading enterprises to Morocco and thence to Africa were planned; in 1553 the Chancellor-Willoughby expedition set sail for Nova Zembla to discover a Northeast passage to the Orient and to begin that intercourse with Russia which was represented by the creation of the Muscovy company. Relations between England and Spain were formally correct under Mary, and, indeed, continued so until ten years after her death; nevertheless it was during this decade that the Guinea trade was looked to by Sir John Hawkins and his friends as a counterbalance to Spanish monopoly.[62] In the fifteen-seventies the desire of patriotic Englishmen was not colonization but breaking down Iberian control of world

64

trade; the thought of colonies had not arisen except in the shape of trading posts on a route to Cathay to be held by temporary residents; and the search was not for lands to be possessed but for waters by which to pierce to the Pacific.

The desired water route might be either to the North or to the South; and the search for the Northeast Passage or the Northwest Passage exhibits not so much the obstinate incredulity of the Tudor mercantile mind as the determination to prevent the slow strangulation of English trade. What may be called the theoretical justification for seeking a Northwest Passage was laid down afresh in 1565 by Sir Humphrey Gilbert in the celebrated *Discourse,* not printed until 1576; [63] and it is notable that in the "Notes framed by M. Richard Hakluyt of the middle Temple Esquire, given to certaine Gentlemen that went with M. Frobisher in his Northwest discoverie, for their directions," [64] the thought of planting is confined to such temporary occupation of seaport or river as will create a trading station rather than to the general occupation of land.[65] The attempts of Frobisher, Lok, Gilbert, and others to force a Northwest Passage are part of a world campaign, but they are attempts which, though important and picturesque in themselves, must be separated in thought, even when "plantations" are involved, from the concept of colony-making which produced Jamestown.

Projects to seize and hold the Straits of Magellan were also part of this commercial campaign. Thus in 1574 a "Petition of Gentlemen of the West parts to the Lord High Admiral Lincoln respecting a voyage of discovery" shows not so much the geographical ignorance of the petitioners, as their shrewd sense of international warfare. This document asks permission to make discoveries in

any landes Islandes and Countries southewarde beyonde the oequinoctial or where the Pole Antartik, hath anie elevation aboue the Horizon, provided these areas are found to be unoccupied by any Christian power, arguing that

the seas and passages as farre as Bresyle, Magelane streightes and the Portugals navigacion to the Moluccas wch all do lie beyonde the zona torrida

are practical.

The aptnesse and as hit were a fatall Convenience [are] that since the Portugale hathe attained one parte of the newfound worlde to the Este: the Spaniardes an other to the weste, the frenche the thirde to the northe; nowe the fourthe to the southe is by gods providence lefte for Englonde, to whome the others in tymes paste haue fyrste ben offred.

Excellent as the providential argument might be, the purpose of exploring the southern end of South America was rather the breaking into Iberian trade, since, besides the "lyklihode of bringinge in grete treasure of golde sylver and pearle into this relme," not to speak of other commodities,

the encrese of the quantitie of golde and sylver that shalbe brought owte of Spaine it self into Englonde when the Commodities comming out of Spaine, by comminge this waie cheper, and so lesse countervaylinge the valewe of o^r clothes caried thyther, the ouerplus shall come more plentyfully hither in treasure.[66]

And how little English interest in the New World was concerned with colony-making and how much it was concerned with seizing any possible bottlenecks for Oriental commerce is interestingly shown by a project dating from about 1580 for seizing and fortifying the Straits of Magellan, the fortifiers to be pirates in English pay!

To the straightes of Magellane may be sent Clerke the pyrott vppon promise of pardon, and to culler the matter he maye goo as of him selfe and not with the countenance of thenglishe state; . . . the Symerones, a people detesting the prowde gouernment of the Spaniardes, will easely be transported by Drake or others of our nation to the straightes, and there may be planted by hundreds or thowsandes, as many as we shall require, and these shall easely be induced to live subiect to the gentle gouernment of the English and to be planted there for the defence of the straightes.

In fact, by employing a few good captains and a few stout ships

there is no doute but that we shall make subject to England all the golden mynes of Peru, and all the Coste and tract of that firme of America vppon the sea of Sur yet not fortefied, and worke the like effect on the hither side of that firme. And for the spaniarde, both for his breedinge in a hote region and for his delicacie in dyett and lodginge, he shall not be able to endure in the coldness of that Climate of the straight.

The projector advocated sending "condemned englishemen and women," if necessary, to hold the straits, who, even if they "there would aspire to gouernmentes of themselues," were preferable to Iberian domination whereby

the spaniard should withe the treasure of that Cuntrie torment all the Cuntries of Europe with warres and practises, as he hathe and will doe if it be not foreseen in tyme.[67]

In fact, so firmly fixed in men's minds was the idea that smashing Spain was more important than planting settlements, that the great stage hero of the epoch, so far as the fame of adventurousness was concerned, was not some founder of colonies, but Sir Francis Drake, whose voyage around the world was intended not only as a raid upon Peru but also as a means of getting into touch with Oriental potentates.[68]

In sum, it was not until the eighties of the sixteenth century that schemes for founding plantations become important, and even then they are subordinate to the larger aim of defeating Spain.[69] To break the power of that empire it was not so necessary that Virginia and New England be settled as it was that military and naval possession be taken of convenient ports and islands. Even before the settlement of Jamestown there were determined efforts to found an English colony in Guiana; and after the settlement of Jamestown both this effort and the endeavor to found a settlement at the mouth of the Amazon which would seal that river against the Spaniards persisted.[70] In fact, almost until the end of the reign of James I, Guiana seemed a more promising location for a settlement than Virginia.[71] Meanwhile the conquest of Bermuda (1609; chartered in 1615) and of the West Indies went steadily forward—St. Christopher in 1624, Nevis in 1628, Montserrat and Antigua in 1632. In 1627 colonists occupied Barbados, which, by 1640, had a population of 18,000; by the end of the seventeenth century British imports from Barbados were worth ten times the imports from New England.[72] If Virginia had thus to compete for attention with South America and Barbados, Massachusetts Bay had to compete with Providence Island and other islands off the Mosquito Coast as a refuge for Puritans.[73] At one time Guiana had been proposed as a place for the Pilgrims.[74]

Had the energetic English moved as directly from discovery to colony-making as did the Spaniards and the Portuguese, the whole history of the colonial impulse might have been different. In that event an immediate territorial conquest by the power of the crown might have swiftly over-run the mainland of North America, and the whole legal and intellectual foundation of the colonies would have differed from what actually took historic shape. In that event English colonization might have resembled that of Spain. Rivalry with Spanish, Portuguese, and French there might have been, but it would have been a rivalry in time for the over-running of an empty land—or at least a land having only its "natural" inhabitants. In place of a series of amorphous and even anarchic little settlements clinging to the Atlantic coast, it is at least conceivable that plans of continental dimension analogous to the Spanish development might have been enforced.

But the English development came slowly; it came not

merely because of over-population, religious expansion, or the search for freedom directly, but only after the lapse of a fateful century, during which England had been almost crushed by the might of the Iberian empire. In place of rivalry with the Spanish being a function of colonization, colonization became a function of rivalry with the Spanish for the trade of the world. Instead of military conquests, mercantile companies were to be the principal instrument of settlement. Instead of launching out into a brave new world, Englishmen were expected miraculously to catch up with, and surpass, the deeds of the Spaniards, the Portuguese, and the French. Having failed in Ireland, they were somehow supposed to succeed in North America. They were to save the souls of Indians not so much from the wiles of Satan as from the wiles of Spain. In short, an outburst of energy more characteristic of Elizabethan England than of the Jacobean age was, on the one hand, to surpass anything the Elizabethans had done, and, on the other hand, to do all that the Tudors had failed to do. The setting of the colonial impulse in the perspective of time is therefore one of the most important aspects of the problem.

5

AMERICAN PROSE STYLE: 1700–1770 *

STYLE is an instrument of thought. It is curious, however, that historians of ideas in America have shown almost no curiosity as to the origins of our prose *qua* prose. Yet, that we have a national prose is patent. It is characteristically marked by a sinewy and simple syntax, swift rhythmic periods, brilliant informality of manner, and freshness (often degenerating into the grotesque) of figure and diction. These qualities tend to differentiate prose here from prose in Great Britain. To be sure, as one works upward along the stream of time, this difference is more difficult to formulate; thus, a critic like Poe reads in his magazine articles like Lord Macaulay. Nevertheless, even in Poe's time one is haunted by the sense that this is American, not British, writing, and though the quintessence of that style is elusive, hesitantly present, and mocking in its ironic duplicity, it is usually there.

A similar differentiation appears even in the eighteenth century. The speeches and state papers of men like Jefferson, Madison, Monroe, the two Adams's, Otis, Dickinson, and others are written in what I may call the revolutionary manner of public statement, and there is nothing in contemporary England quite to match it. Not Pitt, not Sheridan, not Burke, not even writers like Adam Smith or Jeremy Bentham possess the American tang. How did we come by it? One does not know; but because we are so uninformed about the development of prose style in the New World, it is important to record the eighteenth-century debate concerning style. And although even that debate descends from an earlier age, the

* 1934.

growth of the country in the eighteenth century makes that era important in the development of the American manner.

In 1700 the Rev. Cotton Mather sent to England that huge mass of manuscript which, after unauthorized changes by the printer,[1] was published in 1702 as the *Magnalia Christi Americana*. Because the manuscript was completed in 1700, it may be considered a seventeenth-century document; and I quote a passage from the "General Introduction" as an example of what New England practice in literary style had achieved by the year of Dryden's death:

I cannot say, whether the *Style,* wherein this *Church-History* is written, will please the Modern *Criticks:* But if I seem to have used ἁπλουστάτῃ συντάξει γραφῆς, a Simple, Submiss, Humble *Style,* 'tis the same that *Eusebius* affirms to have been used by *Hegesippus,* who, as far as we understand, was the first Author (after *Luke*) that ever composed an entire Body of *Ecclesiastical History,* which he divided into *Five Books,* and Entitled, ὑπομνήματα ατων εκκλησιαστικῶν πράξεων. Whereas *others,* it may be, will reckon the *Style* Embellished with too much of *Ornament,* by the multiplied References to other and former Concerns, closely couch'd, for the Observation of the *Attentive,* in almost every Paragraph; but I must confess, that I am of his mind who said, *Sicuti sal modice cibis aspersus Condit, & gratiam saporis addit, ita si paulum Antiquitatis admiscueris, Oratio fit venustior.* And I have seldom seen that Way of Writing faulted, but by those, who, for a certain odd Reason, sometimes find fault, *That the Grapes are not ripe.* These *Embellishments* (of which yet I only—*Veniam pro laude peto*) are not the puerile Spoils of *Polyanthea's;* but I should have asserted them to be as choice *Flowers* as most that occur in Ancient or Modern Writings, almost unavoidably putting themselves into the Authors Hand, while about his Work, if those words of *Ambrose* had not a little frightened me, as well as they did *Baronius, Unumquemque Fallunt sua scripta.* I observed that Learned Men have been so terrified by the Reproaches of *Pedantry,* which little Smatterers at Reading and Learning have, by their *Quoting Humours* brought upon themselves, that, for to avoid all Approaches towards that which those Feeble Creatures have gone to imitate, the best way of Writing has been most injuriously deserted. But what shall we

71

say? The Best way of Writing, under Heaven, shall be the Worst, when *Erasmus* his Monosyllable Tyrant will have it so!²

Despite Mather's reference to a "Simple, Submiss, Humble *Style*," most readers will regard this passage as learned and even pedantic. The thoroughly seventeenth-century flavor of the paragraph is evident; the profusion of capital letters, italic type, and Greek and Latin quotations, the learned references to Eusebius, Hegesippus, Baronius, and the rest, the wordplay on *polyanthea* and *flower,* the defense of learned citations, and the reference to "*Erasmus* his Monosyllable Tyrant"—all these devices suggest the manner of the prose leviathans from before the flood. From Cotton Mather's point of view, the *Magnalia* was his diploma piece to posterity.

Let me now quote from another, and more familiar, piece of American prose, written seventy-one years after Cotton Mather sent his bulky manuscript to London. The passage is from Franklin's *Autobiography* as reprinted by Bigelow, and is one of the most familiar in that classic work:

About this time I met with an odd volume of the *Spectator*. It was the third. I had never before seen any of them. I bought it, read it over and over, and was much delighted with it. I thought the writing excellent, and wished, if possible, to imitate it. With this view I took some of the papers, and, making short hints of the sentiment in each sentence, laid them by a few days, and then, without looking at the book, try'd to compleat the papers again, by expressing each hinted sentiment at length, and as fully as it had been expressed before, in any suitable words that should come to hand. Then I compared my *Spectator* with the original, discovered some of my faults, and corrected them. But I found I wanted a stock of words, or a readiness in recollecting and using them, which I thought I should have acquired before that time if I had gone on making verses; since the continual occasion for words of the same import, but of different length, to suit the measure, or of different sound for the rhyme, would have laid me under a constant necessity of searching for variety, and also have tended to fix that variety in my mind, and make me master of it. Therefore I took some of the tales and turned them into verse;

and, after a time, when I had pretty well forgotten the prose, turned them back again. I also sometimes jumbled my collections of hints into confusion, and after some weeks endeavored to reduce them into the best order, before I began to form the full sentences and compleat the paper. This was to teach me method in the arrangement of thoughts. By comparing my work afterwards with the original, I discovered my faults and amended them; but I sometimes had the pleasure of fancying that, in certain particulars of small import, I had been lucky enough to improve the method or the language, and this encouraged me to think I might possibly in time come to be a tolerable English writer, of which I was extremely ambitious.[3]

With Franklin it is obvious we are in the full tide of the best eighteenth-century prose. Truly, this is an astonishing change from the *Magnalia,* a change the more remarkable when one remembers that it took place in less than three-quarters of a century, under the conditions of American provincial life—the relative lack of general education, the want of books and periodical literature, the distance from London, and the fact that there was in eighteenth-century America no assured place for a professional literary man. So remarkable a revolution in style requires more detailed explanation than the happy accident of an ambitious young printer finding an odd volume of the *Spectator.* The purpose of this paper, therefore, is to trace certain aspects of the development of prose style in the American colonies in the period between Cotton Mather and Benjamin Franklin. The material offered in evidence is largely drawn from the Wilberforce Eames collection of pamphlets in the Huntington Library.[4]

In one sense the change is easy to explain. The American colonies were part of the eighteenth-century world. They were part of the literary empire of Great Britain; and naturally, as intercourse between the two continents expanded, as the colonial booksellers imported more and more books, the change in prose style in London would have its effect in America. We know that the periodical essays which multiplied with the expansion of the colonial press were almost invariably modeled upon the *Spectator* and kindred works. We know that books and pamphlets by colonial authors were sometimes first printed in the mother country, and often reprinted there; whence it follows that, to be effective at all, the colonial author would have to write within the canons of the polite world of English letters.

But let us assume for a moment a condition contrary to fact. Let us suppose that American intellectual life had been cut off from Europe. Let us suppose it to have remained more or less static, so that the attitude of mind commonly associated with the Mathers persisted throughout our colonial history. The American author would not then have been able to address the eighteenth-century British public in its own terms unless he could master what would have been from his point of view a foreign and artificial idiom. If one can imagine Robert Burton trying to write a pamphlet which would please the taste of Lord Chesterfield, one can see how painful the situation might have been. Of course, nothing of the kind took place. American prose developed on its own line, strongly influenced, of course, by British theory and practice; and it is to certain elements in this development that we now turn.

Styles of expression do not customarily change except in response to changing demands upon language, due to the necessity of expressing new ideas and new aesthetic ideals. The researches of scholars have made us aware of the great debate over the structure of prose in seventeenth-century England. This debate was a function of new artistic ideals and of the rise of a new scientific ideology. Properly to trace the change in colonial prose one should begin by tracing the rise of new intellectual forces in the colonies; but, since to do this would require a detailed essay on the history of colonial culture, one can at this time only indicate certain facets of the changing theories. And, putting aside many really eloquent passages in seventeenth-century American prose, I shall

74

assume that the movement of progress is the movement in the direction of plainness and lucidity—in the direction which Franklin represents.

Those who think of the colonial sermon as mainly a pedantic exercise in casuistry may be surprised to learn that one of the powerful forces making for the new prose in America was the colonial pulpit itself. Those, however, who are familiar with the work of Mitchell and Miss Richardson [5] will be interested to discover that the movement for simplicity in the British pulpit is paralleled in America.[6] The movement of lucidity was a revolt from two sorts of encumbrances upon "plain teaching": one being learned quotation, pedantic discussion, and superfluous erudition, and the other being ornate rhetoric, euphuism, "witty" preaching, and fantastic style. In Great Britain the movement of lucidity was complicated by the struggle between Ciceronian and Senecan prose, sectarian differences carried into styles of preaching, and the struggle between theology and the "new" science. Fortunately for the investigator, the American situation was simpler. Cotton Mather seems to have been the only important colonial aware of the difference between Ciceronian and Senecan prose; sectarian differences play little part in the development of a simpler preaching style in the colonies; and we shall do little injustice to the facts if we assume that the American problem was to create from the general syntactical complexities and diffuse ornament of seventeenth-century prose the plain and lucid manner of writing which distinguishes the style of the great Revolutionary leaders.

Neglecting other points of difference, we may say that Calvinism demanded a learned ministry, and that, in the selection from Cotton Mather already given, one sees the learned manner in America at its best—or worst. The first point to note is that pressure was soon brought to bear upon the colonial divine to distinguish between the ornate scholasticism with which he might properly address his learned peers, and the perspicuous and simple language in which he was expected to "teach." We may illustrate from Increase Mather. In 1674 he published a group of sermons entitled *Some Important Truths about Conversion*.[7] The famous John Owen contributed a preface, in which he said that

> Whatever else the Author aimed at, it is evident that *plainness, perspicuity, gravity* in delivering the Truth, were continually in his eye; nor hath he come short of attaining his Design. . . . he hath in this Discourse abandoned all Additional Ornaments whatever.

Of his father's preaching Cotton Mather said in the *Parentator:*

> He much despised what they call *Quaintness,* . . . Though he were such a *Scholar,* yet his *Learning* hindred not his Condescension to the Lowest and Meanest Capacity: aiming to shoot not over the *Heads,* but into the *Hearts,* of the Hearers. He was very careful to be *understood,* and *concealed* every other *Art,* that he might Pursue and Practise that one *Art* of *Being Intelligible.*[8]

Both quotations point to the ideal of plainness and simplicity; and that they are not due merely to ministerial propaganda or filial piety, that the ideal is Increase Mather's own, is evident from his *A Call from Heaven To the Present and Succeeding Generations* (Boston, 1679), in the preface to which the elder Mather says:

> As for the ensuing *Discourse,* if the Reader expect any thing rare, or curious therein, he will find himself disappointed. I neither can if I would, nor am I willing to doe what I can, in such a way. I would rather let the world see, that I am of *Luthers* judgement, who judged him the ablest Preacher, *qui pueriliter, trivialiter, populariter, simplicissimè docet.* And it is a comfort to think, that such *Simple Discourses,* which they that account themselves the Wits of the World, look upon as *Babling,* will either be blessed by Christ for the Conversion and Edification of Souls, or turn for a Testimony to the Speaker.[9]

But why, it may be asked, with this paternal precept before him, did Cotton Mather write the preface to the *Magnalia* as he did? The younger Mather consciously practised two distinct prose styles, one which he greatly admired and thought worthy as the expression of his culture, and one which the conditions of "teaching" compelled him to adopt. He regretted, says his biographer and kinsman, the Rev. Samuel Mather, that

> *those Composures he wrote with the least Trouble and Care, found a Passage into the World, while many of his elaborate Composures lay by him.*[10]

But, though he regretted the fact, he wrote at times according to the demands of the day. The prose style of the "Political Fables" is like that of Franklin. Many pages of the *Magnalia* are relatively simple and straightforward. In one of his works he acknowledges that the best preacher is he who

> accommodates the Truths of the Gospel, unto his Hearers, that even the *Little Children* may *mind* them when they hear them, and grow sensible of them.[11]

He could, on occasion, refer contemptuously to those *"Insipid"* passages "which the Funeral Orations on the Professors in the Universities are commonly Stuffed withal." [12] When he wrote this plain kind of prose, its note is commonly moral earnestness; and the conflict between his desire to do good and his desire in such *"Composures"* to exhibit all his skill as a penman, is amusingly shown in a passage from the *Essays to Do Good:*

> I don't find that I have spent so many Weeks in Composing the Book, as *Descartes,* tho' a Profound *Geometrician,* declares he spent in Studying the Solution of one *Geometrical Question.* Yet the Composure is grown beyond what I desired it should have done; . . . Tis a Vanity in Writers, to Complement the Readers, with a, *Sorry 'tis no better.* Instead of *that,* I freely tell my Readers,

77

I have Written what is not unworthy of their Perusal. If I did not
Think so, truly, I would not Publish it.[18]

As an artist and a scholar, however, Cotton Mather preferred
the ornate style. Speaking of his ancestor, John Cotton, he
says admiringly that he was

One whose *Consecration* was *the Filling of His Hand,* and whose
Composures all *Smelt of the Lamp;* [14]

and he remembered with pleasure the "copious and florid
Oration" [15] which Urian Oakes delivered at Mather's college
commencement. Consequently, Mather was perpetually running counter to the current of his time, and so putting his
biographers in a difficult position. A year after the great man's
death, the Rev. Samuel Mather wrote that

we need not wonder to find in his Books so *many learned Allusions* and *References;* for it is next to impossible, that a Man
should keep from *writing learnedly,* and as if he were acquainted
with Author's and their Sentiments, when his Mind is stored with
their *various Ideas* and Images, and he is a compleat *Owner* of
them.

Family pride compelled the Rev. Samuel to enter a defense
of this aspect of his kinsman's style:

There are indeed a Set of *Witlings,* who for Fear of *Pedantry,*
and hurting a Period, would not quote a *Greek* or *Latin* Sentence,
however weighty and pregnant it may be; but, instead of the
massy Sense in the Expressions of *others,* chuse *their own easy
Flow of Words, and gliding Vacuity of Tho't.*

He describes Mather's treatises as *"stuck with Jewels,"* though
"not *burthen'd* with them: . . . a strong & easy *Splendor."* [16]
But even family pride could not prevent the biographer from
hinting that there might be "a Fault in endeavouring and
straining for far fetch'd, and *dear bought* Hints, and *cram-
ming* a Discourse with them." [17] This reluctant criticism is
evidence how far the revolution in taste had gone.

Two years before his death Cotton Mather published his *Manuductio ad Ministerium,* a book of directions for the young minister. In this occurs a digression on prose style, the full implications of which have not, I think, been pointed out. The gist of the passage lies in Mather's attempt to reconcile opposites: to fuse the later demand for a plain and easy style with his own belief that the way of the artist in prose is the older manner of the seventeenth century. He was, I think, attempting to find a golden mean between the manner of the new century, which he rather disliked, and the manner of the old century, which his contemporaries were reluctant to continue. Accordingly, one finds him advising the young preacher to study French because

There is no Man who has the *French Tongue,* but ordinarily he speaks the neater *English* for it;

and directing the candidate:

Instead of Squandering away your Time, on the RHETORIC, whereof no doubt, you tho't, your *Dugard* [18] gave you enough at School; . . . My Advice to you, is, That you observe the Flowers and Airs of such *Writings,* as are most in Reputation for their *Elegancy.*

Like Swift, he repudiates textbooks in logic because "The Power and Process of *Reason* is *Natural* to the Soul of Man"; and the direction to try one's hand at a (verse) epigram to "polish your *Style*" is like Franklin's turning prose into verse for the same purpose.[19] The notes of elegance and rationalism in this part of the program are, so to speak, eighteenth-century; and Mather's directions so far make for the new prose.

But the discussion of style itself is soon seen to waver between the two ideals; and Mather's desire is clearly to save as much of the older elaborate and learned manner as he can, and at the same time satisfy the newer ideals:

There has been a deal of ado about a STYLE; So much, that I must offer you my Sentiments upon it. There is a *Way of Writing,*

79

wherein the Author endeavours, that the Reader may have *something to the Purpose* in every Paragraph. There is not only a *Vigour* sensible in every *Sentence*, but the Paragraph is embellished with *Profitable References*, even to something beyond what is *directly spoken*. Formal and Painful *Quotations* are not studied; yet all that could be learnt from them is insinuated. The Writer pretends not unto *Reading*, yet he could not have writ as he does if he had not *Read* very much in his Time; and his Composures are not only a *Cloth of Gold*, but also stuck with as many *Jewels*, as the Gown of a Russian Embassador.[20]

Vigor in the sentences and something to the purpose in every paragraph are ideals to which Franklin would subscribe, and the art that insinuates information is certainly not to be despised. But Mather goes on to strike out at modern critics of the older style:

This *Way of Writing* has been decried by many, and is at this Day more than ever so, for the same Reason, that in the old Story, the *Grapes* were decried, *That they were not Ripe*. A Lazy, Ignorant, Conceited Sett of Authors, would perswade the whole Tribe, to lay aside that *Way of Writing*, for the same Reason that one would have perswaded his Brethren to part with the Encumbrance of their *Bushy Tails*. But however *Fashion* and *Humour* may prevail, they must not think that the Club at their *Coffee-House* is, *All the World*; but there will always be those, who will in this Case be governed by *Indisputable Reason*: And who will think, that the real Excellency of a Book will never ly in *saying of little*; That the less one has for his Money in a Book, 'tis really the more Valuable for it; and that the less one is instructed in a Book, and the more of Superfluous *Margin*, and Superficial *Harangue*, and the less of *Substantial Matter* one has in it, the more tis to be accounted of.

He carries the war into Africa in the following passage:

The Blades that set up for *Criticks*, I know not who constituted or commission'd 'em!—they appear to me, for the most part as *Contemptible*, as they are a *Supercilious* Generation. For indeed no Two of them have the same *Style*; . . . But while each of them, conceitedly enough, sets up for the *Standard of Perfection*, we are entirely at a Loss which *Fire* to follow. Nor can you easily find any one thing wherein they agree for their *Style,* except perhaps a perpetual Care to give as Jejune and Empty Pages, without such *Touches of Erudition* . . . as may make the Discourses less *Tedious,* and more *Enriching,* to the Mind of him that peruses them.

So far Mather seems to defend the older manner, but now he returns to an awareness of new standards, and the necessity of yielding something to them:

Every Man will have his own *Style,* which will distinguish him as much as his *Gate:* And if you can attain to that which I have newly described, but always writing so as to give an *Easy Conveyance* unto your *Idea's,* I would not have you by any *Scourging* be driven out of your *Gate,* . . . since every Man will have his own Style, I would pray, that we may learn to treat one another with mutual *Civilities,* and *Condescensions,* and handsomely *indulge* one another in this, as *Gentlemen* do in other Matters.[21]

In other words, if the moderns argue that every man should follow his natural *"Gate"* in choosing a style, Mather sees no reason why the same indulgence should not be extended to him!

The *Manuductio* contains, I think, the most interesting single passage on style in eighteenth-century America before Franklin's *Autobiography*. It reveals Mather as a transition figure who sought to unite the ideal of *"Easy Conveyance"* of ideas with the ideal of *"Substantial Matter"* bejeweled like "the Gown of a Russian Embassador." But it was a compromise which could not be successful; and the necessity of instructing young ministers how to teach the people was, ironically enough, the very force which defeated it. Samuel Mather noted in 1729 that Cotton Mather

did not make his *Sentences* or Periods too extended for the [shorthand] *Writers* to take them readily, or for the *Hearers* readily and easily to have the sence of them,[22]

when he preached; but the Reverend Thomas Prince was probably nearer the truth when he remarked that Cotton

Mather's *"Style* . . . was something singular, and not so agreable to the Gust of the Age," though he hastened to add that "like his *manner of speaking,* it was very *emphatical."* [23] At any rate, a long line of ordination sermons insists upon the need for the easy conveyance of ideas, but fails to insist upon the desirability of a style incrusted with verbal jewels.

For example, the Rev. John Tucker of Newbury, inducting the Rev. Edmund Noyes into the pastoral care of the First Church in Salisbury, advised him that, the business of ministers being to instruct the ignorant,

they should be well acquainted with Language; and able to use those Forms of Speech which are *most expressive* of what's intended, as well as *suited* to the Capacities of their Hearers. I am sensible, indeed, that such is the odd Turn of some Men's Minds, that they are never *better pleased,* nor think themselves *more edified,* than when they hear what they *do not* understand. . . . the surest Way to gain the Applause of such, is for the Preacher, at least frequently to use the most obscure Terms, and talk *very unintelligibly.*

Mr. Tucker also thought that ministers should avoid

a low grov'ling Stile, . . . as it *disgusts* the Minds even of common Hearers, and brings *Contempt* upon this sacred Office.—Wisdom here, and that Skill in Language, a Preacher of the Gospel must be suppos'd to have, will direct to the *happy Mean* between these two Extreams.[24]

The *"happy Mean"* of the Rev. Mr. Tucker is, however, a mean between colloquialism and elegance, and not between the easy conveyance of ideas and a bejeweled splendor.

Two years later the Rev. Samuel Phillips addressed a convention of ministers in Boston in very similar language, and told them that they should speak plainly:

'Their Style and Language may not be either vainly nice, or meanly negligent, but manly and grave,' and suitable to the Capacity of the Hearers in general, lest they darken, instead of

82

explaining, the Counsels of God. . . . Ministers of the Gospel shou'd beware of wrapping up the Truths of God's Word in dark and uncertain Expressions, which may be interpreted diverse Ways.[25]

In 1755 the great Jonathan Mayhew, publishing a volume of fourteen sermons, said:

. . . I have conceived, That the end of speaking, especially of preaching, was to express, not to disguise, a man's real sentiments: Tho' I know that I, herein, differ from many of my own Order![26]

But if there were "many of my own Order" who held contrary ideals, they certainly were not vocal about them; on the contrary, the emphasis is almost uniformly upon plainness and lucidity. In the same year the Rev. Ebenezer Gay, at the ordination of the Rev. Mr. Smith into "The Work of the Gospel Ministry, in Sharon," told him it should be the concern of preachers

to speak in a clear and distinct Manner, and to adapt their Discourse and Language to the Understanding of Men, and the Capacities of their Hearers. . . . Ministers should . . . in their *Pulpit Discourses,* study *Plainness of Speech;* not, indeed, in Opposition to that which is correct, decent, graceful, nervous, and pungent, but to that which is obscure, lofty and unintelligible, loose and incoherent.[27]

The previous year the Rev. Marston Cabot, a great believer in Greek, Latin, and Hebrew, inducting young Mr. Brown into the pulpit in Kellingley, thought that there were many tropes, such as metaphors, metonymies, ironies, and hyperboles in Scripture, for which a knowledge of grammar is necessary, but he would use logic only

for analysing, defining, dividing, and [achieving] more clear and fair resolution of a Text; Also, for Argumentation and defence of the Truth against an Adversary. Tho a curious trifling and playing with words in a Pulpit is vain, yet it is the part of a skilful Teacher, to order, methodize and distribute truth in it's proper place.[28]

"Cast your publick Discourses," wrote the Rev. Samuel Buell a year later,

into the most regular and becoming Scheme; observe a steady Strain of Thought, good Connection, and natural Transitions through the Whole of them; while you make Use of Art to conceal Art, and endeavour to avoid antiquated multiferious Divisions, and the dry Exactness of metaphysical Accuracy of Distinctions: Labour also to avoid meer loose Harangue, and a confus'd Huddle of Words, shuffl'd together in a wild and incoherent Manner. Let so much of distinct Method be observable to your Auditory, (at least to the Judicious) as that they may be able to commit to the Memory, the main Branches of your Discourse, or the leading Point in View; least nothing be fix'd in the Mind for after-Improvement, and the Sermon be lost as soon as heard: Good Order hath Power and Beauty in it. Let your Stile and Diction be correct, masculine, nervous and striking; make use of such Words and Phrases, as will exhibit the most clear and bright Ideas of Truth, and answer the best Purposes. There is a Plainness, Simplicity, and Majesty of Speech that is most useful, beautiful, and most acceptable also, to the Bulk of our Auditory. Dress not up divine and glorious Truths, in a coarse and contemptible Garb; nor give them such Polish and Ornament, as does not conduce to their Usefulness: Remember you are a Preacher of the Gospel of him, who was the crucified Jesus; and that your Stile must be so far crucified as to be level to the Capacities of the Unlearned and Unskilful: Let not your Stile affect the Pomp and Magnificence of the Theatre, since that is inconsistent with that Gravity which becomes the Pulpit.[29]

That the movement for plainness and lucidity was not confined to the non-Anglican faiths is evident when one discovers the Rev. William Smith of Pennsylvania condemning before a body of Episcopal clergymen those

who, in their Preaching, betray a marvellous Littleness of Genius, and Barrenness of matter. They are ever upon minute distinctions, Party-Shibboleths, perplexing definitions, and nice modes;

and he compares such ministers to scientific smatterers, and says their preaching is usually attended "with Revilings and

Cursings and Anathemas against all others differing the least from them in persuasion, . . ." [30] This was in 1762. The Rev. Samuel Mather, in a sermon preached to the annual convocation of ministers in Boston in May of that year, was saying much the same thing, advocating the diligent preparation of sermons and the careful choice of sound words in which to deliver them to the people.[31]

Two years later, in one of the longest discussions of prose and preaching among the ordination sermons, the Rev. Samuel West of Dartmouth supported the same doctrine:

To abound in too luxuriant and affected a diction, and to run into scholastick niceties, is far from being a likely method to promote the knowledge of christianity, . . . Too much paint and varnish hinder the truths of the gospel from shining out in their genuine lustre and brightness.

West defines a variety of false styles:

. . . such is an affected diction, abounding with *great swelling words of vanity,* and those pompous high-flown metaphors, which under the pretence of containing some very sublime mysteries and profound sense, are only a jingle and play of words.

This, he says, "is the common fault of enthusiasts, and men of too warm an imagination." Equally one should avoid

mere addresses to the passions; without taking any care to inform the judgment and understanding: . . . to set their [the hearers'] passions to work when the judgment and understanding are not convinced; is only a turning religion into a mere piece of mechanism.

Preachers who do so are

not endowed with understanding and common sense. The same may be said of those who abound in nice and refined speculations; such as barren points of controversies, dry and critical observations, or philosophical disquisitions, or any refinements in divinity,

85

which do not level to the capacities of the hearers. . . . How many will contend with the utmost earnestness about a parcel of nice scholastick phrases, as if they were the grand points of religion, when either they are only about a set of vague and insignificant terms, being words without ideas, or mere verbal contentions; or if there is any real difference, 'tis meerly speculative, and such as does not affect practice, or else about something left doubtful and ambiguous in scripture, or of such a nature, that we have not faculties sufficient to determine on which side the truth lies, or at most of but small importance to religion and the souls of men: yet these are often contended for, in such an ill-natured and unchristian manner, as greatly to disturb the peace of churches.[32]

In truth, the business of the pulpit was increasingly held to be pastoral rather than controversial. Said the Rev. Jason Haven at North Yarmouth that same summer:

The faithful and judicious preacher will not affect any great pomp and parade of language; sensible that these serve rather to amuse the mind, and please the fancy, than to convey the weighty truths of the gospel, with life and energy to the heart. . . . A plain easy and familiar style; free from a vain flourish of words, on the one hand; and a slovenly incorrectness, on the other, seems most agreable to the nature of the gospel, and most conformable to the example of inspired writers. . . . It is not the business of the public teacher to seek to discover any new truths, or doctrines, but to collect, adjust and range, in an instructive order, those which lie scattered with a noble profusion, in the sacred scriptures: just as the skilful gardiner is not expected to form any new plant or flower, but to place in a beautiful order and symmetry, those which are sown, in a beautiful disorder, by the God of nature. . . . His sermons should not resemble those cabinets, which are stored with useless rarities, and curious amusements.[33]

Avoid, counsels the Rev. Edward Barnard the following year,

whatever being sordid and boisterous offends the judicious, or that excess of the florid stile, and theatrical action, which by tickling the fancy, and captivating the eye, make an audience forgetful of their solid business.[34]

86

And Andrew Eliot writes in 1766:

I have greatly wondered, when I have heard ministers distinguish and refine, till they have lost both themselves and their hearers; . . . Abstract reasoning is seldom of use in the pulpit, because but few can understand it, and no man can profit by a discourse he doth not understand.[35]

A biography of Nathanael Hooker, published in 1770, remarks that Hooker's pulpit style

was bright and lively, somewhat of the *imagery,* always natural, striking, and to the purpose. He had a peculiar talent to raise striking images in the mind. He knew how to paint things very much to the life; could rouse the passions, and raise the affections; and at the same time his stile and composition were calculated to enlighten the understanding.

The biographer calls him one of the best preachers and one of the "most excellent sermonizers at this day."[36]

Said John Hunt in 1772:

[Sermons must be] calculated to command a close attention, to strike the conscience, to warm and affect the heart,

and therefore

scholastic niceties, and a fine spun thread of reasoning, ought never to be pressed into the service of the Pulpit, unless to . . . adjust some intricate dispute: But we must guard against the *opposite* extremes; pompous descriptions, bold images, and luxuriant flights of fancy, although they may feed the imagination, seldom convey wholesome food to the mind; . . . [Metaphors] resemble the windows in old Cathedrals, in which the painting keeps out the light.[37] Neither are we to endeavour to entertain our hearers with confused incoherent composition, and rambling excursions delivered in a low grovling style: We should beware of offering that to God which costs us nothing, . . .[38]

And the Rev. Samuel Locke remarked:

It is also a point which ought carefully to be attended to, by public teachers of religion, that they accommodate themselves, in language, images, and method, as well as in the depth of their argumentation, and refinement of their metaphors, to the capacities of their hearers.

Jesus "imitated . . . the dignity and simplicity, the uniformity and variety of nature" in the parables, and the minister should do the same.[39]

It would be possible to add quantitatively to the evidence adduced to illustrate the movement away from the ornate prose and intellectual subtleties of the seventeenth century to the plainer prose one associates with Benjamin Franklin. Enough, however, has appeared to show that the distance between the *Magnalia* and Franklin's *Autobiography* was not cleared in a single leap. On the contrary, this by no means exhaustive examination of colonial sermons reveals a continuing movement in the direction of a simple, dignified, and lucid style. The ministers achieved this style oftener than is realized; an examination of these forgotten pamphlets discovers an ordered intellectual substance, a command of dignified cadence, and an accuracy of diction which are part of that "plain easy and familiar style" that these ordination sermons, these discourses before bodies of the clergy, hold as ideals. Colonial congregations were critical of sermons; and there can be little doubt that the improvement of pulpit discourse in dignity, clearness, and simplicity accustomed colonial Americans to expect from their writers that easy command of language which places Franklin and Adams, Jefferson and Hamilton, among the great masters of political prose in the eighteenth century.

But there were ancillary tendencies as well. Not merely the desire to preach plainly, but also the desire to avoid controversy, is part of this movement. Popular historians of the period have succeeded in impressing the general reader with the idea that sectarian controversy in colonial America was continuous and bitter. Such views are colored by partisan accounts of episodes in Massachusetts history, like the persecution of the Quakers and the banishment of Roger Williams. Even better scholars do not always stop to realize that the Quakers who invaded seventeenth-century New England were persons of a different order from those pictured in song and story; and few have read enough of the Roger Williams controversy to realize that it was begun with reluctance and carried on with considerable courtesy on both sides.

What is more important for present purposes, however, is to remember that the leaders of seventeenth- and eighteenth-century New England saw with alarm the rise of theological controversy, and did what they could to check it by striving to discover its causes. One of these causes, as they soon learned, was the Idol of the Market Place, or at least of the theological market place. They learned the truth of Bacon's phrase: ". . . the ill and unfit choice of words wonderfully obstructs the understanding . . . words plainly force and overrule the understanding, and throw all into confusion and lead men away into numberless empty controversies and idle fancies." [40] And accordingly they sought, by clearness in writing, to avoid occasion for controversy.[41] It does not follow, of course, that because a man writes a complicated style he is a disputatious fellow; and I am aware that all who enter theological disputations protest their love of peace and charity, and find fault with their opponents' English. Nevertheless, between 1700 and 1775, one begins by and by to note an interesting correlation of two facts: the appeal for the avoidance of controversy or (viewed from its positive side) for toleration; and the appeal for a simple, lucid, and direct prose style. The colonials apparently came to the conclusion that in proportion as they avoided ambiguity of expression they would avoid controversy over meaning; and so the classical ideal of sweet reasonableness even in matters of religion has as its counterpart a decent propriety in diction and syntax.

This correlation is explicit or implicit in some of the citations

89

already included, but to make the matter perfectly clear let me return once more to Cotton Mather. We have seen him wavering between two styles in prose. Equally one sees him wavering between a greater or less degree of toleration. As his intolerant side has been sufficiently stressed by those who have discussed him, let me simply note that in 1717 one finds him expressing an ideal of reasonable toleration in religion:

A Man who is a Good *Neighbour,* and a Good *Subject,* has a *Right* unto his *Life* and the Comforts of it. It is not his being of this or that *Opinion* in *Religion,* but his doing something which directly tends to hurt *Humane Society,* by which this *Right* can be forfeited. And therefore, *Blasphemies,* and attempts to poison People with *Atheism,* come not into the Catalogue of Things that may sue for a *Toleration.* . . . But a Good *Neighbour,* and a Good *Subject,* has a claim to all his *Temporal Enjoyments* before he becomes a *Christian.* It is very odd, That he should lose his claim, from his embracing of *Christianity;* and because he does not happen to be a Christian of the *uppermost Party.* . . . For an *uppermost Party* of Christians, to punish Men in their *Temporal Enjoyments,* because in some *Religious Opinions* they *dissent* from them, or with an exclusion from the *Temporal Enjoyments,* which would justly belong unto them; 'Tis downright *Robbery.*[42]

It is not germane to the present point to argue whether Mather really meant what he said, or whether this is a piece of special pleading; the point is that the theory of reasonable toleration being thus established could not be easily destroyed. Incidentally, the next year, Mather gave practical force to his doctrine by saying in the course of his ordination sermon for a Baptist clergyman, the Rev. Elisha Callender:

How much *Gall* would be taken out of our *Ink,* if the *Maxims* of PIETY dictated what passes thro' our *Pens* into the World? . . . [Consider calmly] That on both sides, pleading for your *Different Sentiments,* you are to the best of your Judgments, but pleading the Cause of that very PIETY, which you are both *United* in. . . . I pray, we may not be so unnaturally Rude, as to treat churlishly the *Members* of that *Body,* into which all our comfort lies in our being *Incorporated?* [48]

Obviously the minister who preaches piety instead of theology is less likely to employ an involved style and less likely to fall into controversy than one who continues to sever and divide.

An example from secular life will illustrate the union of the desire to avoid controversy, and the ideal of a proper eighteenth-century style. When Thomas Cushing, speaker of the Massachusetts House of Representatives, died, the Rev. Thomas Prince preached the funeral sermon, in which he said that Cushing had been tolerant of every denomination of Protestants, and remarked that

He had a clear Voice, a lively and natural Way of Speaking, a proper Style, and in Affairs of Moment wou'd express Himself with decent Courage and a suitable Pathos. . . . when a *Point* of *Great Importance* laboured, and He was apprehensive of Hurt or Danger to the Publick . . . He would rise in Voice and Argument to a great Degree of noble Warmth:—But not so as to discompose Himself or disconcert his Views.[44]

In other words, Cushing kept to the ideal of a decent composure of mind and a decent composure in speech, and this is the ideal which was increasingly stressed as the century wore on.

Thus one finds the Rev. John Tucker insisting that young ministers should use

those Forms of Speech which are *most expressive* of what's intended, as well as *suited* to the Capacities of their Hearers,

and in the same sermon he pleads for the ending of sectarian controversy. If it is, he says, our duty and privilege in religious matters to investigate for ourselves,

shall we not allow *this Liberty* to *others,* and shew ourselves of a Catholic and Charitable Temper? Upon this free Enquiry, which every Christian has an undoubted Right to, . . . tho' we may hope Men will be generally agree'd in the *more in'tresting* and *important* Things of Religion, . . . yet as it cannot be expected but that in Matters of smaller Moment, there will be a *Diversity* of Sentiment, . . .[45]

If sectarian controversy abandoned this ideal of reasonableness in matter and tone, the clever debater scored heavily by pointing out the deficiency of his opponent. For example, during the controversy over the Anglican establishment in the colonies, the Rev. John Beach observed of his opponents' style:

. . . if, instead of offering the Reasons of our Opinions with Meekness, and speaking the Truth in Love, we use the most provoking and insulting Language we can invent, and rake every Dunghill to find Scandal to fling at our Adversaries, and care not whether it be true or false, so it be but spiteful and disgraceful, if instead of rectifying their Mistakes we try to blast the Reputation of those who differ from us, and represent them as hateful and ridiculous, as Men of no Conscience or Reason, and strain their Expressions to such an ill Sense as was never intended; though this kind of managing Controversy may make Sport for Fools, yet it must needs do a World of Mischief by *souring* Men's Tempers, and propagating Malice and Ill-Nature, which is the very Temper of the Devils; and so making Men much more the Children of Hell, than they would be, if they did remain ignorant of the Truth in Contest.[46]

For additional proof of the correlation between the doctrine of toleration and the ideal of simplicity in style, we have but to turn to that eminent controversialist, Jonathan Mayhew. We find him proclaiming in an anniversary sermon of 1754 that, good morals being the end of government,

Protection is, in justice, due to all persons indifferently, whose religion does not manifestly, and very directly, tend to the subversion of the government. . . . a general toleration, with this single exception, is so far from being pernicious to society, that it greatly promotes the good of it in many respects;[47]

and saying the next year that he has himself searched the Scriptures "without a zealous attachment to, or prejudice against, the opinions of Others," and that his theological doctrines are not disguised by any kind of artifice: They do not just peep thro' the mask of studied, equivocal, and ambiguous phrases; nor skulk in the dark, as it were from a consciousness of what they are, and a fear of being detected: . . . For I have conceived, That the end of speaking, especially of preaching, was to express, not to disguise, a man's real sentiments.[48]

The ideal of clarity led him to state that

It is infinitely dishonourable to the all-good and perfect Governor of the world, to imagine that he has suspended the eternal salvation of men upon any niceties of speculation;

or that any virtuous seeker for truth "shall be finally discarded because he fell into some erroneous opinions."[49]

Scorn all bigottry, party-spirit, and narrowness of mind in religious matters; and allow to all men that liberty herein, which you take yourselves, without hating or reviling them, merely because they differ from you in opinion,

he urges elsewhere—a sentiment the more remarkable because one finds it in a sermon *apropos* of the Boston earthquake of 1755.[50] Mayhew did not always live up to this standard of sweet reasonableness, of course; he was capable of addressing John Cleaveland in language like this:

Can you then possibly think it became you, an obscure person from another province, and one so unletter'd as you are; an outcast from the college to which you was a disgrace; for some time a rambling itinerant, and promoter of disorders and confusion among us; so raw and unstudied in divinity; one hardly ever heard of among us, but in the frequent reports of your follies and extravagances, . . . to turn author . . . ?[51]

But he could recognize good temper even in an Anglican, and say of an anonymous opponent that he was

doubtless a person of excellent sense, and an happy talent at writing; apparently free from the sordid, illiberal spirit of bigotry; one of a cool temper, and who often shews much candor; well acquainted with the affairs of the Society [for the Propagation of the Gospel], and, in general, a fair reasoner. . . . There is much good sense, good temper, candor and christian catholicism discovered in various parts of his Tract.[52]

Disputing with an Arian in 1757, the Rev. Aaron Burr introduces his argument with the following passage setting forth his ideal of controversial style:

The main End of Speaking and Writing (especially when any Thing of a religious Nature and Importance is the Subject) should be, to be thoroughly understood.—And this End (I am bold to affirm) is what I have aim'd at, how far soever I have miss'd it in what follows. . . . I have carefully avoided those labour'd Distinctions, Criticisms and Niceties, which tend to bewilder and confound, rather than in the least to instruct, by far the greater Part of Mankind; who are Strangers to scholastick Niceties, and the various Methods and Arts of Sophistry; and are often easily puzzled and imposed upon by the mere Charm of Words, which either have no Meaning at all, or the true Sense of which they never come at. What I have principally consulted is, to discover Truth; and express it in a Manner plain and intelligible, even to the lowest and most vulgar Capacity.[53]

So, too, the Rev. William Smith prefaces six discourses intended to advocate the Protestant religion and civil liberty, with the hope that

the Occasion will generally justify the Manner. He always endeavours to suit his language to the subject; and thinks he has no where offered to address the Passions, till he has first endeavoured to convince the Judgment.[54]

Three years later the Rev. Thomas Barnard was instructing the young minister that the wise pastor

will avoid Contentions and Censures respecting the jarring human Explications of any of the great Doctrines of the Gospel, of which tho' some Constructions must be false, yet all have by Turns been strove for with the bitterest Zeal. He will leave out of his Divinity, (that is his scriptural Divinity, which he is called to manifest) those abstruse Propositions, concerning GOD and his eternal Counsels, the Liberty of the human Conduct, the Influence of Matter upon Spirit,

for, if he writes or preaches upon these perplexed topics,

what Wonder, if instead of manifesting the Truth, he 'darken Counsel by Words without Knowledge'?

Let him follow the dictates of simplicity in style:

In Reasoning the Terms should be clear, precise and of a known Meaning; the Construction of Sentences, plain and unperplexed, as much as the Subject will allow. In relating Facts, the Manner should be simple, the Collection of the Evidence of them naturally arranged; [55] the Use to be made of them obvious. [56]

Refuting in nine sermons the errors of the Baptists, the Rev. Joseph Fish hoped he had been fair:

If I have, in any instance, mistaken *facts,* or misrepresented *persons* or *things,* (which is not impossible, though I am not conscious to my self that I have,) I desire it may be corrected, and hope it will be look'd upon and treated, as a simple, undesigned mistake. . . . [If there is] any one *expression* or *word,* in the following sheets, rightly understood and duly weigh'd, that so much as *savours* of a contrary spirit, it has escaped my notice—I condemn it, and desire it may be corrected: for I abhor such a spirit, towards my separate brethren.

But he adds, amusingly enough, "my provocations have been uncommonly great." [57]

The provocations of controversy are usually "uncommonly great," and I do not for a moment believe that the controversies, theological and political, which racked the colonies, were all conducted on the high plane of the ideal set forth in these passages. The Rev. Henry Caner in 1763 told Jonathan Mayhew that he observed "no measures of decency or good manners" in his writing, but sacrificed "the meek and gentle spirit of the Gospel to the gratification of a licentious and ungovern'd temper." [58] The Rev. John Beach described a pamphlet by the Rev. Mr. Hobart as "a bundle of . . . hideous and monstrous slanders." [59] No ideal is ever attained; and it would be naïve to pretend that when the Americans gave up seventeenth-century mannerism they therefore ceased to argue. Passages setting forth the newer ideal are naturally more casual in controversial writing than the passages in ordination sermons which instruct the young preacher how best to teach; and the newer ideal is sometimes implicit rather than explicit even in such passages. Nevertheless, when pamphlet after pamphlet suggests that the language of controversy shall be both perspicuous and good-tempered, when sermon after sermon declares that it is idle for the minister to indulge in

a long circumlocution, or series of argumentation, in various heads, observations, divisions and subdivisions, . . . [since] Such a method . . . rather tends to perplex and bewilder the minds of most readers,[60]

the conclusion seems irresistible that the spread of the feeling for tolerance (and good temper) has something to do with the spread of the feeling for style; and that the movement for classical clarity in diction is, in this respect, a function of the movement for the recognition of right reason. Certain it is that, among the fathers of the republic, none assailed his opponents with the personal invective which Milton and Salmasius lavished upon each other.

But it is not alone in this fashion that the new prose received support in theological quarters—it found proponents also among the historians of the colonial eighteenth century. Most of the controversies depend upon history for their facts; and the need of setting forth historic facts objectively was evident. As an ideal, objectivity is claimed by most historians, and sobriety of statement in historical matters is as old as American literature itself, the writings of Bradford and Winthrop owing much of their grave dignity to the desire of these authors worthily to record the truth of history. But it is one thing to have an ideal of objectivity in historical writing, and another to find the right style to body forth that ideal; and the confusion into which the seventeenth century sometimes fell is once more exemplified by Cotton Mather.

I have already quoted from the *Magnalia*. The most stupendous American historical work undertaken in the seventeenth century, Mather's masterpiece was intended, he says, to

Report the *Wonderful Displays* of His [God's] Infinite Power, Wisdom, Goodness, and Faithfulness, wherewith His Divine Providence hath *Irradiated* an *Indian Wilderness*.

Mather devotes considerable space to explaining what he proposes to write and how he proposes to write it. His ideal is, of course, impartiality:

'Tis true, I am not of the Opinion, that one cannot merit the Name of an *Impartial Historian*, except he write bare *Matters of Fact*, without all *Reflection;*

yet it is in the question of *"Reflection"* that the ambiguity lies.

I have not *Commended* any Person, but when I have really judg'd, not only *That* he *Deserved* it, but also that it would be a Benefit unto Posterity to know, Wherein he deserved it.

But wherein do the deserts of the deserving lie? His history is frankly a church history, a Protestant church history, written to a thesis, which he sets forth:

It may be, 'tis not possible for me to do a greater Service unto the Churches on the *Best Island* of the Universe, than to give a distinct Relation of those *Great Examples* which have been occurring among Churches of *Exiles*, that were driven out of that *Island*, into an horrible *Wilderness*, meerly for their being Well-willers unto the *Reformation*.[61]

His theory of history is that of Cicero: *"Historia est Testis temporum, Nuntia vetustatis, Lux veritatis, vita memoriæ, magistra vitæ."* His book is religious history teaching by example, and he summons up all his stylistic ingenuity worthily to present his great theme. He adduces Moses and twenty or thirty other writers to prove that history is important. He cites Polybius, Lucian, du Maury, Tacitus, Lipsius, Salmasius, Pope Zacharias, Schlusselbergius, Heylin, Chamier, and various other worthies to show how difficult it is to avoid praising good men and condemning bad ones. He refers to thirty or more authors while discussing the fact that he himself has not had sufficient time to write his history well; and he sprinkles his introduction liberally with learned citations and stylistic "quaintnesses," when he expresses the hope that he will not be too severely criticized and that his work will redound to the glory of Christ in America. As for the style, the passage with which this study began shows Mather pleading for the use of learning and decoration. Here is a second characteristic discussion:

Parve (sed invideo) ne me, Liber, ibis in Urbem.

Luther, who was himself owner of such an Heart, advised every Historian to get the *Heart of a Lion;* and the more I consider of the Provocation, which this our *Church-History* must needs give to that Roaring Lion, who has, through all Ages hitherto, been tearing the Church to pieces, the more occasion I see to wish my self a *Cœur de Lion.* But had not my Heart been Trebly Oak'd and Brass'd for such Encounters as this our History may meet withal, I would have worn the Silk-worms Motto, *Operitur dum Operatur,* and have chosen to have written *Anonymously;* or, as *Claudius Salmasius* calls himself *Walo Messalinus,* as *Ludovicus Molinæus* calls himself *Ludiomæus Colvinus,* as *Carolus Scribanius* calls himself *Clarus Bonarscius,* (and no less Men than *Peter du Moulin,* and Dr. *Henry More,* stile themselves, the one *Hippolytus Fronto,* the other *Franciscus Palaeopolitanus.*) Thus I would have tried, whether I could not have Anagrammatized my Name into some Concealment; or I would have referr'd it to be found in the second Chapter of the second Syntagm of *Selden de Diis Syris.* Whereas now I freely confess, 'tis COTTON MATHER that has written all these things;

Me, me, ad sum qui scripsi; in me convertite Ferrum.[62]

If the substance of the *Magnalia* scarcely suggests Gibbon, the style is equally remote from Goldsmith.

Less than a quarter of a century later, another clergyman, the Rev. Hugh Jones of Virginia, published a history of that commonwealth, entitled *The Present State of Virginia*. No contrast can be greater. None of the books about Virginia, says Jones, "descends to the present State and Circumstances of this Colony"; and because mankind entertains "very erroneous and monstrous Thoughts concerning the Country, Lives, Religion and Government of the *Virginians*," he has resolved to write:

I have industriously avoided the ornamental Dress of Rhetorical Flourishes, esteeming them unfit for the naked Truth of historical Relations, and improper for the Purpose of general Propositions.[63]

Three years afterward the Rev. Experience Mayhew, writing a series of biographical sketches of pious New England Indians, enunciates an equally simple standard of historic truth. The testimony in his book, he says, is

my own Fidelity and Concern for Truth in this Performance. . . . I have not in this History imposed on others any thing which I do not my self believe; [64]

and he has known the persons described, or has carefully inquired of reputable witnesses, or taken accounts of those who lived before his own time — from his father, his grandfather, or other worthy persons. Mayhew enunciates no theory of style, but it is striking that the biographies thus carefully guarded against error are plain and direct in manner. He was aided in this project by the Rev. Thomas Prince, who, in 1736, edited an edition of Mason's *Brief History of the Pequot War*, a book then a century old; a modern editor could not be more concise, clear, and direct than was Prince in this undertaking.

Prince was also the compiler of the invaluable *A Chronological History of New-England In the Form of Annals* (1736), the preface to which expresses his theory of historical writing; and the point for us is not his belief that Governor

Belcher will "take a noble and useful Pleasure" in the actions of his predecessors, but in the passage which follows:

It is the *orderly Succession* of these Transactions and Events, as they precisely fell out in Time, too much neglected by our Historians, that for some years past I have taken the greatest Pains to search and find, . . . not in the specious Form of a *proper History,* which admits of artificial Ornaments and Descriptions to raise the Imagination and Affections of the Reader; but of a *closer* and more naked REGISTER, comprizing only *Facts* in a *Chronological Epitome,* to enlighten the Understanding.[65]

This repudiation at once of history-teaching by example and of "artificial Ornaments and Descriptions" is the antithesis of Mather. It is followed by some charming paragraphs in which Prince tells how he got his materials, Chamberlain's account of the Cottonian Library having been the spark "Which excited in me a Zeal of laying hold on every Book, Pamphlet, and Paper . . . that have any Tendency to enlighten our History." "It is *Exactness* I aim at," he says, "and [I] would not have the least Mistake if possible pass to the World"; and, though "I am on the side of *pure Christianity,* as also of *Civil* and *Religious Liberty;* . . . I am for leaving every one to the *Freedom of Worshipping according to the Light of his Conscience;*" and above all, he hopes he is accurate.[66] The three ideals of a plain style, a reasonable toleration, and an exact historical method meet in Prince's volume.

Samuel Mather's *An Apology For the Liberties of the Churches in New England* (Boston, 1738) is, like Prince's *History,* written after a careful consultation of first-hand authorities, but Mather says nothing on the question of style.[67] A year later, John Callender's history of Rhode Island, one of the most impartial of all the colonial histories, furnishes us with another glimpse of the historian at work:

I hope there are few or no Errors in the Matters of Fact related, or the Dates that are assigned; to prevent any Mistakes, I have carefully reviewed the publick Records, and my other Mate-

rials; . . . I designed to have put all the Additions and Enlarge-
ments, in the Form of Notes for my own Ease, but have been
perswaded to weave as many of them as were proper into the
Body of the Discourse.

His model, he says frankly, is Prince, whose stylistic ideal to
avoid "artificial Ornaments and Descriptions" he obviously
shares.[68]

One of the most curious passages among the colonial historians is that in which William Stith records the genesis of
his *The History . . . of Virginia* (1747). He tells us that his
uncle, Sir John Randolph, originally planned to write a preface
to the laws of Virginia, and collected materials for that purpose, which he never carried out. Stith thinks "such a Work,
well performed, must naturally be a great Satisfaction, and
even Ornament, to our Country," since, save for the "excellent
but confused Materials, left us in Captain *Smith's* History,"
every other work is "empty and unsatisfactory." Stith wishes
some one else would write the book, that he might be saved

the Trouble, of conning over our old musty Records, and of
studying, connnecting, and reconciling the jarring and disjointed
Writings and Relations of different Men and different Parties.

He bids the "inquisitive Reader" perceive how much of his
own book is founded on Smith, whose writings he found
"vastly confused and perplexed, and took me more Labour
and Pains to digest . . . than I at first expected." Stith's own
account is "founded on the express Testimony, and the incontestable Authority, of our Records in the Capitol, and the
Company's Journals," for

I take it to be the main Part of the Duty and Office of an Historian, to paint Men and Things in their true and lively Colours;
and to do that Justice to the Vices and Follies of Princes and great
Men, after their Death, which it is not safe or proper to do, whilst
they are alive. And herein, as I judge, chiefly consist the Strength
and Excellency of *Tacitus* and *Suetonius*.[69]

If Stith does not directly discuss the question of style, and if his ideal of historical writing is a curious blend of Cotton Mather's and that of the eighteenth century, he yet insists upon the ideals of order and clarity, of the rational weighing of authorities and the statement of events in succession which distinguish Prince, whom he also resembles in avoiding "artificial Ornaments and Descriptions."

Recording certain French and Indian encroachments upon the colonies, the Rev. Benjamin Doolittle, in a manuscript published in 1750, opens his brief, dry, but impressive narrative with the statement:

> My Purpose is only to relate Facts, as near as I am capable, from the best Information I could get: But it is probable there may be some Mistakes from Misinformation, arising from the different Apprehension Men have had concerning Facts, and the different Interests Men have in View: . . . Which makes it difficult in every Case to obtain an impartial Account.[70]

His recital, by reason of its objectivity and direct style, is in striking contrast to the rhetorical dress in which the horrors of French and Indian warfare are usually described.[71] Doolittle, however, though he practises the newer plainness of style, does not expatiate upon it. The Rev. Samuel Hopkins, writing a biography of John Sergeant, missionary to the Indians, says in 1753 that he designed a faithful account, that his work has been delayed by the necessity of consulting Sergeant's letters, and that he has not sought *"Eloquence"* but a plain narrative of facts intelligible to all.[72] But with William Smith we reach another full-dress discussion of historical style.

Smith's *History of the Province of New-York* was written to correct British ignorance of colonial affairs. The author says he has tried to examine the public documents pertinent to his subject from the beginning; and sets forth his historical ideal in the following interesting passages:

> My Design is rather to inform than please. He who delights only in Pages shining with illustrious Characters, the Contentions of

Armies, the Rise and Fall of Empires, and other grand Events, must have Recourse to the great Authours of Antiquity. A Detail of the little Transactions, which concern a Colony, scant in its Jurisdiction, and still struggling with the Difficulties naturally attending its infant State, to Gentlemen of this Taste can furnish no Entertainment.

His narrative, he says, is in this sense not history but

only a regular Thread of simple Facts; and even those unembellished with Reflections, because they themselves suggest the proper Remarks, and most Readers will doubtless be best pleased with their own. The sacred Laws of Truth have been infringed neither by positive Assertions, oblique, insidious, Hints, wilful Suppressions, or corrupt Misrepresentation. To avoid any Censures of this Kind, no Reins have been given to a wanton Imagination, for the Invention of plausible Tales,

for Smith chooses to be "honest and dull" rather than "agreeable and false."

With Respect to its Style, the Criticks, in that Branch of Literature, are at full Liberty to condemn at their Pleasure. The main Use of Language is to express our Ideas. To write in the gay, pleasing, Pomp of Diction is above my Capacity. If any are disposed to blame me for being too verbose, let it be remembered that this is the *indefeasible* Right of my Profession, . . . Perspicuity is all I have endeavoured to maintain, nor am I at Leisure to study any higher Attainments in Language.[73]

I do not know whether that forgotten small masterpiece, *An Essay on the Invention, . . . of making . . . Iron, from black Sea Sand,*[74] is properly discussed as history or not, for it contains a little of everything from humor to scientific speculation, but, inasmuch as it is an account of an episode in Eliot's life by which he set great store and the historical importance of which he felt to be very considerable, it seems pertinent to cite him here. This lively example of colonial prose at its best and brightest includes a discussion of style:

Some may say, that such trivial Stories, and a long Detail of minute Particulars concerning a little Bag of Sand and a Bar of

Iron, is really below the Dignity of Writing. I do not know what such Persons intend, by Dignity of Writing, unless they can Mean, that when a Person is to write a Letter or a Book, he must ascend into the Clouds, think himself going about something quite different from the common Actions of Life: That he must divest himself of that Sociability, that easy Freedom, that Familiarity which is so much the Support and Pleasure of Conversation; must now put on a distant and forbidding Air, assume a solemn Mein, a formal Stiffness, as if clad in Buckrum; and being thus equipt is in Appearance like a Hog in Armour, very different from the inimitable Sir *William Temple,* who relates the common Incidents of Life, in such an easy agreeable Manner, as to engage the Attention, captivate the Mind, and excite the Admiration of every Reader.[75]

How remote is this from the "Buckrum" manner of Cotton Mather!

To sharpen one's sense of the long journey of the colonial mind in search of a style which would "engage the Attention, captivate the Mind, and excite the Admiration of every Reader," let me conclude by placing side by side two portraits by colonial writers, the first from 1697, the second exactly sixty years later. In the first, Cotton Mather is describing that excellent characteristic of Phips that "he would speak of his own *low beginning* with as much Freedom and Frequency, as if he had been afraid of having it forgotten," on which follows this paragraph:

It was counted an Humility in King *Agathocles,* the Son of a *Potter,* to be served therefore in *Earthen Vessels,* as *Plutarch* hath informed us: It was counted an Humility in Archbishop *Willigis,* the Son of a *Wheelwright,* therefore to have *Wheels* hung about his Bed-Chamber, with this Inscription, *Recole unde Veneris,* i.e. *Remember thy Original.* But such was the *Humility* and *Lowliness* of this *Rising Man!* Not only did he after his return to his Country in his Greatness, one Day, make a splendid Feast for the *Ship-Carpenters* of *Boston,* among whom he was willing at his Table to Commemorate the Mercy of God unto him, who had once been a *Ship-Carpenter* himself, but he would on all Occasions *Permit,* yea, *Study* to have his *Meannesses* remembered.[76]

These learned references to Agathocles and Willigis, carefully balanced against each other, the conscious treatment of cadences, the opposition of *"Lowliness"* and *"Rising Man,"* and the conclusion, *"Study* to have his *Meannesses* remembered"— all stamp this passage as belonging to the style of the *grand rhétoriqueur* of seventeenth-century New England. But here now is William Livingston striving to paint the portrait of John Pownal in 1757; the subject is again a colonial "statesman," albeit Livingston, unlike Mather, does not admire the character in question:

> This gentleman . . . is something of a scholar, but a confused reasoner; and in his stile perplexed; and in that usefullest of all sciences, the knowledge of mankind, he is a mere novitiate: without the latter, your Lordship knows that other acquirements are comparatively of small account, in the management of public business. To be only learned, is frequently to be vain, ostentatious, and obstinate; such a one, in a word, as Tertullian describes the most learned among the heathens, 'an animal of glory.' This gentleman is fond of being considered *in an important light.* Insatiable of praise, he can not only hear himself flattered; but, what is more unaccountable in a man of tolerable sense, can flatter himself. He is a person of uncommon application, and a good memory. . . . He is for galloping into preferment: and so intent on the contemplation of his future grandeur, as to lose all patience in earning it.[77]

Livingston is addressing a nobleman, and his style is therefore a touch more genteel than the common run of eighteenth-century American prose. Nevertheless, how remote is this writing from the "Buckrum" manner! The solitary allusion to a learned work is such as a virtuoso might make, and conceals rather than parades scholarship; the structure of the sentences is of the kind we instinctively associate with Chesterfield or Bolingbroke, and the antitheses are intellectual rather than rhetorical.

To pass beyond 1770 into the revolutionary decades is to pass to a separate problem. Indeed, not even all the elements affect-

ing eighteenth-century colonial prose have here been analyzed
—for example, the theory of education which emphasized
training in English rather than in Latin and Greek worked
towards informality and simplicity. But enough has been
shown to illustrate how deep-rooted in our national history is
the avoidance of fustian prose, how old is the emphasis upon
plainness, how ancient is our distrust of inkhorn terms, a distrust expressing the average man's lack of ease in the presence
of the scholar. Notable, too, is the drive against contentious-
ness, itself an aspect of a deep-seated belief in fair play. And
if none of these elements in the stylistic controversy I have
studied is peculiar to America, they indicate in their totality
that we must push back the supposed origin of some of our
intellectual and moral traits, we must see that the colonial
periods originate much that we have unthinkingly referred to
the so-called "national" period. Prose style has its modest part
to play in the history of ideas in America.

6

THE DRIFT TO LIBERALISM IN THE AMERICAN
EIGHTEENTH CENTURY *

THE topic before us is "Classicism and Romanticism"; and
ranged as this topic is under the larger heading "Authority and the Individual," it suggests that in the conflict between authority and the individual, classicism and romanticism
have their part. I propose to inquire how far the terms in
question are applicable to American literary history.

I shall not attempt to define either term,[1] though it is important that no literary historian has spoken of a classical age
in American literary history, those portions of the seventeenth
and eighteenth centuries which are elsewhere known as classical, neoclassical, or Augustan being called the Colonial and
Revolutionary periods. As for romanticism, recalling Professor
Lovejoy's warning that we should discriminate among romanticisms,[2] I shall begin by touching upon the confused uses
of the word by American literary historians.

In the first place, it is notable that a number of histories of
American letters having considerable philosophical weight,
published between 1887 and 1936, do not find it necessary to
discuss or distinguish a "romantic period."[3] Other books
formally recognize a "romantic period" under a variety of
names, but do not agree as to the extent of the era involved.
Thus Parrington entitled his second volume *The Romantic
Revolution in America: 1800–1860;* Leisy entitles his third

* A contribution to the symposium on Classicism and Romanticism at
the Harvard Tercentenary Conference of Arts and Sciences, 1936.

chapter "The Romantic Impulse," and discusses literature from Irving to the metropolitan poets; Blankenship believes that "America of the early nineteenth century accepted" the ideas of the romantic school "as if they were of unquestionable validity," and extends romanticism from the early 1770's to the Civil War; Dickinson thinks the romantic period runs from 1789 to 1855; McDowell confines the "romantic triumph" to the years 1830–1860; Miller tells us that the literature of romantic America extends from 1800 to 1850; and Taylor extends "romantic art in an agrarian republic" to 1870.[4] These authors are not so generous as the late George Edward Woodberry, who, though he told his readers on one page that American literature "has been sundered from the great movement of romanticism abroad," told them elsewhere that "America was romantic from the first," that "romance has been our genius," and that American literature has been controlled "by the academic, artistic, and romantic spirit."[5]

Such is the chronological perplexity; what may be called the geographical confusions of American romanticism are also noteworthy. There is general agreement that romantic literature was written sometime in New England; but one writer says that this movement democratically "emphasized the worth of human nature"; another, that on the whole "the aristocratic tradition persisted more strongly in literature than in most other fields of life"; a third, that Unitarianism accomplished a "wide dissemination of eighteenth-century French liberalism" in New England; a fourth, that this writing exhibits "reactionary tendencies of thought, Utopias, and a refuge in history and mediaevalism"; a fifth, that a wave of Wordsworthianism "swept gently over New England and here and there found a mind which was . . . refreshed"; a sixth, that if "Emerson and Whitman were pure Romanticists, then none of the various definitions of Romanticism so far formulated is adequate"; and a seventh dubs the whole thing an "Augustan age" when "gentlemen pursued literature in a seemly fashion."[6] As for the South, the inquirer will find it asserted that the Southern planters cherished "a romantic dream," and that classicism is "a distinctly Southern trait"; that, "landing first in Virginia in the early seventeen-seventies, [French romantic theories] met with a hospitable reception from the generous planter society," and that "the heritage of the pre-Civil War South from feudal mediaevalism by way of the eighteenth century was inevitably expressed in reactionary thinking"; that the favorite reading of the South was Scott, Bulwer, Byron, and Moore, its lyrical poets being "disciples of the romantic poets of England," and that early nineteenth-century Virginia writers were anti-romantic, and Charleston, that influential intellectual capital, was a place dominated by the Addisonian essay, the heroic couplet, and a classical education. Not unnaturally, in view of these contradictions, one historian concludes that "in literary advancement, the South stood in 1860 where America as a whole stood at the beginning of the century"![7] In the earlier nineteenth century New York or Philadelphia is variously described as romantic or conservative, depending on the book one consults;[8] and the frontier is alternately a source of romanticism and a mistaken adopter of it.[9]

What are the inciting causes, origins, beginnings, initial impulses, or backgrounds of American romanticism? In other words, what started it? There is a rich variety of theories. One may learn that American romanticism is due to French rationalism,[10] mysticism,[11] Puritanism,[12] the revolt against Puritanism,[13] a belief in the innate goodness of man,[14] a Puritanical absorption in sin,[15] post-Kantian idealism,[16] travel,[17] closeness to nature in America,[18] the search for foreign themes,[19] an interest in the American rather than in the European past,[20] industrial expansion,[21] the fact that we were not an industrial but an agrarian society,[22] optimism,[23] an unconscious return to Jonathan Edwards,[24] a slavish following of Wordsworth, Coleridge, and others,[25] pride in our new-found independence,[26] the frontier,[27] the romantic charm of Spain,[28] the fact that Channing visited Virginia,[29] a thirst for greater culture,[30] primitivism,[31] and the absence of primitivism from American literature [32]—they all had something to do with it! A movement thus heterogeneously "founded" is necessarily equipped by scholars with a wild disorder of qualities, but these I shall not pause to enumerate.[33]

Since by "romanticism," "the romantic revolt," "the romantic triumph," "the romantic impulse," and similar phrases, historians of American literature mean so many things, we can clarify the situation by discriminating among meanings. One may pass over such naïve confusions as that of "romance" in the sense of a form of fiction with "romanticism" as a literary philosophy and such vague generalized uses of the term as appear in phrases like "the romantic New World"; one may note in passing that if Fichte, Schelling, Coleridge, and the like are to be denominated romantic philosophers, the same adjective can not be consistently applied to rationalists, sceptics, and materialists like Voltaire, Diderot, Holbach, Helvétius, and D'Alembert; and one may find the literary historian referring to some one or other of the following meanings of American romanticism:

1. *Generalized Romanticism.* He may mean that American writers, especially poets, frequently adopt the literary themes and the literary rhetoric of European romanticism (usually British) without at the same time adopting or expressing any philosophy or system of ideas significantly or primarily romantic.

2. *The Romantic Treatment of History.* He may refer to writing which sets forth real or imaginary events in the American past, so narrating or describing these events through a more or less romantic rhetoric as to emphasize their ideal, colorful, "poetic," dramatic, melodramatic, or heroic qualities at the expense of historical or psychological realism in the contemporary sense of realism.

3. *Romanticism as Escape.* He may refer to "escapist" literature written by Americans, mainly in the nineteenth century, who, dissatisfied with the actual conditions of American existence, sought aesthetic or emotional satisfaction in the contemplation of lands and cultures, real or imaginary, remote in time or space from the actual United States and interpreted by these writers in terms primarily conditioned by their dissatisfaction with the actual conditions of American life.

4. *Romanticism as Philosophy.* He may refer to a phase of American intellectual development primarily theological in its origins, centering in New England, supposed to begin as a revolt against Calvinism and to culminate in the transcendental writers, and influenced to an undetermined degree in the later phases of its history by German transcendental philosophy, French eclecticism, and the philosophical outlook and aesthetic standards of such British writers as Wordsworth, Coleridge, and Carlyle. Writers associated with this movement do not customarily express themselves in the same rhetorical fashion as those in group one.

5. *Romanticism as Political or Economic Theory.* He may refer to a movement in political and economic theory primarily libertarian in character, expressive of political and economic individualism, supposed to have its intellectual bases in the polemics of the American Revolutionary period, and presumed by some historians to be influenced to a degree not ascertained by a group of eighteenth-century French theorists vaguely denominated the French radical, revolutionary, or romantic philosophers. For some theorists other bases of this movement are supplied by the Newtonian world order, deism, rationalism, primitivism, and a "return to nature" in the sense of a cosmic order benevolently directed towards economic abundance.

6. *Romanticism as Nationalism.* He may refer to the expression in literature, usually through a romantic rhetoric, of a nationalistic spirit in one or more of the following senses:

(a) American "democratic" life poetically, or at any rate unrealistically, conceived as *per se* superior to life in the Old World; (b) the American landscape conceived as unspoiled, wild, grandiose, sublime, strange, or beautiful, and fertile in plants, animals, and, I may add, Indians; (c) "pioneer" life poetically, or at any rate unrealistically, conceived as the resultant of the interplay between democratic existence and the natural setting of that existence, the absence of European and of urban culture making for the release of primary or elemental virtues, and therefore, in a somewhat unusual sense of the word, primitivistic. The origins of this phase of American literary expression are left chronologically indefinite, but its ending is usually placed in the 1870's.

Though these categories are neither exhaustive nor mutually exclusive, one may confidently say that American romanticism in senses one, two, and three offers little difficulty. We should agree, I think, that in style and substance American lyricists of the last century are romantic rather than classical in the main; that a poem like "Paul Revere's Ride," a novel like *The Last of the Mohicans*, and a play like *Shenandoah* offer romantic versions of historical events; and that "escapist" literature is romantic. But senses four, five and six—romanticism as philosophy, romanticism as political or economic theory, and romanticism as nationalism—offer greater problems because it is precisely to these more intellectualistic concepts that the terms "romantic revolt" and "romantic triumph" are applied. If there was a revolt, against what was it directed? If there was a triumph, in what respects was it a victory? In older literatures, the romantic movement is conceived as a departure from classicism; but the failure of literary historians to distinguish a classical movement in American letters robs us of this easy dichotomy. And yet one writer assures us that at the turn of the last century the romantic revolution laid hold of men's minds [in America], consuming the stubble of eighteenth-century harvests, sweeping away the drab realisms of a cautious past, and offering in their stead more alluring ideals; [34]

a second, that "the romantic revolution,"

affecting everything from our verse form to our conception of man's place in the universe, was probably the most influential and widespread intellectual force ever liberated in the United States; [35]

and a third, that

Freneau's religion, the religion of nature and humanity . . . illustrates the neglected transition from Puritanism to deism and from deism to Unitarianism and pantheism [and] motivates . . . [the] political and . . . poetical interests [36]

of the "father of American poetry" and therefore presumably serves as the focal point in a revolution wrought for subsequent American verse.

Now my objection to language of this sort is that it is not justified by the facts of American intellectual development and that it gives a distorted and over-dramatized picture of what actually occurred. The scholar who describes a romantic revolution "consuming the stubble" of the eighteenth century places Thomas Jefferson in the center of the stage and makes much of the influence upon him of French "romantic philosophy," so called, despite the fact that the most careful biographer of Jefferson's intellectual development assures us, not once, but over and over again, that Jefferson owes almost nothing to the French. "The Jeffersonian democracy," Chinard says picturesquely, "was born under the sign of Hengist and Horsa, not of the Goddess Reason." [37] But passing over these aberrations, I should like to examine the idea of nature as set forth in Freneau in order to illustrate the difference between the concept of a literary revolution and the concept of a slow, organic growth in the American mind.

Since "nature" in the sense of the cosmos, however interpreted, is on the whole for the transcendentalists by some historians supposed to be "good," [38] and since "nature" in the sense of created nature is by some historians supposed for the Calvinists to be "bad," it has seemed necessary to explain this reversal in point of view, and the deism of Paine, Freneau, and Jefferson has been put forward [39] as a middle term of the "revolution" wrought. Thus we are told that deism

> found congenial soil on the American frontier, an environment inculcating freedom, self-reliance, and optimism in place of determinism, passivity, and gloom; [that] Freneau reverently tells us that the "Great Frame of the Universe"—its "exact design," a "structure complete in itself"—teaches "the reasoning human soul" to infer an "author of the whole."

in contrast to the deity of this "good" universe our author places the *New England Primer*, the bloody deity of Increase Mather, and Jonathan Edwards' deity contemplating sinners in hell.[40] "One can understand," says this scholar, "how this sort of thing would annoy Presbyterians." [41] I can understand that deism annoyed Presbyterians, and it is regrettable that Jonathan Edwards' God was not more gentlemanly, but it seems odd that if frontier conditions in the eighteenth century produced "freedom, self-reliance, and optimism," analogous conditions should in the seventeenth century have inculcated "determinism, passivity, and gloom"; and I am compelled to point out that there is little in Freneau's interpretation of the universe as rational order which Calvin could not approve and which was not a commonplace in American thought long before Freneau.[42]

Calvin, it is true, says that Adam "ruined his posterity by his defection, which has perverted the whole order of nature in heaven and earth," [43] but this does not mean that the glorious rational order of the cosmos has been warped, only that man's nature has been fatally affected. As he tells us at the opening of the *Institutes*:

Of his wonderful wisdom, both heaven and earth contain innumerable proofs; not only those more abstruse things, which are the subjects of astronomy, medicine, and the whole science of physics, but those things which force themselves on the view of the most illiterate of mankind, so that they cannot open their eyes, without being constrained to witness them. Adepts, indeed, in those liberal arts, or persons just initiated into them, are thereby enabled to proceed much further in investigating the secrets of Divine Wisdom. Yet ignorance of those sciences prevents no man from such a survey of the workmanship of God, as is more than sufficient to excite his admiration of the Divine Architect. In disquisitions concerning the motions of the stars, in fixing their situations, measuring their distances, and distinguishing their peculiar properties, there is need of skill, exactness, and industry; and the providence of God being more clearly revealed by these discoveries, the mind ought to rise to a sublimer elevation for the contemplation of his glory. But since the meanest and most illiterate of mankind, who are furnished with no other assistance than their own eyes, cannot be ignorant of the excellence of the Divine skill, exhibiting itself in that endless, yet regular variety of the innumerable celestial host,—it is evident, that the Lord abundantly manifests his wisdom to every individual on earth . . . the composition of the human body is universally acknowledged to be so ingenious, as to render its Maker the object of deserved admiration.[44]

"The structure and organization of the world," says Calvin, "and the things that daily happen out of the ordinary course of nature," "bear a witness to God which the dullest ear cannot fail to hear" (*Institutes,* I, v, 1, 3, 7; II, vi, 1); the "light that shines from creation while it may be smothered, cannot be so extinguished but that some rays of it find their way into the most darkened soul" (*Institutes,* I, v, 14);[45] and long before the deistic movement of Freneau, Paine, and Jefferson, seventeenth- and eighteenth-century Americans had taken up with especial ardor those branches of natural science which enabled them to penetrate "further in investigating the secrets of Divine Wisdom." Of the innumerable instances which might be given, I shall cite only one: a sermon or two by that excellent Presbyterian clergyman, the Rev. Benjamin Colman, preached in Boston three-quarters of a century before Freneau's first book appeared. His subject was the incomprehensibility of God.[46] The incomprehensibility of God, he argued, is no reason why fallen man should not try to understand his nature. "The true Pleasure and blessedness of the Intelligent Creature lies in the Knowledge of the Creator," he said. And the learned Presbyterian surveyed "nature" with all the ardor of a deist:

It is the *fixt Opinion* now of *Learned Men,* from what they do see and know of the Creation by *Telescopes,* that there may be and in all probability are many such *Worlds,* as this which our Eyes view, when we take the compass of the Heavens with them. And if it be so, how does it *Enlarge* the Creation to us, and the Greatness of the *Creator?* [47]

Colman admires the great frame of the universe and the "exact design" of the heavens; then he fixes his attention upon the earth, hanging like a ball in the air, and exclaims over the wonders of it:

. . . the *Living Creatures* in the Air, Earth and Sea are an Inexpressible *Variety* of Divine Workmanship, both of *beauty and use,*

he says, reviewing the furs of beasts, the feathers of birds, and the scales of fishes. The wonders of the microscope are "astonishing," and so is the human body, and he bids his hearers:

Look thro' the Visible Creation, and see the Provision made thro'out it all for the Entertainment of Man, his Soul and Body! Immense Stores from the Divine Fulness and Munificence! What Wonders of Wisdom for our musing *Minds?* What Beauties for our gazing *Eyes?* What Pleasing Sounds for our *Ears?* What Delicacy of Food for our Palates? What a Paradise the Earth. . . . The Law of *Nature* is a very *Sacred* Law, and the Light of Nature a very *great Light*: to *live up* to it is a very great thing; and to *quench* it by Lust, or wilfully to Sin against it is a very *high Guilt.* . . . [God] has given *Man* the *Dominion* over and *Use* of the Inferior Creatures, and puts them under our *Feet*; and it becomes us not to *trample* either in Pride or Carelessness on a very *Worm. . . .*[48]

From this rhapsody by a leading Presbyterian on the wisdom and benevolence displayed in nature, I have omitted one phrase. Colman wrote: "What a Paradise the Earth—if by our Sins we had not blasted it?"—which means, not that the cosmic order is evil, but that man misuses his opportunities for wisdom and happiness offered by a rational and benevolent universe. Calvinist and deist differed as to the nature of man; I am unable to see that they differed importantly as to the order, beauty, and benevolence of the cosmos *qua* cosmos. And when, on the basis of the theory set forth by Moore that in British poetry the romantic "return to nature" is, to a large degree, based on deism,[49] American scholars argue that Freneau's deism "marks the starting-point in America of this all-important trend toward the concrete in poetry," [50] I find myself simply bewildered. Was a Calvinist denied the opportunity of calling a thing by its right name? Here is William Morell writing in 1625 of "Deare or Bever, with the hayreside in"; Anne Bradstreet referring to blackbirds, thrushes, kids, lambs, pears, plums, apple trees, grass, primroses, violets, a "clocking hen" and "chirping chickins," cherries, peas, strawberries, double pinks, roses, honey bees, cowslips, oak trees, elm trees, the grasshopper, and the cricket; here is Benjamin Thompson writing satirically of mud and turf, pick-axes and wagons, pies and tarts, in 1675; here is Nicholas Noyes in 1702 comparing his thoughts to "a swarm of *Bees,* That fly both *when* and *where* they please"; here is Nathaniel Evans, missionary of the S.P.G.A., talking in 1722 of the yellow finch and linnet blue on the banks of the Schuylkill river; here is Joseph Green in 1733 lamenting the loss of his cat; and so on indefinitely.[51] And it is scarcely necessary to say that from the travel books, diaries, histories, letters, and even from the sermons of colonial American literature written by

Calvinists and other varieties of Christians, one can cull an indefinite number of passages in which natural objects are referred to specifically because they were the subject of curious admiration and wonder.[52]

If the history of certain themes in the work of Jefferson and Freneau thus suggests a reasonable doubt as to the extent of the intellectual revolution supposed by some to be wrought by the deistic view of nature at the turn of the eighteenth century, one may also note that, although some writers have spoken of transcendentalism as a revolt against Calvinism, an intellectual revolution, or what not, others have, I think more wisely, traced its sources upward to the seventeenth century. Into this vexed problem I shall not enter further than to quote three paragraphs, the authorship of which I shall specify in a moment:

THERE is nothing in the World more clear to ME, than This; That I have in me a *Principle*, which does not meerly *Receive Idea's* (as a Looking-Glass may *Images*,) but also *Perceive* them, and make *Remarks* upon them; and has a certainty of *it self*, and of what *is done* in itself. . . . An *Indivisible Being*, and yet what can Embrace and Contain the *Universe!* No Bounds can be set unto the Number of the *Objects* which it can *successively* take a Cognisance of. . . . The *Body*, which is *Matter* in such and such a *Figure*, cannot Affect the *Immaterial* SOUL, nor can the SOUL, which has no *Figure*, Command the *Body;* But the Great GOD having established certain *Laws*, that upon such and such *Desires* of the SOUL, the *Body* shall be so and so Commanded, HE 'tis, who by His *Continual Influx* does Execute His own *Laws;* 'Tis to His *Continual Influx* that the *Effects* are owing.

Though we suppose, that the existence of the whole material Universe is absolutely dependent on Idea, yet we may speak in the old way, and as properly, and truly as ever. God, in the beginning, created such a certain number of Atoms, of such a determinate bulk and figure, which they yet maintain and always will, and gave them such a motion, of such a direction, and of such a degree of velocity . . . all the ideas that ever were, or ever shall be to all eternity, in any created mind, are answerable to the existence of such a peculiar Atom in the beginning of the Creation . . . God . . . causes all changes to arise, as if all these things had actually existed in such a series, in some created mind, and as if created minds had comprehended all things perfectly. And, although created minds do not; yet, the Divine Mind doth; and he orders all things according to his mind, and his ideas.

Three problems are put by nature to the mind; What is matter? Whence is it? and Whereto? The first of these questions only, the ideal theory answers. Idealism saith: matter is a phenomenon, not a substance. Idealism acquaints us with the total disparity between the evidence of our own being, and the evidence of the world's being. The one is perfect; the other, incapable of any assurance; the mind is part of the nature of things; the world is a divine dream, from which we may presently awake to the glories and certainties of day. . . . Yet, if [idealism] only deny the existence of matter, it does not satisfy the demands of the spirit. It leaves God out of me. It leaves me in the splendid labyrinth of my perceptions, to wander without end. . . . The world proceeds from the same spirit as the body of man. It is a remoter and inferior incarnation of God, a projection of God in the unconscious.

Putting aside obvious differences in style, most readers would say, I think, that this little essay in three paragraphs is not too bad a sketch of philosophical idealism; yet the first paragraph was written by Cotton Mather, the second by Jonathan Edwards, and the third by Ralph Waldo Emerson! [53]

The nineteenth century is not the eighteenth; romanticism is not classicism; the universe of the transcendentalist differs *toto caelo* from the Newtonian world-machine; and the deistic view of human nature contradicts at every turn that of high Calvinism. I do not wish to confuse these clear distinctions. But I submit that our anxiety to equip American literary history with its complement of "periods" and "factors" has led us to indulge too liberally that false power by which we multiply distinctions. A saltatory conception of American literature, with its easy opposition of romanticism to something ever left undefined, its talk of "revolt" and "revolution," its picture of a libertarian ideology opportunely arriving from Europe to free the American mind from its theological prison-house like the angel liberating Paul and Silas—this it is which has produced the confusions I have sketched. And I suggest that if we are to understand the historic function of the various American "romanticisms," we must turn to that epoch of American literary history, which, since the days of Moses Coit Tyler, has scarcely been explored; we must begin by discovering what the nineteenth century really owes to the colonial period. For it seems obvious that the problem of American romanticism can not be solved merely by enumerating European influences: what is borrowed, after all, is determined by what is wanted; and we can not discover what was wanted until we know what we had. And much penitential reading in the obscurer printed material of the colonial period, especially that of the eighteenth century, leads me to present a simple but suggestive hypothesis—an hypothesis, indeed, implicit in the work of Tyler [54]—which may serve, however tentatively, to place American romanticisms in a more understandable, if less theatric, light.

Our culture is a Protestant, and not a Catholic, culture; it is a Protestant culture begun in dissent and retaining dissent as its chief characteristic for decades, as the failure of either Anglican or Catholic authoritarianism [55] decisively to influence that culture testifies. The essence of dissent lies in the appeal to private judgment, that is to say, to the individual reason; and one of its primary philosophic interests is the problem of the relation of the individual to God. I suggest that the central problem in American thought, at least until late in the nineteenth century, is the problem of the moral order of the universe—a problem so primary as on the whole to subordinate almost all other philosophical and aesthetic considerations to this central question. [56] For the Americans until recent times the metaphysical problem has been characteristically a problem of teleology rather than of ontology, a problem not of being, but of doing—and doing rightly. From their point of view the question of classicism and romanticism is not primarily a metaphysical or an aesthetic question, but a moral problem; and they have adopted the patterns of classicism or of romanticism not as aesthetic or metaphysical absolutes, but as instrumental aids towards solving the problem of the moral order. Thus it is (to work for a moment rapidly backward) that in general the Americans have accepted European romanticisms only as they have appealed to the moral sense; that American transcendentalism stresses ethics rather than epistemology or aesthetics; that American literary criticism between 1810 and 1835—the only period concerning which we have sufficient knowledge to judge [57]—owed allegiance to Kames, Blair, and Alison—that is to say, to critical principles which fused the question of taste with that of morality and which led the critic to think of himself as "the watchdog of society"; [58] that the official philosophy of the period was that of the Scotch school of "Common-Sense"; and that deism, largely because of its ethical and theological weaknesses, failed to make any lasting impression on the national mind. [59] Do we not, in fact, instinctively feel, under whatever definition we choose to set up, that the nearest analogue to American romanticism is not found among the wits, rebels, and mystics of the Regency; not among the wild and picturesque young men of Paris in 1830; not among the Erste Romantische Schule nor yet the writers of young Germany; but rather among the earnest idealists of Victorian England? [60] Not rebels, but reformers, not iconoclasts, but moralists, the American romantics, with but few exceptions, assumed that the central problem of thought was the problem of the moral order of the universe—that is to say, they were men who subordinated aesthetics to ethical ends and sought to make their version of reason and the will of God prevail. [61] Even in their most rebellious moments the appeal is neither to cynicism, anarchy, nor despair, but always to a higher law. [62]

If, then, American romanticism, considered as philosophy,

as politics, or as nationalism, is best understood as the final phase of a slow evolution in thought beginning in the colonial period, what of the eighteenth century out of which, in a sense, it emerged? In older cultures romanticism was a liberalizing force directed against decadent classicism; but in America, as I have hinted, historians have failed to distinguish a classical period to overthrow. The obvious failure of the colonial centuries to produce a great classical genius, a great classical work of art, or an influential classical aesthetic; the failure of the colonies to create a genuinely classical education—a failure due, on the one hand, to theological preoccupations, and on the other, to a utilitarian misvaluation of "dead languages"; [63] the fact that the colonies were never a part of the ancient world and were separated by immense distances from the European heirs of the Roman empire—such were the fatal obstacles to the flowering of a classical culture in colonial America. But if in Europe secular thought was liberalized by a romanticism seeking to overthrow a senescent classicism, in America thought and expression had first to be made secular; and it was the historic mission of that aspect of the classical world-view men call the Enlightenment to liberate American thought and expression from theology in the very decades when the young romantic movement in Europe was seeking to liberate European thought and expression from the Enlightenment! This paradox is, of course, only approximately true; but it becomes understandable when one remembers that there was a cultural lag between the New World and the Old, so that, whereas from 1760 to 1800 the great monuments of a new European literature are to be found in the writings of Rousseau, the *Kritik der Reinen Vernunft*, the earlier emotionalism of Goethe and Schiller, Burns's poems, and the *Lyrical Ballads*, the great monuments of the American intellect in the same decades are the writings of Franklin, of Hamilton and Jefferson, of Otis, the two Adams's, and Tom Paine.

For if one conceives of classicism with Professor Lovejoy as meaning in its widest sense the assumption that, "in each phase of human activity, excellence consists in conforming as nearly as possible to a standard conceived as universal, static[,] uncomplicated, uniform for every rational being," the story of eighteenth-century American development is the story of the slow fusion of a culture founded in Protestant dissent with certain of the secular ideas of classicism. The Lockeian psychology, the contract theory of government, the Newtonian world-view, the theory of progress, experimental science, cosmic optimism, deism [64]—these were some of the forces with which theology had to struggle; the result was, on the whole, a secular, but not a sceptical, victory—that is to say, the transfer of the problem of universal order from the theological to the moral sphere. The documents in this war of liberation are a vast polemic literature in which the remotest village pulpit echoed with contending arguments; until we explore this literature more thoroughly than we have done, we have little right to theorize about a romantic "revolution" or a romantic "triumph."

In sum, the discussion of American romanticism has been extraordinarily confused because of the failure to distinguish terms. In what may be called the rhetoric of belles lettres, this confusion is relatively unimportant; but when it is argued that a romantic movement in America enshrines the monuments of an intellectual revolution in the philosophcal or political sphere, closer examination of the evidences does not seem to justify so dramatic an interpretation. In the sphere of political action a romantic revolution in European terms was at once tautological and irrelevant; tautological, since, by the terms of its own "democratic" revolution, America *was*, politically speaking, the romantic revolt; [65] irrelevant, because the return to throne and altar, which is the romantic phase of the European reaction, was meaningless in a Protestant and democratic republic with no medieval past. In the intellectual sphere many of the ideas associated with American romanticisms have roots deep in the national past; and romantic literature in this country for the most part represents but the final phase of a statement of the moral order—final, because the impact of Darwinism ended the older teleologies. In this view emphasis must be given to the struggle between theology and the forces of the classical Enlightenment in the earlier centuries, for the paradox of the American situation is that on the whole the secular phases of classicism served as the original force to liberate the American mind from theological authoritarianism.

7

THE INFLUENCE OF EUROPEAN IDEAS IN
NINETEENTH-CENTURY AMERICA *

CALVIN COOLIDGE once wrote a history of the United States in five hundred words. If to discuss in a short paper the influence of European ideas in nineteenth-century America is equally preposterous, justification lies in the need of correcting theories of American cultural development now current. The vogue of economic determinism and over-emphasis upon elements like the frontier have undoubtedly falsified cultural history. Turner's classic essay was necessary in its time, but when one finds enthusiasts discovering a frontier element in the novels of Henry James, it is time to remember, with Siegfried and Schönemann,[1] that the United States is a part of the west-European cultural hegemony, and that its civilization results from the inter-play of American *and* European forces.[2]

By reason of the passage of time the investigator of nineteenth-century intellectual relations is confronted with more difficulties than one meets in the eighteenth or seventeenth century. Forces of European thought at work in the New World from the earliest decades are necessarily still operative. Such influential ideas as deism, Newtonianism, primitivism, Calvinism, the rights-of-man philosophy, and the stake-in-society theory of economics do not conveniently die out in 1800, but, allying themselves with new modes of thought, turn up to confuse the inquirer. For example, Puritanism did not invent the economic virtues, but the Puritan rationalization of life could be applied to business activity; and, in the

* 1935.

125

nineteenth century, such ethical concepts as frugality, thrift, and industriousness adapted from Puritanism (with some help from Franklin) by the middle-class New Englander and applied to the nascent industrial order, became synonymous with "Americanism," and in this form led directly into that conflict with the mores of French and Irish Catholics which appears in politics as the Know Nothing party.[3] Similar transmogrifications of ideas once rooted in European soil confront the investigator of nineteenth-century ideology at every turn.[4]

A second difficulty arises from the increasing specialization of knowledge. Briefly, the development runs from the omniscient natural philosopher of the seventeenth century to the modern laboratory technician. The language of the first usually requires no special training to be understood; the vocabulary of the other is commonly beyond the comprehension of the layman. Eighteenth-century science had not developed the mass of technical diction and technological information which overwhelms the historian of the nineteenth century. In that earlier period the inquirer may survey thought without falling into important errors; whereas, in the nineteenth century, the mere historian cannot hope to avoid mistakes due to his ignorance of techniques. Moreover, since most scientists are not interested in the history of their own disciplines, information is lacking, or must be gleaned from elementary treatises or diffuse and badly documented essays. If the situation makes for humility, it does not make for confidence.

A third difficulty lies in the vast increase of European immigration during the century. In the eighteenth century the cultural pattern of the future republic is still dominantly British. Until about the middle of the nineteenth century it remains British, but thereafter the arrival of increasing thousands of immigrants bringing with them their own culture patterns greatly complicates the problem. Historians of these movements usually make extravagant claims for the contributions of such groups, which cannot be accepted without investigation; yet to ignore these nationals, and to study only the importation of European ideas through book, letter, voyage, or magazine, among the "Anglo-Saxon" part of the population is equally erroneous.[5] We cannot deal adequately with this portion of the problem until we have impartial appraisals of the cultural contributions of foreign-language groups.

A fourth difficulty lies in the question: what is meant by a European idea? The history of ideas cannot be a bloodless dance of the categories; ideas must have been put to work; they must have contributed historical effects. But what constitutes an effective idea? Shall we, for example, include inventions? The creation of railways is a prime fact in American history; shall we point to this fact as the result of a chain of ideas running from James Watt to George Stephenson? Merely to debate the priority of inventions is idle. On the other hand, if we exclude inventions, shall we also exclude techniques? Samuel Slater brought Arkwright's idea of a cotton mill to the United States, and so created the textile industry—is that an example of an influential European thought? Or if cotton mills are too pragmatic, what shall we say of the creation of American scientific laboratories on European models, with all their far-reaching intellectual consequences? If we exclude techniques, if, for example, we turn to the importation of European philosophy, as in the case of New England transcendentalism or of Hegelianism in St. Louis, are we not struck by the fact that though these matters are of significance for literature and metaphysics, their importance in the total history of the country is relatively minor? Again, shall we class artistic influences among ideas? Where the ideology of an art movement is clear and precise, as in the case of the importation of European realism, no difficulty appears; but when the artistic influence is diffuse, as in the fact that leading American sculptors living in Rome during the first part of the century were subjected to innumerable shaping influences, the terms of the problem are changed, so that, whereas the connection between Hamlin Garland's fiction and his reading of Taine is tolerably easy to define, the relation of the work of Greenough and Powers to the art of Rome is much more difficult to trace.

Each of these inquiries, which could be increased in number, gives rise to endless debate. The careful inquirer must weigh arguments pro and con, and yet, while the debate goes on, our inquiry stands still. There is in truth no general principle which can be established; the utmost that one can hope to accomplish is to offer general suggestions, conscious that there is no statement in so difficult a query but can be controverted. The first need is for simplification.

For the sake of clearness I shall divide the century at the decade of the sixties and discuss only the first of the two periods. In this period, then, I suggest that the thousand influences pouring in upon the United States from Europe tend to be polarized about two foci of intellectual influence. The first of these I shall describe as post-Revolutionary or post-Napoleonic rationalism; the second I shall call the dynamic view of nature. As with all such dominant ideas, the two in question tend to blend into each other: the dynamic view of nature was the result of the rationalism I have in mind, and, on the other hand, the postulates of rationalism were reconditioned by the dynamic view of nature. I turn first to rationalism.

II

Generally speaking, the difference between rationalism before the French Revolution and rationalism after it, is that its absolute sanctions disappear. Before Napoleon, it is possible to speak of a religion of reason; after Napoleon, rationalism is not so much dethroned as delimited.[6] In one area, the awakened spirit of nationalism checked the cosmopolitanism of the eighteenth century, placing patriotism among the mystic virtues and beyond skeptical questioning.[7] In another, the obvious need of religious reconstruction ended inquiries which had seemed to result in materialism, atheism, or cynicism, so that in both Catholic and Protestant countries the fundamental tenets of religion were placed outside of inquiry.[8] The Age of the Enlightenment had ended in the blood-bath of 1793; consequently, out of the long agony of the Napoleonic struggle, the concept of the relativity of rationalism replaced the concept of the absolute reason. Rationalism was thus not ended, but redirected;[9] for if the tenets of the philosophers had seemed to lead to the débâcle of a world war, it was evident, on the other hand, that rationalism had produced such indisputably useful results as the French school of mathematicians, the new political economy of the British classical school, new modes of investigation in history, archaeology, and anthropology, surprising discoveries in chemistry, physics, geology, and other natural sciences, and (as applied reason) the profitable inventions which began the industrial revolution. A tyrannous master, rationalism was nevertheless a good servant, and, in the light of experience, the new age proposed to employ the servant and dismiss the master. In the relation of the thought of Kant to that of Hume we may see an almost algebraic symbol of the mode by which rationalism was, for a time, to be circumscribed.

In the United States meanwhile an analogous shift of emphasis was taking place. American opinion came to condemn the French Revolution and to share the British view of its probable origin in the godless intellectualism of the Enlightenment.[10] A rising religious reaction smothered the deism of the elder generation both intellectually and emotionally,[11] and rolled westward to the frontier. Like the Lake Poets, the Hartford Wits, the only consolidated literary group in the country in 1800, passed from an eager interest in late eighteenth-century ideas to a theological and conservative point of view.[12] Despite the defection of New England, the War of 1812 increased the spirit of nationalism [13] and in so doing tended to turn Americans away from Europe.[14] To the United States as to England the Continent had been practically closed from 1793 to 1815; unlike the Englishman, however, the American had to cross the Atlantic to reach Europe. Moreover, during these years, Great Britain had been more or less actively hostile to the United States, so that direct British influence upon the republic was checked. The consequences in America were that eighteenth-century rationalism had been more effectually smothered than even in Great Britain itself,[15] and American connections with Europe had, in a sense, to be remade.

Had there been no change in the spirit of European rationalism, had the restoration of the kings meant also the restoration of the *philosophes*, it is possible that the Americans might have cut themselves off from Europe, displaying no more interest in its culture than they displayed in the culture of Hispanic America. This is possible, though not probable; and the actual facts are that, owing to the general ignorance of foreign languages in the United States,[16] owing to the absence of an international copyright act covering the country—an absence which made it easy to reprint British publications—and owing to our traditional cultural alliance with Great Britain, we tended, though in diminishing degree, to look at the continent through British eyes. It was therefore the British version of post-Revolutionary rationalism which had the most vogue in the New World.

Though the constituent elements in this stream of influence tend to spring from a common mode of thought, they are not for that reason necessarily consistent with each other or with their origins. For example, the American magazines which sprang up in the nineteenth century, especially the quarterlies and the "heavy" literary periodicals, generally owe both their form and their spirit to British originals; [17] yet it is precisely in these magazines that American literary warfare against

British criticism was carried on.[18] Antagonism to British superciliousness did not, however, prevent American critics from adopting that "system" of judicial criticism which one associates with Jefferson, Smith, Lockhart, Gifford, Macaulay, *et al.* —a "system" which is essentially the expression of a modified rationalism.[19] Books, domestic and foreign, were haled before the judgment seat in American periodicals as they were in London.[20] In the field of theology one finds Americans combating subversive ideas from German theological faculties (ideas known as "German rationalism") or defending evangelical Christianity against the Romanizing tendencies of the Oxford movement, with weapons borrowed from Scotch or English theologians, the weapons being a cautious logic exercised on behalf of historical evidences, the reasonableness of the Trinity, etc.[21] A more complex problem is presented by Unitarianism, which certainly watered the rigors of Presbyterian logic with sentiment. Yet Unitarianism could not forget its intellectual origins in deistic rationalism; and, in the nineteenth century, it attacked Calvinism with logical weapons, and its intellectual relations with such British thinkers as Priestley and James Martineau were close.[22] Unitarianism must therefore also be listed among the movements which borrowed the weapons of post-Revolutionary rationalism.

If one passes from theology to philosophy, the most striking influence upon American metaphysics in general is that of the Scotch "Common-sense" school, the doctrines of which, taught by Witherspoon, Hedge, Upham, Wayland, Hickok, Seeley, Bascom, McCosh, Porter, and other professors of "moral philosophy," may be considered the official academic belief of the period, furnishing the substance of both lectures and textbooks,[23] and, where it touched on theology, affording a "reconciliation" of teleological concepts with the advance of scientific speculation. The same guarded logic is seen in the American adaptation of European economic theories. It has often been remarked that until late in the century American economic thought derives from the utilitarians and the British classical school.[24] Two elements in this adaptation need, however, to be emphasized. The first is that American economic theory, at least in the first part of the century, was canalized into a teleological, and sometimes even a pietistic, mode of thought; [25] and the second is that, even in those theorists who departed from, or attacked, such "classical" doctrines as free trade, there is no change in the mode of thought, but simply a new interpretation of the logic. The conditions of American life made protectionists of Raymond and Carey; they led Carey to repudiate the Malthusian theory and the Ricardian law of rent, but the intellectual premises are nevertheless those of the classical school. Pragmatism and piety met together; the dismal science of M'Culloch and the American belief in necessary progress [26] kissed each other.

Only a few of the complex relations of American educational policy to European theory fall in this division of the subject. The Sunday school, the infant school, and the Lancasterian and Bell monitorial schools, all borrowings from Great Britain,[27] represent that union of the pious and the useful which was rationally justified under prevailing systems of thought. The pedagogy in these systems was, moreover, mainly catechetical, that is to say, rationalistic. But the influential reports on various European school philosophies,[28] which helped to create the American public school system, are more complicated matter. The obligation of the state to educate its citizens, an ideal which these inquiries found exemplified in Prussia, is a nineteenth-century ideal complex in its origins, and depends upon a quasi-mystical attitude towards the state which differs from the rationalistic concept of government; [29] for this reason it is necessary to distinguish various streams of European influence.[30]

One of the most curious holds of the pragmatic rationalism current in Great Britain, however, is found in the slow development of American mathematical thought.[31] Until about

1820 mathematical books in this country, overwhelmingly British in their origins, were essentially utilitarian handbooks,[32] the brilliant work in theoretical mathematics of the French school being practically unknown (barring Bowditch and Adrian) until, characteristically, it had first spread into Great Britain, and again, characteristically, until the appointment of Crozet to West Point under Thayer in 1817 showed that French mathematical techniques were a necessary part of military engineering.[33] If mensuration is an index of civilization, we may note the significant fact that not until the 1870's did Americans contribute importantly to mathematical theory.[34] A similar tendency toward the utilitarian undoubtedly aided—and hindered—the development of the natural sciences,[35] but the most striking fact in this department is not so much that science was applied,[36] as that it generally rested upon a Christian, or at any rate a theistic, teleology.[37] This assumption was strengthened by American interest in such publications as the Bridgewater Treatises, and American admiration for such pious men of science as Sir Humphry Davy and Michael Faraday.[38] In the first part of the century the professors of "natural philosophy"[39]—significant phrase!— thought of the scientist as one who thinks God's thoughts after him.[40] Science was therefore to be devoted to exhibiting the evidences of design in nature; for that reason, perhaps, astronomy retained its traditional position as the queen of the sciences, since the telescope revealed the majesty of God's works.[41] If geology raised disturbing questions, if palaeontology and anthropology seemed to conflict with the Noachian story,[42] the American scientist strove to keep speculation within proper bounds. The teleological interpretation inevitably led to grandiose theorizing and worked against specialization; thus the prospectus of *The American Journal of Science* defines the field of the magazine as the physical sciences, their application to arts, agricultural, manufacturing, and domestic economy, engineering, and navigation,[43] because "the whole circle of physical science is directly applicable to human wants and constantly holds out a light to the practical arts; it thus polishes and benefits society and everywhere demonstrates both supreme intelligence and harmony and beneficence of design in the Creator." [44] Theology thus strengthened and limited scientific advance, even in medicine; [45] when we trace this theism to its source, we are usually led to post-Napoleonic Britain.[46]

III

It is time, however, to consider the second pole of influence, the view which I have called the dynamic conception of nature. In this interpretation, which lies between Newtonianism and Darwinianism, and which prepares the way for evolution, the universe is seen in terms of creative energy rather than of mechanical motion, its perfection being the harmony of the Divine Artist rather than the unity of a perpetual motion machine designed by a Great Engineer.[47] The mechanistic view yields to the organic,[48] scientific observation gives only a partial view unless coupled with poetic insight,[49] intuition is found equally valuable with impersonal deduction; and, far from awakening terror because of its vastness, the universe reveals a new and stimulating majesty perpetually active.[50] I suggest that this larger concept draws to a focus such subsidiary forces of European influence as literary romanticism, transcendentalism, the doctrine of immanence, the vitalistic concept of life, and a certain expansiveness, an affirmative optimism said to characterize the American attitude toward living. I do not, of course, suggest the dynamic principle as the sole source of these ideas.

The connection of American transcendentalism with various European sources is well established, though the mode of influence is under perpetual debate.[51] Equally, the American adaptation of the romantic conception of art as creative ideality which finds in the imagination a faculty comparable to the creative power of the World-Soul or of God,[52] is part of the same filiation; the question, in either case, is twofold but simple: what elements in the European situation did the Americans accept, and what reject? and what did they do with those elements they accepted? As I have elsewhere suggested,[53] European romanticism entered this country only through the gates of Protestant morality. As a result, though innumerable schemes for the salvation of society were in the air, such as Fourierism, Owenism, Saint-Simonianism, and the like; and though pseudo-scientific cults essentially romantic in their ideology, like mesmerism, phrenology, vegetarianism, hydropathy, and their kind had their little day and ceased,[54] the Americans indignantly repudiated the moral anarchy of romanticism.[55] The consequences were paradoxical: on the one hand, the really great American moralists—like Emerson, Alcott, Thoreau, and Whitman—were stimulated by exciting philosophical discussion from or about Europe; on the other hand, the emasculation of that romanticism in the interests of "morality" encouraged the sentimentalism of American culture.[56] Nor is sentimentalism so remote from the dynamic concept as at first glance it may seem, since, like the stronger doctrine of the transcendentalists, it rests primarily upon a theory of immanence in nature.[57]

A more problematical, but fascinating, question is the development of the American feeling for landscape [58] as it is related to the dynamic conception of the universe. To the earlier explorers the New World landscape was remarkable for its novelty and its fecundity, whereas to the settler both attributes were as likely to be annoying as appealing. In the full eighteenth century, nature was beneficent, its utilitarian aspects being cordially chronicled by Franklin, Jefferson, Crèvecoeur, and others.[59] In the last decades of that century the external "romantic" and "picturesque" entered the national consciousness.[60] In the earlier nineteenth century writers exhibit that "ardent emotional devotion to nature because of her beauty or divinity"[61] which has been noted, but obviously the American situation represents more than the application of romantic theorems to "unspoiled" nature.[62] In the full flood of the new epoch, feeling for landscape did not begin characteristically with genre pictures or local color fiction;[63] on the contrary, because of the size, variety, and mass of the continent, the American movement is expansive and grandiose rather than local. The Hudson River School painted their immense canvases in a vain effort to catch the sweep and movement of the American scene;[64] poets like Bryant leave in the memory an impression of the immensity, the vast forces of nature, in America;[65] in Cooper's novels the characteristic note is not so much that God created the natural world as that the American wilderness teems with an exhaustless variety of types and forms of life. In succession to the Hudson River School, painters like F. E. Church, Thomas Moran, and Albert Bierstadt[66] sought to record an immense dynamism[67] upon their vast panoramas; a man like Catlin went west to paint the "free and vivid realities of life" among the Indians;[68] and the charm of Audubon's bird-pictures for Europeans lay not only in their accuracy, but in their sense of vital life.[69] Mere imitativeness, the ordinary channels of artistic influence alone,[70] are insufficient to account for these extraordinary revolutions; and I suggest that, just as the present age thinks in evolutionary terms, so the earlier period thought in dynamic terms, and that the origin of this dynamic view is European.

To distinguish in the histories of the sciences the ways by which the organic view supplemented the mechanical view in nineteenth-century America requires more expert knowledge than I possess. Among the contributors to natural science, however, two characteristic figures emerge, Audubon and Agassiz. It is significant that Audubon was at once literary man, artist, and naturalist. The dynamic view of nature tempted to intuitional short-cuts; and just as Humboldt drew with no sense of difference upon landscape painting, travel books, poets, and scientists to explain the world, so in Audubon, as John Burroughs says, the "love of nature and of copying natural forms, rather than the love of science, was the mainspring of his career." [71] His drawings were intended to endow "his animals with all the moving energy of which they were capable" [72]—again one notes the vitalistic prepossession —and though the lines of his intellectual filiation are not clear, one finds him admiring Thomson's *Seasons*, longing for the pen of Walter Scott, and accepting the friendly interest of Professor Jameson in Edinburgh, and of Cuvier and the younger Geoffroy St.-Hilaire in Paris.[73] He, too, insists upon the dynamism, the endless fecundity of nature;[74] he, too, seeks in it a grand and simple vital force.[75] But Audubon was a nature-lover rather than a scientist; it is in the person of the immensely influential Agassiz, pupil of Oken and Schelling, the friend of Humboldt and Hugh Miller,[76] that one finds the most influential channel of the dynamic concept. An opponent of evolution, Agassiz yet argued for a ceaseless form of development of plan as expressed in structure (as opposed to the change of one structure into another) and spoke of "an invisible thread" which "unwinds itself throughout all time, across this immense diversity, and presents to us as a definite result, a continual progress in the development of which man is the term." [77] When Adam Sedgwick wrote him in 1845 that he was pained by the "turgid mystical bombast" of the evolutionists and their "cold and irrational materialism," Agassiz cordially replied that the biological phenomena of the changing earth were due "to the direct intervention of a creative power," and that the only source of species was "a creative purpose manifested in space," "emanating from a creative power, the author of them all." [78] He devoted the Lowell lectures to the plan of creation; and in his influential *Geological Sketches* argued for a dynamic force in nature which was not evolutionary.[79] If the "organic" point of view overthrew Newtonian mechanism, it retarded the acceptance in America of the Darwinian hypothesis; and the personal popularity of Agassiz was such as vastly to extend the boundaries of his influence.[80]

The dynamic view, translated into the doctrine of immanence, had also its powerful influence in American religion. The change in Christian theology wrought by men like Bushnell, Theodore Parker, and Henry Ward Beecher [81] and carried forward by Theodore Munger, George A. Gordon, Washington Gladden, and William A. Brown in following decades, had its roots in European theology. In revolt against Calvinism, the movement began with Parker's sermon *On the Transient and Permanent in Christianity* (1841)[82] and Bushnell's *Christian Nurture* (1846); it held, in Bushnell's phrase that "growth, not conquest" is "the true method of Christian progress," [83] and argued that theology is not "a scheme of wise sentences," but "a Living State." The Christian student "will be a man who understands God as being indoctrinated or inducted into God, by studies that are themselves inbreathings of the divine love and power." [84] Popularized by the revival methods of Charles G. Finney, the "New Theology," preached from a thousand pulpits, seemed to enlist the doctrines of immanence, of the creative Logos, in the service of progress, of expansiveness, of the exploitative and optimistic life of the nation: [85] the go-getter was to have the authority of theology behind him. On a lower level, the same religious expansiveness appeared among the innumerable religious prophets, sects, communities, and crazes of the period, a large number of which have their origins in Europe.[86] Half social, half religious, these foreign transplantations added to the urge, the sense of divine guidance, the belief in the manifest destiny of American life.

Here I must conclude, leaving most of the story untold. Even in the period I have been able to discuss a hundred questions arise. What new elements, for example, entered American education from European theories, half mystical, half realistic? How far was the American notion of nationalism strengthened by European historical theory of the progress sort? When did the Americans adopt the institutional economics of the mid-century? How far was the concept of the national state strengthened by the coming in of foreigners and of foreign thought? In what degree was the woman's rights movement dependent upon European ideas? Is the careless exploitation of national resources purely an American philosophy? What does the nineteenth-century concept of democracy owe to Europe? These and similar problems readily occur. In post-revolutionary rationalism and in the dynamic concept of the universe I find two important poles from which European influences tended to emanate. I believe the influences I have sketched are of fundamental importance to the historian of American culture.

8

THE RENAISSANCE AND AMERICAN ORIGINS *

I BEGIN with the historical truism that the Renaissance
corresponds generally to the interval between the effective
discovery of the New World and the permanent establishment
of English-speaking colonies in North America. I say "permanent establishment" for two reasons. In the first place, until
the second third of the seventeenth century, it was nip and
tuck whether Jamestown and the Massachusetts colonies
would survive; and in the second place, it is often assumed
that because these colonies were created during the Renaissance, Renaissance culture is directly reflected in their creation. My speculations concern this second assumption. So far
as American culture has been influenced by the Renaissance,
was that influence immediate in time, or has that influence
been more richly felt at some later stage of our national development?

Every age is both cause and consequence. Every age is the
heir of all preceding ages, so that, to paraphrase Emerson,
every fact of history contains all of history. One is aware how
scholarship, rightly curious about origins, ever tends to ante-
date conventional beginnings and therefore to deny the unique
validity of any chronological division. This has been particularly true of that elusive concept, the Renaissance. Some writers
have become so convinced the Renaissance is but a late phase
of mediaeval culture that they would, if they could, abolish
the term. Others point to the Renaissance of the thirteenth
century or to the Carolingian Renaissance as if some fallacy

* 1943.

were involved in talking about what we conventionally call the Renaissance in terms of what we conventionally attribute to it. Doubtless it is laudable to keep a flexible mind, but it is also confusing; and there comes a time when it is well to retreat upon a kind of Macaulayan common sense and say flatly that the Renaissance exists. By that word one means that the West-European world, beginning about the middle of the fifteenth century and continuing for a considerable space of time thereafter, but not later than about 1660, came to cherish those values, to make those discoveries, and to act in those ways which differentiate the era in question from the earlier middle ages and the later modern times.

I trust this is not shadow-boxing, nor is it another bout of shadow-boxing if I now assert that North America was of the Renaissance, but not in it. I mean by this to point to the paradox of our situation. Whereas the effective discovery of the New World immediately and profoundly affected men's concepts of life in Europe, it is not clear that Renaissance Europe immediately and profoundly shaped life in colonial North America except in the general sense that any age is the heir of the past. In South America, to be sure, things were different. The two great Iberian empires below the Rio Grande were Renaissance cultural achievements of the utmost magnitude, as their literatures, their architecture, their paintings, their modes of life (especially at the upper-class level), their manner of colonial government, and their religious establishments prove. The English colonies were, however, fashioned in the first instance by forces mainly released through the Reformation rather than through the Renaissance, and in the second instance by a commercial revolution in an England that was already forgetting Marlowe and Raleigh in proportion as it was getting ready for Bunyan and Defoe. In some ways, indeed, the colonies were farther along (or farther behind, as one prefers). Milton is still a Renaissance poet, though he died in 1674, and Cromwell has some of the characteristics of the man of *virtù*. There is no American Milton, and there is no American Cromwell, even in colonial terms.

One can, of course, debate endlessly the precise intellectual relations of the Reformation to the Renaissance. The important fact is that they were different phenomena, antagonistic or complementary as one chooses. But if we accept the usual notion of the Renaissance, it is difficult to see that the British colonies owed it very much. As I have elsewhere showed, the very concept of colony-making among the English owed almost nothing to Renaissance thought. There is no Renaissance colonial architecture and no painting. If the man of *virtù* is the supreme expression of Renaissance secular energy, it is evident that men of *virtù* like Raleigh, Gilbert, or Captain John Smith either do not touch our shores or touch them but to return. I suppose the humanist to be the most characteristic expression of Renaissance intellectual and moral values; but though one may admire the erudition of the Mather family or remember that Sandys translated part of Ovid in Virginia, the translation is without significance for American letters, and no one, so far as I recall, ever thought of John Cotton or Increase Mather as a humanist—that is, if Erasmus and Sir Thomas More deserve the term. The New England clergyman was often a precise and lucid thinker and a person of considerable information, but he was a theologian rather than a philosopher, a learned man rather than a cultivated one, an antiquarian rather than a humanist. Again, the Virginia gentry, like the New England merchants or the Carolina planters, often exhibit what Dr. Johnson calls literature and were by no means without graciousness; but it is no derogation from the honest merit of the Brown brothers of Rhode Island to say that none of them quite parallels Cosimo dei Medici, just as it is no derogation from the genial culture of the Byrd family to say that no member of it quite suggests Marsilio Ficino or the Admirable Crichton. I do not regard the Puritans as a crabbed or inferior people, but, religion apart, they were not persons likely to be comfortable in the Vatican of Julius II or the court of the Duchess of Urbino. If colonial historians were the heirs of humanistic theories of history, and if colonial literary men preached or practised a theory of poetry or criticism whose antecedents can be traced to the Latins and the Greeks, it does not therefore follow that they were the direct heirs of the Revival of Learning. A variety of forces may have intervened. He who reads Cicero is not necessarily a Ciceronian.

If I am unjust to the colonies and to the forces that shaped them, the error can be corrected. What is more important is that I may seem to be saying only what is extremely true. More important still is my suggestion that the richest influence of the Renaissance upon American culture is to be found, not in the seventeenth, but in the nineteenth, century, so that, even if my doubts about the direct transplantation of Renaissance values to North America are silenced, I should still hint at the possibility of another, and more revealing, study of cultural relationships.

In the third and fourth chapters of his book on the Renaissance Funck-Brentano discusses the connection between merchants and bankers in Italy, and Renaissance culture. Let me quote or summarize his description of Cosimo dei Medici the Elder, who was, as he reminds us, for thirty years as undisputed a master of Florence as were Peisistratus and Pericles in the cities of ancient Greece.

His bearing and expression in slyness and false affability are strongly reminiscent of Louis XI of France. Both were of the same bourgeois cast. Cosimo's frail body owed its stoop, perhaps, to long hours spent crouching over his ledgers and peering at their spindly commercial script. He had neither beauty nor distinction; in society he was grave and taciturn, speaking chiefly in monosyllables, accompanied by a nod, or in short pithy phrases, but sometimes breaking out into totally incomprehensible speech. Vespasiano says of him that he could read people from their faces alone. In public, he was no orator, but a skilful conversationalist, full of logical subtlety and unforeseen twists of speech, with often a spark of malice or some broad and popular witticism. He had the art of convincing without reasoned argument. In private life he was serious, taking no pleasure in play-actors or buffoons, but his delight was in chess and in his vineyard and garden. He was no warrior. . . . His greatest assets were his subtlety, his indefatigable patience, and his imperturbable cunning. He was as skilful a politician as he was a banker, and the fortune he amassed from banking he used for the furtherance of his political ambitions.

Let me quote some other characteristic sentences: "His will was felt everywhere, in great things as in small, in general policy and minor every-day details, but he himself never appeared." "He was liberal without generosity and conciliatory without ever yielding an inch which he desired to retain; magnanimous to his friends but pitiless to his enemies. . . ." "He cared not a fig for those who spoke of toleration and of liberty. 'Yes, yes,' he would say; 'that is all very well—in principle—but men are not led by paternosters.' " "In his hands taxation became a merciless weapon." And yet Burckhardt calls Cosimo the foremost man in Italy, both because he managed Florence well and because he was one of the principal patrons of art, letters, culture, and charity. He supported Marsilio Ficino. He patronized Della Robbia, Donatello, Castagno, Ghirlandajo, Fra Lippo Lippi, and a dozen more. He rebuilt much of Florence. He housed the Platonic Academy. He gave generously to charity. He was also ruthless and unjust, employing writers to libel his enemies and driving his adversaries to prison or death.

To Funck-Brentano Cosimo suggests Louis XI, but this comparison will not occur to an American. Does not this sketch, with certain omissions, rather suggest one of those millionaires whom an unfavorable historian has called the "robber barons" of the last century—the Huntingtons, the Goulds, the Fiskes, the Clarks, the Stanfords, the Rockefellers, the Carnegies, the Guggenheims, the Morgans, the Pulitzers, the Mellons of the palmy days before the New Deal? The days of economic exploitation, combines, trusts, the Heinz-Daly copper war in Montana, the fight of Jim Hill to dominate a railroad empire in the Northwest, the buying up of courts and legislatures, Senatorial elections and appointments to the Federal bench, the manipulation of stock markets, the use of rebate and simulated panic, of artificially lowered prices and artificially increased taxation to crush competitors—in sum, all the cruelty and epic struggle of the Gilded Age and its aftermath? But does it not also call up the founding of libraries and art museums, hospitals and institutes, the patronage of opera and orchestra, the creation of schools, colleges, and universities, the purchase of newspaper publicity and magazine propaganda, the patronage half scornfully, half enviously extended to writers, musicians, painters, sculptors, decorators, fashion designers and cooks, the beginnings of vast foundations for scholarship, research, medicine, public charity, and education—in sum, all the intellectual benefits that have come to the nation through the fortunes of the robber barons? I have said that the Mathers would have been uncomfortable in the Vatican of Julius II or the court of Urbino; but I find no difficulty in picturing Senator Clark of Montana in easy converse with Cosimo dei Medici, and I suggest that the parallel between the Fuggers of Augsburg and the Rockefellers of New York or the Huntingtons of California or the Guggenheims of Colorado is close and instructive. The robber baron and the Renaissance commercial tyrant managed to combine cruelty and culture, the exploitation of the state and benevolence towards its population, plunder and patronage, the support of private armies and the creation of academies, ruthless individualism and a queer sort of social responsibility. The palaces of Italian cities were in fact often the models of the palaces that once lined Fifth Avenue, and the difference between the Farnese family building the first modern theater in Parma and Mr. Samuel Insull and his friends building a lush, but modern, Civic Opera House in Chicago is not important.

If Florence owes its art galleries to mercantile munificence, Chicago owes its Art Institute to the Hutchinsons, the Spragues, the Ryersons, the McCormicks, the Bartletts, the Fields, the Palmers. Said Gertrude Stein to Mrs. Charles B. Goodspeed of the Windy City: "Never make the mistake of fraternizing with artists—*command* them!" The saying is worthy of the Borgias.

The self-justification of the capitalist has been traced by a succession of writers to the rise of Protestantism, specifically of Calvinism, and therefore to the Reformation, but this is not now my point. Neither is my point the Veblen theory of conspicuous expenditure. It is also true that the merchant princes of the eighteenth century were often patrons of art, philanthropists, and friends of education. There is, however, a profound difference between a merchant prince and a captain of industry; and though the elder Rockefeller is said to have once gravely testified in a Presbyterian church: "I believe the power to make money is a gift from God," I find nothing in Calvinism that leads directly to boxes in the diamond horseshoe of the Metropolitan Opera House at $60,000 a season. Most of us do not confuse Benjamin Franklin with Diamond Jim Brady, Alexander Hamilton with William Randolph Hearst. My point is not that rich Americans did not exist before Appomattox nor that the wealthy failed to patronize culture before 1860; my point is the special quality of the relation between wealth and culture beginning in the second half of the nineteenth century. I suggest that this relation is closer to Cosimo dei Medici than it is to John Calvin.

Is the parallel anything more than curious? Is there reason to suppose that the example of the Renaissance was influential upon American behavior in the Gilded Age? I cannot answer the question with exactness; but I suggest there are indications hinting at a real connection; and I suggest also that no more exciting field for cultural study is open to the student of American affairs.

What are some of these indications?

According to the *New English Dictionary* the word "renaissance" in the sense in which I have been using it does not appear in our language until 1845, when it is used in Ford's *Handbook of Spain*. As applied to art and architecture only, it is first used in 1840 by T. A. Trollope. The first American example is from an essay on Keats by James Russell Lowell in 1854. The first use of the word in a generalized sense— as when one speaks of a renaissance of French nationalism— dates from 1872 when John Morley so used the word in his *Voltaire*. Whatever is true of other languages, the late appearance of this familiar term strongly suggests that the English— and American—concept of the Renaissance is a creation of the nineteenth century.

This paradox finds stronger support. I have checked some characteristic bibliographies in the *Cambridge Modern History*. For Chapter 16 of the first volume—the chapter on "The Classical Renaissance"—11 general items are listed, ten of which date from the nineteenth century. Seventy-three other authorities are given, of which 46 date from the same era. For chapter 17, "The Christian Renaissance," 44 items appear, of which 22 date from the nineteenth century. The bibliography for the first three chapters in volume two, which deal with Medicean Rome, the Habsburgs, and the Valois kings, lists 9 bibliographical works, of which seven date from the nineteenth century; 38 documentary sources, of which 35 were printed in the nineteenth century; 56 contemporary histories, chronicles, etc., of which 24 were not printed until the nineteenth century; and 153 secondary works, of which 108 are from that crucial period. Other bibliographies will reveal similar distributions. That is, putting aside a few twentieth century titles, and putting aside also primary sources printed during the Renaissance, the nineteenth century, as it were, is *par excellence* the period of scholarship about the Renaissance. The number of works dealing with this age and descending to us from the seventeenth and eighteenth centuries is relatively slight. Contrast the history of scholarship about antiquity.

Lord Acton described Burckhardt's *Die Cultur der Renaissance in Italien* as "the most penetrating and subtle treatise on the history of civilization that exists in literature;" yet this profoundly influential volume did not appear until 1860 (at Leipzig). Pater's famous *Studies in the Renaissance,* a book that did much to popularize the concept, was not published until 1873; John Addington Symonds' magisterial volumes did not reach publication until 1875. Let us add that Renaissance scholarship in this country was negligible until about the same decades. Thus the first American edition of Shakespeare of real worth was that of Richard Grant White in 1857-1866; and H. H. Furness's *New Variorum* Shakespeare began publication in 1871. The first thorough treatment of Renaissance art by an American would seem to be *Art Studies: The 'Old Masters' of Italy* (1860) by that neglected talent, James Jackson Jarves, whose influence upon American culture most historians ignore. Isolated dates prove nothing, but it is at least disturbing that the mature interpretation of the Renaissance coincides with the efflorescence of the American millionaire.

Is the coincidence only chronological? Here I suggest investigation is needed. Again, however, there are signs of a real connection; and I urge that a climate of opinion created by John Ruskin and Matthew Arnold, James Russell Lowell, Charles Eliot Norton, James Jackson Jarves, Howard H. Furness, Thomas Lounsbury, Barrett Wendell, Frederick Law Olmsted, Charles Follen McKim, Edmund Clarence Stedman, Richard Henry Stoddard, John Root, Montgomery Schuyler, Augustus St. Gaudens, John La Farge, and many more; the life of the Century Club, the Lotos Club, the Tavern Club, the St. Botolph Club, the Sketch Club of Philadelphia, and others; the efflorescence of university clubs in various eastern cities—all these helped to turn the attention of American wealth to the importance of patronizing the arts and education, research and philanthropy. Article I of the constitution of The Century Association is typical, and reads: "This Association shall be composed of authors, artists, and amateurs of letters and the fine arts," and the charitable phrase "amateurs of letters and the arts" was often broadly interpreted to cover wealth precisely at a period when the practioners of the arts were struck by the parallel between the Italian and French Renaissance and their own times. The curious fascination which the man of culture had for the millionaire is illustrated in the affection of Andrew Carnegie for Matthew Arnold.

As revealing the fresh enthusiasm of the times I suggest a close reading of Lewis Mumford's *The Brown Decades* and Van Wyck Brooks's *New England: Indian Summer* with this hypothesis in mind. Mr. Brooks, for example, notes how, after the Civil War, the old ties of New England with reform and to the soil were loosened, and how a general re-orientation of interest took place, one aspect of which was an interest in things aesthetic. The Museum of Fine Arts was founded in 1870, "the symbol and crystallization of this movement of feeling; and half the domestic walls of Boston blossomed with Fra Angelico angels, with photographs or prints of Mona Lisa, or perhaps The Last Communion of Saint Jerome." The new age was Hellenistic rather than Hebraic; the vogue for travel and the rage for art came in as the old religions weakened.

Young men of means roamed over Italy, inspired with a wish to see sincerely, the fruit of their reading of Ruskin. They copied Roman inscriptions in their pocket notebooks. They studied Sciennese architecture and Tuscan sculpture; and they went to Verona to examine the Lombardic pillars, often with a mounting scorn of all things modern. . . . The Italianate circle was closely connected with Boston, and there the rage for art was all-engrossing. Days that had once been merely misty were described now as "Corot days," and Giotto and Cimabue, as themes of conversation, vied with castled crags and historic landscapes.

Important, I think, was the circle of Charles Eliot Norton, which included men like George E. Woodberry the Platonist, Bernhard Berenson the connoisseur, and James Loeb, who, in founding the Loeb Classical Library, was in a sense carrying on the work of the humanists. Equally important were Norton's summer gatherings at Ashfield, reminiscent of a Renaissance academy, where the problems of art and civilization were discussed in a group limited much after the fashion of the court of Urbino.

"America has a Renaissance," said Rodin of this period, "but America doesn't know it." The vital connection between wealth and architecture, notably the architecture of public buildings, traced by Mr. Lewis Mumford strikes me as very close to Renaissance culture, especially after one has read the books of Jarves and S. G. W. Benjamin, Montgomery Schuyler, and others. In 1883 Herbert Spencer was in New York; being interviewed by the newspaper men, he said:

After pondering over what I have seen of your vast manufacturing and trading establishments, the rush of traffic in your street-cars and elevated railways, your gigantic hotels and Fifth Avenue palaces, I was suddenly reminded of the Italian republics of the middle ages; and recalled the fact that, while there was growing up in them great commercial activity, a development of the arts which made them the envy of Europe, and a building of princely mansions which continue to be the admiration of travelers, their people were gradually losing their freedom.

Do you mean this as a suggestion that we are doing the like? It seems to me that you are.

The fact that Spencer's political prophesy parallels Macaulay's earlier one is not here relevant; what is significant is that this student of comparative cultures interpreted the phenomena as I have just done. One final observation. When the group of artists, architects, sculptors, and landscape designers met to plan the Columbian Exposition of 1893, Saint Gaudens is said to have looked around the board and exclaimed: "Do you realize this is the greatest gathering of artists since the Renaissance?" He could have uttered this sentence at no earlier stage in our history, and his striking remark first suggested this little study.

9

THE AMERICAN SCHOLAR ONCE MORE *

A HUNDRED years have elapsed since the most famous
Phi Beta Kappa address ever delivered was spoken in
Cambridge. Although anything less than a reading of all that
golden essay is to do injustice to it, I shall begin by briefly recalling it to your memory. The scholar, said Emerson, is Man
Thinking; and the principal instruments of his education are
three—nature, books, and action. From nature, rightly understood, he will learn that the laws of the universe are also the
laws of the human mind. The office of books is not to create
book-worms, but independent souls. The life of action is not
to be swallowed up in business, but to translate intellect into
character. And the final object of education is that the soul
may be weaned from a passive clinging to what has been said
and done in the world and prefer instead a vigorous intellectual independence. "We have listened too long," he said,
"to the courtly muses of Europe." The essay concludes with its
eloquent plea for a race of vigorous American individuals—
"the spirit of the American freeman is already suspected to be
timid, imitative, tame;" and the young sage declared to the
young men of 1837: "We will walk on our own feet; we will
work with our own hands; we will speak our own mind."
Everyone will recall how members of that audience went
out from the meeting as if they had listened to a voice proclaiming: "Thus saith the Lord."

I am frequently told that Emerson is outmoded. In the realm

* The Phi Beta Kappa Address, Dartmouth College, March, 1937.

of economic life rugged individualism, it is true, has a quaint, archaeological flavor, but Emerson was not discussing the life of business, but the life of citizenship and the life of thought. I propose now to inquire how far the liberal college in America has been faithful to the program suggested by his address.

In 1837 there were no universities in the United States with their innumerable professional colleges, vocational branches, graduate schools, extension divisions, and correspondence courses. The curriculum of the college was still centered in the humanities—the classics, philosophy, some history, a course in "natural philosophy" which, unlike most modern science courses, was really philosophical, and some training in rhetoric and oratory. The content of that curriculum was, I am afraid, meagre, the instruction was not good, libraries and laboratories were inadequate, and the life of the undergraduate suffered from obsolescent regulations. But the liberal college of 1837 had one advantage over the liberal college of today. It knew what it was doing; and it had a unified concept of college education. It conceived that the humanities were central to the training of an educated man.

A hundred years later the liberal college of Emerson's day has, in effect, almost disappeared. The most characteristic educational institution in the country is the State university; and if we examine the college of arts in any State university, we discover that, though it exists as a formal organization, its intellectual unity has vanished. In its first two years it is trying to do the work which the high schools, under the direction of educational experts, have ceased doing—that is, it is trying to get its students to read and write. It is also offering "service courses" for the benefit of the professional schools which feed upon it—beginning instruction in this or that branch of knowledge which the student must get out of the way before he can fully enter the engineering school or the school of law or the school of medicine. In its last two years it has in fact become a vocational school for the training of teachers of English or history or the foreign languages, or for the training of biologists, chemists, social service workers, archaeologists, and so forth.

It is a commonplace that the multiplication of knowledge has meant the multiplication of courses; and that any unity of aim which the college may once have had has in fact disappeared beneath an avalanche of specialized instruction by specialists. The formal paper requirements of general training in the first two years and specialization in the second, of concentration and distribution, of major subjects and related minor subjects—the phrases differ—though designed to retain what can be kept of the old unified concept, do not in fact achieve their object. And if I select as an example the college of liberal arts in the State university, with which I am most familiar, the same conditions, to greater or less degree, exist in privately endowed universities, and even, to some extent, in what are euphoniously known as the "ivy colleges." Proponents of instruction in the psychology of salesmanship or statistical measurement or journalism claim that their subjects, properly pursued, are as "liberalizing" as literature or philosophy; but where every course is equally humane, the concept of the humanities loses all meaning.

There have been gallant attempts to check or redirect the current of educational development and to revive the concept of a unified humane education in the liberal college. Mr. Meiklejohn headed for a time an experimental college at the University of Wisconsin, in which the students, after directing their energies to Greek civilization, turned their attention to civilization in the United States. If the educationalists are right in supposing that the proper procedure in learning is to proceed from the known to the unknown, this attempt violated the first principle of pedagogy; at any rate, the college has since been closed.

More recently, Professor Norman Foerster, director of the School of Letters at the University of Iowa, has issued a book called "The American State University," in which, after an exhaustive analysis of the evils now existing in the liberal college, he proposes that we shall abandon what he calls the naturalistic view of life and return to the humanistic. Mr. Foerster is somewhat vague as to the details of his curricular reform, but it seems to imply that we should all adopt a dualistic theory of human nature. He submits a list of great books which have been proposed as central to such a curriculum; of the fifty-three authors named, I note with interest that only two have to do with the United States—an item called "American State Papers" and the final name in the list, William James. The list, however, is not of Mr. Foerster's composing; he remarks that the past hundred years are represented by it "somewhat injudiciously" and he says that the present cannot be represented by great books at all—there would have to be "lectures and demonstrations illustrating the principles and modern history of science." But in a general way a curriculum which would center around great names from Homer to William James, provided the writings of these geniuses are interpreted to throw light upon the dualistic nature of man, would have Professor Foerster's approval.

A third interesting experiment is that being carried on at the University of Chicago. With the formal reorganization of the university which has gone hand-in-hand with this change we need not trouble ourselves. The underlying philosophy of the Chicago idea is what concerns us. This underlying philosophy, clearly and emphatically presented by its president, Mr. Hutchins, seeks in effect to return to the mediaeval concept of university training. By cutting through specialization and fact-finding to underlying principles, the proponents of this scheme hoped to alight upon certain controlling instruments in education. The method, at least as it is exemplified by some members of the faculty, depends on Socratic analysis. Rhetoric and grammar, in the sense of the exploration of meaning, receive renewed importance; and the primary business of the college seems to be to discuss principles rather more, and applications rather less, than has been customary in many college courses. "To aid in his understanding of ideas" (I quote Mr. Hutchins) "the student should be trained in those intellectual techniques which have been developed for the purpose of stating and comprehending fundamental principles."

With any attempt to restore unity to the liberal college one must have a certain sympathy. I confess, however, that Mr. Hutchins is over hasty in his scorn of specialists; and I am compelled to inquire, if the principal business of the college student is to learn to state and comprehend fundamental principles, when is the proper time for his beginning to apply them? I am of the philosophy that a fundamental principle remains an airy abstraction until you do something with it or about it; and though I hail with pleasure Mr. Hutchins's insistence upon the desirability of putting first things first, I wonder whether a loving and long perusal of Plato's "Republic" is really going to change the voting habits of American citizens so fundamentally that we can relegate our present departments of sociology and political science to an inferior position in the educational scheme of things. The habit of making metaphysical inquiry into what history or literature or philosophy may be before you get around to the facts of history or literature or philosophy has its weaknesses; and the weaknesses of this educational reform seem to me to be two: it tends to subordinate the genetic study of human institutions to a system of metaphysical absolute; and it tends to turn out students, whose habits of analysis may become so strong as to hinder their habits of action—and action, as Emerson reminds us, is one of three requisites of a humane education.

However this may be, I wish to call your attention to one quality which all three of these reforms of the liberal college have in common. In Emerson's phrase, they have all listened to the courtly muses of Europe. Mr. Meiklejohn did not get around to American life until his students had spent a year on Greek civilization. The list of great names in Mr. Foerster's book contains only two American items out of fifty-three. Mr. Hutchins sets before us the example of mediaeval European universities and urges us to revive the practices of the mediaeval schoolmen.

No one in this audience, I trust, wishes to be a chauvinist. No one can seriously argue that what the world needs is more nationalism. After certain performances by the self-styled patriotic societies, or the drive for teachers' oath bills, or our contemptible attitude towards foreigners, no one but desires less, rather than more, one-hundred-per-cent Americanism. We are accustomed to say that the essence of a liberal education is an acquaintance with the best that has been said and done in the world, and not merely in the United States. Everyone will agree that a knowledge of other times and other nations, other geniuses than American ones, other art than American art, other cultures than our own is indispensable to the humanely educated man.

But at the same time I am impressed by two facts about these reforms of the liberal education. The first is that, given American youth to educate, these outlines of great books, this return to scholastic analysis, this occupation with Greek civilization first and American civilization afterwards, have a curious air of hanging in a vacuum. The connection between the reading proposed, and the fact that the reader is going to live in the United States of America in the year nineteen-hundred-and-something is tenuous and remote. The student is required to accept too much on faith; and the teacher is left with only the vaguest directions as to how this analysis, this reading, this exploration of a remote culture are to be brought to bear upon the civilization into which our student is to be catapulted at the end of four years in college.

I should not so much mind the cloistral air of these programs, were it not that each of the reformers argues that his proposal is directly intended to create better American citizens. Both Mr. Foerster and Mr. Hutchins cite with admiration the ideas of Thomas Jefferson, who in his letter to Peter Carr of 1814, urged that Virginia should establish schools "where every branch of science deemed useful at this day and in our country should be taught." Mr. Hutchins tries to get around this letter by saying that Jefferson did not mean college, when he said college, and university, when he said university, but the uncomfortable fellow will not down: in his discussion of the University of Virginia Jefferson explicitly called for "all the branches of useful science," and when he said "useful," it is clear that he meant those branches of knowledge which would be relevant to the American cultural problem. However much some of our so-called cultured men may dislike the fact (and some of them apparently do), we have to deal with education in the United States; and the second weakness I would point in these schemes is that the American cultural tradition is, in fact, ignored. They are set up as if Europe were the main thing that mattered.

And if it be argued that it is essential for American students to get a world-view from their four years in the liberal college, I can only retort that the reforms in question do not even do that. As H. G. Wells long ago pointed out, European education has agreed tacitly to ignore three-fourths of the human race. I refer, of course, to the civilization and the arts of Asia, not to speak, in lesser degree, of Africa. The return to Europe, which is at the bottom of these representative proposals, is a return to an attitude of mind which Emerson was expressly endeavoring to destroy. "The spirit of the American freeman," he said, "is already suspected to be timid, imitative, tame." "I ask not," he remarks, "for the great, the remote, the romantic; what is doing in Italy or Arabia; what is Greek art, or Provençal minstrelsy; I embrace the common, I explore and sit at the feet of the familiar, the low. Give me insight into today, and you may have the antique and future worlds." If this be chauvinism, I can only say, like Patrick Henry, make the most of it.

The claims of the world and of our own country; the necessity of understanding the past and understanding the present; the desirability of acquainting the rising generation with the works of dead geniuses, and at the same time not inducing in them what scholarship too often induces—a lack of sympathy for present art, an attitude of superiority towards the American experiment, and a disdain for democracy—how shall we solve a problem so complex?

I suggest we return to the practice of the Greeks. The ancient Greeks were unfortunate in that they had no college presidents, no professors of anything, and no schools of education to instruct them in the desirability of knowing the best that had been done and thought in the world; but I am impressed by the fact that these Greeks whose sagacity we today so much admire, placed their own culture foremost as an object of study. Plato's "Republic" is not a vague attempt at comparative political science; it is a rather practical inquiry into what can be done to improve the Greek city-state. Thucydides is not writing the history of the world; he tells us he is writing the history of the greatest thing that ever happened to Hellas. The inquiries of Aristotle are not into what other people thought, but, to a remarkable degree, into what the Greeks thought.

I am not now interested to inquire whether the great Greek thinkers might have taken a world-view of civilization, and did not—they might certainly have told us more about the Egyptian and Persian cultures than they chose to; I am not now inquiring whether their attitude towards the *barbaroi* was provincial; I am merely saying that on the basis of an exploration of their own culture they created a body of literature to which we have ever since been recurring. Neither do I propose that, in our search for a central point around which to build a humane education, we should so far imitate the

Greeks as to concentrate on the United States and throw everything else out the window. What I am saying is this: first,
the supposition that humane education is necessarily an anti-
national or un-national education is a supposition which, in
the case of the Greeks, clearly breaks down; and second, a
study of one's own culture, a preparation to live in the state
to which birth has consigned one for better or worse, would
seem to offer a center around which a humane education could
conceivably be built.

And I further point out that the French, who are in the
modern world sometimes considered the successors of the
classical peoples, in their educational system do precisely what
the ancient Greeks may in a sense be said to have done. The
French tradition is central in French education. The calm
assumption that French thought and French literature are the
most civilized thought and literature in the modern world
is an assumption which has its amusing aspects; but I suspect
that the solidity of the French intellectual tradition owes more
to the refusal of the Frenchman to be diverted from his fine
belief in the superior validity of his own tradition than our
more enthusiastic advocates of educational cosmopolitanism
are willing to admit. In the very last paragraph of his great
Histoire de la Littérature Française, perhaps the finest history
of a national literature ever written, M. Lanson, after speculat-
ing on what the future of that literature may be, concludes that
there will still be masterpieces, reading which future Frenchmen will find in them "le visage de la France éternelle."

I have yet to hear any member of an American English department assure his class that future American literature will
mirror "le visage de l'Amérique éternelle." And before we
smile at an idea which may seem incongruous, I think we had
better first inquire why we are willing to accept M. Lanson's
dictum as entirely proper, and why we treat the same idea as
satirical by-play when it is applied to a republic whose government has outlasted every European government save two,

the history of whose country extends backward to the invention of printing, and the study of whose civilization is seriously pursued over the entire civilized world.

I cannot too often insist that I have no desire whatsoever to cut off American students from the fullest possible knowledge of the thought and culture of other lands. But I am continually impressed by the fact that among the humanities we seem to stress the importance of an acquaintance with every great culture except our own. In the single field of literature in English, for example, note the casual treatment of our own literary history. It is a subject which is almost invariably at the bottom of that heap of miscellaneous courses which constitute the curriculum of the English department. Thousands of college students are annually graduated who have no knowledge of their own literary tradition whatsoever. Thousands more are graduated with no knowledge of the history of their own country. Those who know anything about American philosophy or American religion or the American theatre or the history of painting or architecture or music in their own country are negligible.

I wonder whether we shall ever make headway with the humanities, so long as we insist, as in fact we do insist, that an understanding of American civilization is the last thing that we are going to teach. Is it any wonder that alert minds are drawn into economics and sociology and science and schools of pedagogy and engineering and law, when those in charge of the humanities persist in their refusal to bring to bear upon the problems of life in the United States what they have to offer? I see no use in scolding young America because it finds a seminar in capital and labor vital in the nation in which young America has to find a job. The depopulation of the classics departments, the drift out of philosophy into social problems, the complaint that our best minds do not go into the study of modern languages—these are symptomatic of a deeper malady than the urge for vocational study—they

161

are symptomatic, I believe, of the profound fact that the undergraduate wants to understand his own country, and that the humanities have mainly failed to show him how they could help him to comprehend it.

It is one thing vaguely to summon the student to learn the best that has been done or said in the world; another thing to summon him to the problem: through what inquiries into the past and present can I best understand the country in which I am going to live? When Emerson says in his oracular way: "Give me insight into today, and you may have the antique and future worlds," he does not mean we are to discard past times and foreign countries, but rather that the value of past times and foreign countries is that value which they have towards the enrichment of life in present-day America. I submit that we are altogether too vague about how we propose to secure these values. I submit that intelligent citizens are not created by a mere passive exposure to the past. I submit that teaching the humanities in America is not the same thing as teaching America the humanities.

While the humanities have been exploring the sources of Ben Jonson's comedies or Greek art or the epistemology of Duns Scotus—all of which, I freely admit, are admirable things in themselves—the social studies, so-called, have moved into the American field. The one thing that we can be reasonably sure of in the present state of the liberal college is that if the student has any acquaintance with the interpretation of life in his own country, it will be an economic interpretation. Even the historians have, in a number of cases, swung over to economic determinism. But the economic interpretation of history or of society, though a valuable interpretation, is fundamentally a rather naïve one.

Since the days of Thorstein Veblen, that scarecrow of the British classical school the economic man has been wonderfully dressed up, but he still remains economic man. According to those who first brought him into being, economic man was a very simple creature. He was motivated by a single and selfish desire—the desire to seek pleasure and avoid pain. He had a supernaturally intelligent mind. For example, he always bought in the cheapest market and sold in the dearest, which is more than most business men have been able to do. His sole reading matter seems to have been Ricardo's book on rent and Malthus's essay on the increase of population. His life was devoted to economic gain; and what he did in his spare time, if he ever had any, I haven't the slightest idea. He must have married and begot children, because Malthus worked out what would happen if he had too many children and the wheat crop didn't go around, but how he ever fell in love, or how he proposed to his girl, or whether he mislaid the ring at the wedding I do not know. I assume he was once a boy and that he eventually grew old, and that he was filled with dreams and memories—probably of the time he bought pigs in one town and sold them at a slight profit in another, but it seems more probable that he was created full-grown, at about forty-two. His world must have had starlight and moonrise and the scent of flowers in it, but like a well-educated pupil of Adam Smith, he determinedly paid no attention to these things; and if he was ever actuated by rage or hate or love or passion, quickened by a drumbeat or awed by an ocean storm, there is no record. He was not English nor American nor Chinese; he had no legends, no tradition, no customs; he was simply economic man.

Now when you strip the merely sociological interpretation of the modern world of its manifold variations, it is surprising how often—I do not say always, but often—you will find that you are dealing with economic man—economic man multiplied into masses or nations, but fundamentally very like the imaginary being whom Ricardo and Malthus created for their calculations. Within the limits of the proper frame of reference, this concept of human nature is very useful; but just as it is difficult to conceive of economic man writing

"Hamlet" or painting the Sistine Madonna, so it is difficult in a nation "explained" only by economic forces also to explain the style of Emerson or the wide appeal of the "Gettysburg Address."

The advances made by the social sciences in the last few decades have my profound admiration. Their exponents are to be commended for having made America their laboratory. They are not in the least to blame because they have done their job extraordinarily well. No competent social scientist but admits as a matter of course that sociology is not all of existence, that economic motives are not even three-fourths of life. But when in the social sciences the student learns, or thinks he learns, that present-day America is in the grip of vast economic forces; while the humanities are off somewhere else talking about the sources of Chaucer or mediaeval scholasticism or the art of Cimabue, the practical conclusion which the student is likely to draw is either that the humanities have no place (except a decorative one) in the present United States or that humane arts and letters are something practised long ago by persons who are now excessively dead. And if I seem to speak with momentary disrespect of the labors of the classicist, the metaphysician, the philologian, or the literary historian, it is only because I am trying to see things from the point of view of the American undergraduates, the majority of whom, I am convinced, come to college because they are genuinely desirous of a better comprehension of the age in which they live. The difficulty of the humanities seems to be that they too often manufacture only meek young men in libraries; but man thinking, Emerson sternly reminds us, must not be subdued by his instruments.

It may be that a return to the methods of the scholastics will prove of lasting benefit at the University of Chicago. It may be that Mr. Foerster will convert enough persons to a philosophy of dualism to enable him at Iowa to reduce laboratory techniques to their proper subordination and get rid of the courses which now clutter up the curriculum of the college of liberal arts. It may be that someone somewhere sometime will be able to make ancient Greece so exciting a topic that American undergraduates will abandon the New Deal for the Peloponnesian War. I am, however, skeptical that the college of liberal arts can be permanently unified around a method, a system of ethics, or a return to a civilization over twenty centuries in the past. I think that Emerson, with the uncanny penetration of genius, saw more deeply into the problem of national education than the educators do. And I venture to suggest that a living core of interest around which the liberal college could once more be given a vital unity is the study and comprehension of American civilization.

I can see the classicist turn pale, and the professor of Chaucerian scholarship wince, while the metaphysician who has just completed a monograph on the monadism of Leibnitz utters faint sounds of inarticulate distress. The entire body of foreign language teachers rises in anguish, or would rise, I am sure, if the conventions of polite conduct did not restrain them. Yet I am suggesting only that we do what the ancient Greeks did; and proposing that we improve on their practice. I do not suggest that the present curriculum be abolished, or that we begin insisting that all good Americans shall remain sublimely ignorant of the effete monarchies of Europe—as Jefferson once thought that they should. I am merely proposing that the problem of American civilization, instead of being placed obscurely in the rear of our studies, shall be placed somewhere near the front. If we are really interested in educating American citizens for an intelligent participation in American life, I suggest that the liberal college might seek out ways and means of bringing before its students a far richer and more comprehensive knowledge of the American heritage, not only in the field of economic existence, but in those areas we vaguely call culture, than it has yet attempted to do. And when I speak of the American heritage I do not in the least propose that the New World shall neglect what it owes to the Old.

What I am seeking is not an administrative reorganization nor a required course nor a curricular upset nor an absorption with the immediate and the contemporary, but a point of view. The liberal college has been too eclectic, not merely in the sense that it has admitted all kinds of courses, but in the sense that its courses in the humanities themselves have been without any governing philosophy, any genuine educational aim. They seek too often to produce imitation Europeans, and imitation Europeans are always inferior to the genuine article. We try to bring America to Greece or Rome, Italy or France, instead of discovering what it is that Greece and Rome and France and Italy have to bring to America. I return once more to Emerson, when he says: "I look upon the discontent of the literary class as a mere announcement of the fact that they find themselves not in the state of mind of their fathers, and regret the coming state as untried; as a boy dreads the water before he has learned that he can swim." "It is," he says, "a mischievous notion that we are come late into nature; that the world was finished a long time ago." We cannot forever tacitly insist that the humane values are found everywhere but in the United States. We do not necessarily need to abandon what we are teaching, but we need to teach it in a different way. Goethe did not become a Hellenist first and a German afterwards; it was when he discovered that an artificial education had quite unfitted him to understand the significance of his own cultural traditions that he embarked upon that remarkable career of self-improvement which made him the greatest German of his age.

Let us remember that the United States is also a very large and important part of the world. Let us sharply remind the nationalist and the one-hundred-percent patriot that he is merely the heir of an immense period of historic time which requires patient study, but let us not at the same time forget

166

that if the humanities are to dwell upon the virtues of Herodotus or Chaucer, they cannot therefore neglect the virtues of Whitman and Henry Adams. If there is culture in France, there is also civilization in the United States. The best corrective of American provincialism is not merely a knowledge of Europe, but also a richer knowledge of the struggle of the republic to become what it has dreamed of becoming. I do not desire to drive Europe out of the colleges, I merely insist upon the necessity of putting America in. How long can we safely permit our students to believe that the rise of industry is all there is to the story of American life? We have faced backward and turned to Europe in the humanities; cannot we sometimes turn westward and appraise our own accomplishments? The spirit of Emerson is likewise America. We have neglected the resources of our own spiritual life too long—I trust we shall not have to pay dearly for our neglect, in the materialism of which so many now complain, or in a narrow and extravagant nationalism, which, uncorrected by an understanding, not only of the spiritual struggle of mankind at large, but also by an understanding of the larger purposes of life in this republic, may yet obliterate the America of Emerson in the America of Ford.

IO

NOBILITY WANTED *

IN a revealing article in the *Saturday Evening Post* Mr. Arthur Train, whose Mr. Tutt is the delight of many readers, had this to say of the literary world: "I have read my own stuff in print for nearly half a century—forty-eight years, to be exact. During that time I have seen authors 'made' like movie stars, rise to glory, and, like the latter, fall; magazines in myriads appear, only to vanish into space; revolutionary changes in public taste; the honored names of one decade become the hissing of the next, again to achieve the later approval of critics; the art of writing often sink to a trade and authorship to big business."

To many persons Mr. Train's paragraph will seem a sufficient diagnosis of the ills which afflict American publishing. Some of these ills are universally recognized and deplored, but nobody seems to want to do anything about it. For the first time in its history, publishing faces redoubtable competition from other inventions—the motion picture and the radio; and it is natural, perhaps it is inevitable, that publishing should, in its effort to survive, adopt the weapons of the enemy. The movies advertise in superlatives, the radio plays up "personality appeal." Hence the adoption of phraseology from the circus in advertising books; hence the "making" of books and authors by commercial ballyhoo, the whirligig rise and fall of magazines, the elaborate contracts covering serial rights, motion-picture rights, radio rights, reprint rights, and recita-

* Founders' Day Address, Wheaton College, 1938.

tion rights; hence, in fact, everything that Mr. Train complains of.

But, though I admire Mr. Train's modesty (for he does not describe himself as a misunderstood genius), I doubt whether he has got at the root of our difficulties, which seems to me to be this: why, about twenty-five or thirty years ago, did American literature break with a hundred-year-old tradition, and what can be done to get it back into the tradition to which it belongs? For literature is still a powerful imaginative medium which can support, or fail to support, the democratic tradition in the United States, and for something over a quarter of a century it has in the main unconsciously failed to support that tradition.

Over and against the paragraph from Mr. Train let me place a quotation from De Quincey. The passage is found in De Quincey's discussion of the literature of knowledge and the literature of power. Here it is:

It is in relation to these great *moral* capacities that the literature of *power* . . . lives and has its field of action. . . . Tragedy, romance, fairy tale, or epopee, all alike restore to man's mind the ideals of justice, of hope, of truth, of mercy, of retribution, which else (left to the support of daily life in its realities) would languish for want of sufficient illustration.

And, a little later:

It is certain that, were it not for the literature of power, these ideals would often remain amongst us as mere notional forms; whereas, by the creative forces of man put forth in literature they gain a vernal life of restoration and germinate into vital activities. The commonest novel, by moving in alliance with human fears and hopes, with human instincts of wrong and right, sustains and quickens those affections.

The essay of De Quincey was published in 1848; Mr. Train's article appears ninety years later. Like Mr. Train, De Quincey was a professional writer—one who earns his living by his pen.

The essays which a solitary student now and then opens, to marvel, one hopes, at the richness of their music, were contributed on the ordinary bargain-and-sale basis to the commercial periodicals of the nineteenth-century world. They were written from the same profit motive which leads the contemporary novelist to sell his manuscript to the highest bidder and to bargain shrewdly with Hollywood over the movie rights.

Mr. Train refers to his own writing as stuff in print. He tells us that the art of writing sinks into a trade, and authorship into big business. He says that the reputation of authors, like that of movie stars, is commercially made, and vanishes when commerce is satiated. De Quincey, on the other hand, does not refer to literature as stuff. So far as he is concerned, publishers and literary agents, authors' contracts and serial rights, do not exist. They are the means to literature, not the end of writing. Literature is eternal. Its purpose is to restore to man's mind the ideals of justice, of hope, of truth, of mercy, of retribution. Lest we hastily judge he is talking about the difficult air of the iced mountain's top where Milton is supposed to dwell, he brings the argument down to the commonest novel, which, moving in alliance with human fears and hopes, sustains and quickens the affections.

Now it is easy to dispose of De Quincey by saying he is a Victorian. The opening sentence of my quotation gives him away at once. He speaks of the literature of power as having "its relation to the great *moral* capacities of man." It is of course axiomatic that everything moral is Victorian. We have given up the word as obsolescent. We no longer speak of the moral nature of man; we talk about his reactions. We do not think of human nature as something equipped with ideals of justice, of hope, of truth, of mercy, of retribution; we equip it with social attitudes, a psychological slant, endocrine glands, and a set of conditioned reflexes. Juxtapose Wordsworth and any book by Mr. Faulkner or Mr. Hemingway or Mr. Farrell, and we see how wrong De Quincey was in talking about the vernal life of restoration in literature.

The commercialization of letters is no new phenomenon. There are passages in Horace which hint that Roman poets occasionally sold out to the highest bidder; and anyone who reads a biography of John Murray, the great bookseller of De Quincey's day, will learn that the Napoleon of publishers had a canny eye for a profitable cookbook.

And yet the tinge of sorrow in Mr. Train's observations is not mere sentimentalism. A deep, ineradicable instinct tells us that there is more to literature than bargain and sale, adjectives and excitement. We think better of the muse than to bind her to Mercury, god of business. We assume that publishers exist for authors, and are a little ashamed to be told by Mr. Train that authors frequently exist for publishers. We were brought up to think of literature as something fine and a little mysterious, like classical music and the old masters.

To be sure (and in his essay De Quincey points this out) the word "literature" is, as the Congressman so unfortunately said, like Cæsar's wife—all things to all men. If by "literature" we mean only the literary classics we read in school in order that we may safely forget them, these do not arouse the ballyhoo in publishers. And at the other end of the scale, if the writers of sensational serials want to be ballyhooed, it is of no consequence whether they are ballyhooed or not. But between these extremes there are scores of authors possessing talent and sincerity, just as there are scores of publishers loyal to the fine traditions of an honorable trade, who are swept regretfully before the flood. If they are to survive, they must give the public what it wants; and what the public wants is apparently determined by those who take the most advertising space to tell the public in startling adjectives that it wants what they want the public to want.

There is no harm in repeating a story of the days when Harold Bell Wright was sweeping the bookstores with his tales of ineffable cowboy virtue. Ellen Glasgow had just completed another of her admirable novels of Virginia life when a representative of her publishers came to see her. "Ellen," he asked, "why don't you write an optimistic novel about the West?" Miss Glasgow's reply was prompt and efficacious. "If there is anything I know less about than the West," she replied, "it is optimism."

II

That the direction of American letters, especially the direction of American fiction, has been away from De Quincey's assumption is a fact so patent as to require no demonstration. Our literature has at the moment many virtues,—wonderful dexterity, high technical accomplishments, humor of a satiric or ironical order, truth to life (or at least the appearance of truth to certain aspects of life), a laudable interest in social amelioration, intellectual daring,—but it lacks, as Newman would say, the note of nobility. It lacks, in other words, precisely the quality which is central to De Quincey's observation that literature should restore to our minds the ideals he enumerates, and I now wish to inquire into the causes of this situation.

At first sight the inquiry seems both vast and superficial. A thousand extraneous forces press upon the writer, to which he sensitively responds. We are living in an ignoble and savage time: why should we expect of literature more than the age itself can give? We live in a century which has seen the importance of man to the universe dwindle into nothingness; why should anyone attempt to reinstate him upon his old, imperial throne? We live in an age of big business and ballyhoo, the loud-speaker, the extravagant movie, flaring billboards, startling crimes, enormous crowds, hysterical propaganda, and mass emotionalism; the frail voice of the muse is naturally inaudible among these gigantic alarms. Why should the poet think well of the human race? Ours is an age of gigantic collapse, of enormous armies, of catastrophic wars, of world-wide depressions, of international bitternesses—to call upon nobility, to retreat into fatuous art, is simple cowardice.

These are powerful considerations, but I shall not discuss them. I shall turn instead to consider certain aspects of our own cultural development.

When this republic was founded, there was no doubt in the minds of many intelligent men that a new and better era had dawned. A new nation, founded in liberty and justice, its government the result of rational discussion, its fundamental tenet the principle that every active citizen should count as one and only as one—this meant that, set free from the old errors, modern civilization would flourish as never before. The hopefulness with which the Russian Revolution was first received among liberal minds is a modern parallel to this expectancy.

Civilization was felt to include the arts as well as commerce, and the art of literature was richly to develop when the new republic unchained men's minds from the fatal delusions of Europe. Having this purpose in mind, the first formal literary group in the country, the Connecticut Wits, sought diligently to create a literature worthy of the new nation. They sang the virtues of the American farmer. They celebrated the American landscape. In *The Conspiracy of Kings, A Poem Addressed to the Inhabitants of Europe from another Quarter of the Globe,* Joel Barlow castigated monarchical vice and eulogized republican virtue. Because the epic was the noblest form of literature, they sought to create the great American epic, and poems like *The Conquest of Canaan* and *The Columbiad* obediently appeared. The work of the Connecticut Wits is unread, their literary canons are obsolete, their style is often in the worst fashion of Regency periphrasis. But all literary fashions fade; what is now important is that they were sustained by the sincere belief that a noble original literature should be created in the United States.

About thirty years after the publication of the final version of *The Columbiad*, Emerson delivered his famous Phi Beta Kappa address, *The American Scholar*. There he summed up a discussion which had been going on for a quarter of a century. His address is based on a noble trust in American life. "I read with some joy," he said, "of the auspicious signs of the coming days, as they glimmer already through poetry and art, through philosophy and science, through church and state." He did not repeat the mistake of the Connecticut Wits; he did not think that epic poetry was the only proof of literary nobility. "One of these signs," he said,

is the fact, that the same movement which effected the elevation of what was called the lowest class in the state, assumed in literature a very marked and as benign an aspect. Instead of the sublime and beautiful; the near, the low, the common, was explored and poetized. That, which had been negligently trodden under foot by those who were harnessing and provisioning themselves for long journeys into far countries, is suddenly found to be richer than all foreign parts. . . . I ask not for the great, the remote, the romantic; what is doing in Italy or Arabia; what is Greek art, or Provençal minstrelsy; I embrace the common, I explore and sit at the feet of the familiar, the low. Give me insight into today, and you may have the antique and future worlds.

We have been embracing the common and sitting at the feet of the low almost continuously since the American acceptance of European naturalism, but does our literature give us that insight into today for which Emerson was ready to sacrifice the antique and future worlds? It gives us partial insight, to be sure, but most people do not find glimmering through it the poetry and art, the philosophy and science, which Emerson had in mind. Perhaps Emerson was mistaken; or perhaps, when one considers his serene belief that American literature would have the note of nobility, we have not understood what Emerson had in mind.

A little more than a quarter of a century after *The American Scholar* Whitman published *Democratic Vistas*. In this redundant but striking performance Whitman reaffirmed his belief in the nobility of our literary ideals. Here are some of his sprawling sentences:

In the prophetic literature of these States (the reader of my speculations will miss their principal stress unless he allows well for the point that a new Literature, perhaps a new Metaphysics, certainly a new Poetry, are to be, in my opinion, the only sure and worthy supports and expressions of the American Democracy,) Nature, true Nature, and the true idea of Nature, long absent, must, above all, become fully restored, enlarged, and must furnish the pervading atmosphere to poems, and the test of all high literary and esthetic compositions. . . . What is I believe called Idealism seems to me to suggest, (guarding against extravagance, and ever modified even by its opposite) the course of inquiry and desert of favor for our New World metaphysics, their foundation of and in literature, giving hue to all.

Whitman uses words like "nature," "idealism," and "metaphysics" in senses peculiar to himself; and, even after one understands his full meaning, it is possible to bring against him, as against Emerson, the objection that his intellectual assumptions are outmoded. But one nevertheless observes that he too thought that the nobility of the democratic ideal implies the nobility of a literary ideal; he agrees with his predecessors that there is a working relation between the republican experiment and the reinvigoration through a noble literature of the moral nature of man.

I turn next to a representative of the most despised and rejected of our literary groups, the writers of the genteel tradition. Critic after critic has made merry at their expense. The year after the essay was published which I am about to cite, the late John Macy wrote sardonically: "The American spirit may be figured as petitioning the Muses for twelve novelists, ten poets, and eight dramatists, to be delivered at the earliest possible moment." And of the genteel group the emptiest, in the opinion of some critics, was Professor Brander Matthews. Yet in an essay printed in 1907, entitled "Literature in the

New Century," Matthews described with startling accuracy the principal elements which have shaped American letters since that time. These were, he said, the scientific spirit, the spread of democracy, the assertion of nationality, and the cosmopolitan spirit. By the assertion of nationality he meant an interest in the melting-pot theory of the national life. By the spread of democracy he referred to the inclusion in literature of the lowest of mankind. By cosmopolitanism he had in mind the acceptance of European experimentation in order to avoid parochialism.

But what interests me even more is the conclusion of his essay, which runs: "It is the spirit of nationality which will help to supply the needful idealism. It will allow a man of letters to frequent the past without becoming archaic and to travel abroad without becoming exotic, because it will supply him always with a good reason for remaining a citizen of his own country." Expatriate writers in the last twenty-five or thirty years have not convinced themselves of the soundness of Matthews's statement. Matthews was a university professor, and it is notorious that university professors are amiable gentlemen who cultivate a well-bred distress because there are not more nice books. Having read widely in the literature of the world, however, Matthews nevertheless joins the procession of witnesses in defining a tradition—the tradition that American literature should think well of the democratic experiment and, thinking well of it, become something admirable and fine.

III

The line of my argument hitherto has seemed to carry me into a stubborn hostility towards the world of contemporary books. This hostility is only apparent. It would be as foolish to condemn all recent writing as it would be to assume that all dead authors are good authors. American literature is today the most interesting literature in the English-speaking world—the British Empire has nothing to compare with it.

And there is no one having even a fragmentary knowledge of recent American literature but knows that it does not wholly lack the note of idealism. A poet like Sandburg is in the tradition of Lincoln and Whitman. A poem like *John Brown's Body* would have pleased the Connecticut Wits, it is so magnificently what they wanted to create. A novel like Mr. Foster's *American Dream* holds steadily before the reader the implication of its title. The fiction of Ellen Glasgow or Willa Cather is in the tradition. The excellence of our historical tales is that they show how the common man during crucial epochs of the past fought for and maintained liberty, as the books of Mr. James Boyd beautifully witness. From the left wing come Mr. Granville Hicks's volumes, *The Great Tradition* and *I Like America;* and it is not necessary to subscribe to Mr. Hicks's political philosophy to see that he is trying to define American idealism and make it a force for social justice and great art. Even the hardboiled school may plausibly claim that it is picturing violence and frustration and cruelty in order that the American conscience may be shaken by a sense of wrong. There is not a reader of this essay who could not add examples to those I have cited.

But, though the note of nobility is now and then overheard, the total effect of American literature upon disinterested criticism during the last twenty or thirty years can scarcely be defined as an effect of idealism. I do not mean merely that the commercial spirit (which Mr. Train deplores) is rampant; I think the malady lies deeper. And I offer the suggestion that a principal cause of our lost innocence has been the careless acceptance of powerful European influences without at the same time making the necessary adjustment of these forces to what seems to be the American tradition about the function of literature in the republic.

What have these influences been? They have principally been the influence of European realism and naturalism; the influence of European theories of the psychological nature of man, notably the influence of Freud; the influence of European politico-social theories, an example being Marxianism; the influence of European inventions in technique, from free verse to the fictional method of James Joyce; and the influence of intellectualist criticism, most familiar in the work of such expatriate Americans as Mr. Ezra Pound and Mr. T. S. Eliot. When, for example, Mr. Eliot proclaimed that he is conservative, Catholic, and royalist, he may have uttered a philosophic truth of profound importance to himself, but he clearly put himself out of line with the Connecticut Wits and Emerson and Whitman and Brander Matthews.

It is, of course, true that these influences brought with them notable gains. Realism and naturalism broke down artificial barriers and got rid of a genteel veneer. Anyone who passes from the novels of Howells to the novels of Mr. Dos Passos must see that fiction has been immensely invigorated. American interest in the psychology of the subconscious and the unconscious has permitted novelists, poets, and dramatists imaginatively to explore the rich chaos of inner life. American communism, the most literary of our political movements, has developed interesting critics, poets, and playwrights, and compelled us to rethink the problem of the relation of literature to society and of propaganda to art. The adoption of European techniques has widened the scope and the subtlety of our writers. Intellectualist criticism has raised the level of critical discussion and helped to make this century the richest century in critical writing the country has ever known.

But these gains do not hide a fundamental weakness in the situation. That weakness is the failure to integrate what was gained with the substance of the American literary tradition. Perhaps an analogy from painting will make clear what I mean. Since the foundation of the republic, American painters have gone abroad only to return neither European nor American. As a consequence, with a few exceptions like Winslow

Homer, American painting has been an awkward compromise between the necessity of choosing themes suitable to painters trained in a European tradition and the desirability of selecting subjects expressive of American life. The problem of light in our climate is, for example, a problem apparently different from that offered by the climate and atmosphere of various European art centres, and—I speak under correction—it would appear that the same technique will not do for both. Such, at any rate, is the conclusion I draw from the work of painters like Grant Wood and Thomas Benton, who have, it seems to me, submerged or thrown away European technique for the presentation of vitality so direct that we do not exclaim, on seeing one of their pictures, "This is as good as anything in Europe of like kind," but rather, "This is truly American life."

The error of the strange European conquest of American literature which is characteristic of the last twenty-five years is not at once apparent for the reason that it has been paradoxically disguised as a realistic approach to the actualities of the American scene. Twentieth-century literature has been consciously and even violently regional and "American." For the first time in history American writers have been awarded the Nobel Prize—for example, Sinclair Lewis and Eugene O'Neill. For the first time our literature has such vigor and richness as quite to overshadow the pale culture of the genteel tradition.

Have writers not concentrated upon area after area in the United States? We had not known the whole truth about New England until the rise of Mr. O'Neill. We had not known the whole truth about the Middle West until the arrival of novelists ranging from Sherwood Anderson through Mr. Lewis to Mr. Farrell. The South, formerly romanticized by Page and Cable, is now more truly pictured by Mr. Faulkner, Mr. Erskine Caldwell, Mr. Carl Carmer, and that perennial drama, *Tobacco Road*. The West was not rightly analyzed in Owen Wister's *The Virginian;* but in such a novel as *Slogum House,* in such poems as those of Mr. Robinson Jeffers, it is truthfully presented. Why talk about the glories of our blood and state when Columbia is a land containing a cemetery like Spoon River, a town like Zenith City, a murder like *An American Tragedy,* a population which includes the idiot whose submental processes are set forth in *The Sound and the Fury* and the gentle nitwit whose desire to play with a woman's hair leads to murder in *Of Mice and Men?*

In 1910 the idea of democracy was something we took for granted, and iconoclastic writers were correct in furiously reproaching us for our complacency. We failed to perceive that the American way of life had not brought happiness to thousands and thousands of our citizens. But now that the concept of democracy is threatened by militant barbarism in Europe and Asia, the question is no longer whether the American way of life is imperfect, but whether the democratic way of life offers any security at all in the darkness of mankind.

For, as force and brutality and unreason and horror increase, intelligent men, and many who are perhaps not so intelligent, are beginning to ask whether the idealism of the founders of the republic, of Emerson and Whitman, of Lincoln and Lee, of all those who, here or abroad, fought and died that liberty of conscience and conduct might become commonplace, was not a futile idealism. On the whole the majority of Americans do not yet incline to believe that it was futile. But when American readers are continually assailed through the imagination with pictures of life which in fact deny that intelligent living is anywhere possible, they may find it difficult to keep faith with the democratic ideal.

There is a profound disharmony between the assumptions of naturalism (including much psychological theory), as these are imaginatively worked out in literature, and the assumptions of democracy. If men are more or less able to make intelligent choices, democracy will work. But if man is merely a stupid creature whose supposed intelligence is operated in fact by forces over which his volition has no control, a mechanism motivated by primitive urges, an atomy subject to insane moments of cruelty and fear which it is the chief concern of the artist to register, an irrational being incompetent to manage his own life, yet highly competent to ruin the lives of others, faith in the possibility of the democratic way of life becomes well-nigh impossible.

If, to take a concrete example, the poems of Mr. Robinson Jeffers set forth the basic truths about human nature, democracy cannot work. The only government which can rule in the world he pictures is a government of force, because only a government of force can suppress and control the outrageous beings that we are. We confront once more the dilemma of the seventeenth century—the old dilemma which faced Hobbes and Locke. Either life is a *bellum omnium inter omnes,* a warfare even more savage than Hobbes imagined it to be, in which case we might as well be ruled by Leviathan, the corporate state; or it offers some opportunity for the average man to be both master of his fate and captain of his soul, in which case government may conceivably rest upon the rational consent of the governed.

The state of the world requires that we reaffirm our faith in the possibilities of the democratic way of life. Literary men have fought for and mainly won relatively complete liberty to write as they please. But when the result of this freedom is an imaginative literature which powerfully demonstrates that freedom is an illusion and volition a fraud, I am puzzled to know where the imaginative defenses of freedom are to be found. Sitting at the feet of the low and embracing the common seem mainly to result in the conviction that the high and the noble are shams, and that if we believe in rationality we are self-deceived. I do not desire a literature of propaganda, God knows; I ask nobody to surrender his honest convictions;

I have no patience with that milk-and-water optimism which futile persons mistake for moral idealism, and I am not interested in the didactic. But writers who cry out against oppression here and abroad do not stop to realize that, when novel after novel is devoted to picturing the helplessness of man, the imaginative inference which readers eventually draw, however noble the writer's original purpose may have been, is that man is helpless. Surely the time is ripe for some inspiriting word; surely our artists, themselves believers in democracy, owe us some firmer expression of that belief than we have had in most of the poetry, the fiction, and the drama which have appeared in the twentieth century.

IV

We were once naïvely proud of being different from the effete monarchies of Europe. This belief had its parochial weakness, and those who insisted upon giving literature a wider and more cosmopolitan range were right. In the nineteenth century it was agreed that the problem of American letters was to create a noble literature expressive of the idealism of the republic. Now that our literature has passed beyond parochialism, by a strange paradox, the note of nobility is lost in discord. If optimism was our fault as late as 1910, may it not be that cynicism is our fault in 1939?

The implication of the American experiment and of American letters until recently has been that man, imperfect though he is, may consciously struggle towards justice and rationality. When, however, one examines many of the European influences which I have enumerated, one observes that their implications point in the opposite direction. The implication of naturalism is that men are the products of hereditary and environmental forces they are helpless to control. The implication of Freudianism, as it has influenced American letters, is that the irrational is the most powerful urge in life. The implication of the Marxian theory of literature is that the class to which a human being more or less helplessly belongs conditions all that he does and all that he thinks. The implication of intellectualist criticism is that literature—true literature—is the property of a samurai class (the intelligentsia), which may properly ignore the vulgar herd. The implication of the American literary tradition, as I understand it, is, on the contrary, that in a democracy forces of reason and justice are released, and that literature, reflecting the ideals of society rather than merely mirroring its defects, will also insist that the human struggle has its nobler side.

It will of course be said that the powerful books of disillusion and despair which have appeared among us are really the products of a noble aim. Our humility would not be so low were our aspiration not so high. But, though this is something the writer may feel, it is not something he necessarily conveys to the reader. The paradox of our situation is, indeed, vast if this is the best defence that can be offered for ignobility!

Our writers seem, in truth, to be democratic by temperament, but anti-democratic in method. They cry out, to be sure, for liberty, equality, and fraternity, but their books too often brilliantly demonstrate that men are incapable of freedom, sympathy, or brotherhood. They have enriched letters by many borrowings, but they have not always seen where the logic of their imitation was leading them. They rightly praise Thomas Mann, but they seem incapable of his simple and eloquent assertion of the democratic principle. What is the good of getting up meetings to denounce the fascist conquest of democratic Spain, and at the same time writing books to demonstrate that democracy is a failure in the United States? For democracy has not yet failed, though it has been weakened, and the principal reason why it is still a going concern, though battered and wounded and deserted by authors who should rally to its standard, is that there is a vast deal more idealism and good will among ordinary Americans than ever get pictured in the books that are written about them.

No one ever accused the late E. A. Robinson of being a sentimental optimist. No one looked deeper than he into the abysses of despair. Yet, skeptic though he was, his poetry does restore to man's mind the ideals of justice, of hope, of truth, of mercy, of retribution. I am by no means certain that my analysis is at all points correct, but perhaps I cannot do better, to indicate what I am trying to get at, than to quote from "Man Against the Sky":—

> Shall we, because Eternity records
> Too vast an answer for the time-born words
> We spell, whereof so many are dead that once
> In our capricious lexicons
> Were so alive and final, hear no more
> The Word itself, the living word
> That none alive has ever heard
> Or ever spelt,
> And few have ever felt
> Without the fears and old surrenderings
> And terrors that began
> When Death let fall a feather from his wings
> And humbled the first man?
> Because the weight of our humility . . .
> Falls here too sore and there too tedious
> Are we in anguish or complacency . . .
> To pity ourselves and laugh at faith?
> What folly is here that has not yet a name?

Emerson, Whitman, Robinson, Frost, Sandburg, MacLeish, and other poets have heard

> The Word itself, the living word
> That none alive has ever heard
> Or ever spelt.

Dramatists are exploring the American way of life and finding in the American story kindness and hope as well as frustration and horror. Novelists over and beyond those I have hastily cited live in the traditional belief that democracy is not an illusion and ethical idealism a mockery. May we not gently require of other writers that, in the old Roman phrase, they take care lest the republic come to harm?

184

I I

AMERICAN LITERATURE AND
THE MELTING POT *

A MONG the pressing problems which confront the United
States, none is more important than that of racial relationships. By this I do not mean merely the ability of the white
man and the black man to live peaceably together in the same
republic; I refer to that larger problem of fusing into a common nation and a common culture the immense variety of
races, nations, cultures, and customs which have their representatives among us. And I call it important because until the
problem is truly solved, the republic will always be threatened
by disruption from within.

We used to call it the problem of the melting pot, and it is
one of our oldest problems. It is a problem which we have
nowhere perfectly solved, and which we have in some instances badly solved. Upon its right solution depends what
we vaguely call the democratic way of life. And even though
the flood of immigration into the United States has been reduced to a mere trickle, the problem presses upon us more
dramatically than ever. The reason is quite clear. Whether
we formally declare war on the Axis powers or whether we
do not, we are, by the mere fact of their existence, at war
with them; and they are at war with us. It is irrelevant to say
that we do not seek this struggle. It is immaterial to say that
sincere Americans wish to avoid an armed conflict. The fundamental, the basic, the elementary fact is that there is not

* An address delivered at Southern Methodist University, 1941.

185

room in the world for both the dictator state, animated and driven forward by a special interpretation of race, and the democratic state, animated and driven forward by an interpretation of mankind totally at variance with that held in contemporary Germany.

What is the fundamental disharmony between these two interpretations of mankind, which thus sets them at eternal variance? In this country we hold that men are bound together into a civil polity by the common denominator of their humanity. This concept is as old as the Stoics and as universal as Catholic philosophy. It is a concept which was powerfully at work in the minds of those who wrote the American Constitution. That document does not anywhere use the word race. When the Constitution refers to the men and women who make up the American nation, it considers them collectively as *people* and individually as *persons;* it makes no reference to their biological inheritance. The same rights are guaranteed to all men; and the great dream of those who created the Constitution was of a nation in which men of every race might forget themselves into Americans. To be sure, in certain states legislation has made a difference between the white man and the black man in respect to transportation and schooling and similar matters, but even these laws, where they are constitutional, require that equal facilities shall be provided for both races. That these facilities are not always equal is a patent fact, but thoughtful men are everywhere at work to make the situation better; and the philosophic ideal of the founding fathers—namely, that every individual in the human race shares equally with every other individual certain rights, duties, and privileges—is, with us, as yet unshaken and unchanged.

What, now, is the German idea? The modern German idea is that the race to which a man belongs is more important than the fact of his being a man, and that this supposed truth divides humanity into two great and unequal divisions. In one of these divisions the Nazis place the Germanic peoples, of whom they are, they say, the perfect representatives; and in the other division they place everybody else. Europe has been inhabited by so many races that even in Germany persons of pure Teutonic origin are not as common as theory demands; but this fact does not prevent the Nazis from asserting that they are a *Herrenvolk*—that is, a race specially commissioned by history to dominate the world. The destiny of this *Herrenvolk* is to reduce all other races to appropriate subordination; and such devices as an alliance with the Japanese, not a Germanic people, or a pact of friendship with Soviet Russia, a country made up of innumerable races, few of them Teutonic, or a military compact with Italy, a country inhabited by a thoroughly miscellaneous population—these are temporary expedients. The foundations of this special doctrine of race were laid in the nineteenth century, and some of the ideas upon which it depends are at least as old as the American Constitution, but until recent decades these speculations were regarded as harmless eccentricities. We know now that they are not harmless. Either the Nazi leaders will succeed in gaining the overlordship of the world, or they will not. If they succeed, the constitutional theory of the American republic will not matter, because we shall be subordinated to them. If they are not to succeed, however, and if we really believe in the American constitutional theory, we must protect and defend the American theory of man in opposition to the Nazi theory of race.

Our people have on the whole instinctively recognized the impossibility of living in a world dominated by a Germanic *Herrenvolk;* and they have been, and are now, doing all they can to help Great Britain and her allies defeat Germany and its friends. Because this has thrown us into an attitude of hostility toward the Hitler regime, Germany is engaged in doing all it can to make our aid to Great Britain as ineffective as possible. Now the Nazi theory of warfare is a very old one, a theory successfully practiced by the ancient Romans: *divide et impera*—that is, split up the enemy in every possible fashion and then you can lord it over him. And by the methods of propaganda the Germans have done and are doing all they can to destroy the unity of the citizens of the United States. They have done all they can to set race against race in this republic. They have said that the American treatment of the Negro race belies our pretensions of constitutional equality and justifies their treatment of the Pole and of the Jew. They have tried to create resentment on the part of the Aryan against the Jew, and they have encouraged an attitude of suspicion in the Jew toward the Aryan. In the First World War they tried to incite the Mexican against the Anglo-Saxon. In the present crisis they are deliberately encouraging Germans in this country to defeat the American aim of aiding Britain and, through Italy, their ally, they are attempting the same tactics with respect to our citizens of Italian origin. It is to the credit of many Americans whose racial origins place them in one of these categories, or into others equally useful for *Herrenvolk* propaganda, that they have steadily resisted this sort of suggestion; but it is not to the credit of the republic that other Americans, not German or Italian by racial origin, have taken opportunity to promulgate anti-Semitic or anti-Catholic or anti-Negro propaganda.

As the great majority of Americans are unalterably opposed to any such doctrine as that of a master race, we work for the defeat of Hitler; but in the meantime, by way of preventing the spread of pernicious propaganda, it behooves us not merely to give an example of tolerance and good will toward each other, but to take more positive action by exploring the basis of our own culture and our own beliefs. It is my present purpose to inquire whether the history of American literature helps or hinders us in our desire to hold firmly to the faith that the doctrine of man is stronger than the doctrine of race. Has American literature done all it could to fuse into a common nation and a common culture the immense variety of men now represented among us?

At first glance, this looks like an idle question. Our immediate inclination is to say, "Of course it has." American literature includes the essays of Tom Paine and the Gettysburg Address and the poems of Walt Whitman. American literature means the individualism preached by Emerson and Thoreau and Amos Bronson Alcott. American literature is made up of the wide charity of Lanier's doctrine of love and the wide sympathy of Mark Twain's denunciation of cruelty. American literature, especially in the form of drama or of fiction, has been one of the principal means whereby we have come to understand ourselves, so that the life of a steel worker is imaginatively familiar to a reader of novels in the Arizona desert, and the mind of a Scandinavian farmer in the Dakotas is revealed to a reader living on Park Avenue in New York.

The Germans, however, are in certain respects a very shrewd people, and their views of life in the United States sometimes startle the reader by an uncomfortable penetration. For example, some eight or nine years ago Professor Eugen Schoenemann, who has often visited the United States and who has, I am informed, accepted the Nazi philosophy of life, published a thick two-volume work called *The United States*. And the American way of life, as set forth by Professor Schoenemann, is very different from the American way of life as interpreted by Thomas Jefferson. What are the facts of American life, according to Professor Schoenemann? The facts are, he says, that a tremendous racial struggle is going on in the United States, a struggle in which the Anglo-Saxon minority, once a numerically dominant group, is fighting to maintain its control over subject populations composed of the men and women of other races. For this purpose it is waging war with every weapon at its command. It has position, power, prestige. It has imposed its own forms of culture, characteristically deriving from England, upon a nation the citizens of which do not, in the majority of cases, derive from England; it has imposed its own code of ethics, which Professor Schoenemann thinks is not only Protestant but also Calvinistic, upon a miscellaneous population, about 35 per cent of whom are Roman Catholics and most of whom are not Calvinists. And it has imposed its own notions of education and of literature upon a nation of 135,000,000, most of whom come from races and nations and cultures having quite different educational traditions, and literatures in what we regard as foreign tongues.

It is the Abbé Dimnet, a Frenchman, who warns us to beware of looking for anything, for we are sure to find it. Professor Schoenemann, of course, found what he was looking for. He has twisted some of his facts out of their natural meaning; he has not allowed for the amalgamating powers of such experiences as the draft or the public schools; and there are a good many other things that are wrong in his interpretations. Nevertheless, everyone knows that prestige attaches to being descended from one of the Mayflower families or to being one of the F.F.V.'s; everyone knows that the process of Americanization means the learning of the English language, the acceptance of newspapers, magazines, and books which are not merely written in English but which belong to a particular cultural tradition of publishing and of literature; everyone knows that little Susan Shimultowski doesn't make the society page when she gets married and that Doris Duke Cromwell does; everyone knows, in short, that one of the problems before any large new American group in this country—the Irish, say, or the Italians or the Jews or the Poles or the Bohemians— is how to acquire status in a land customarily spoken of by its enemies as part of the Anglo-Saxon bloc.

Now when we turn to our literary tradition, the important fact is not that American literature is written in English; the important fact is that it began as a transplantation of British literature. It began as a colonial literature; it went on to become a provincial literature; it became a sectional literature; and only recently has it been a national literature. Let us look briefly at this literature in its several phases and inquire what treatment has been given by it to Americans of non-English stock.

When the Declaration of Independence was signed, the colonial experiment which was to become the United States had been going on for about two centuries. The majority of the colonists were of English descent. We must remember, however, that a rich miscellany of racial stocks was even then to be found in North America. Swedes and Finns had settled in Delaware, New Sweden had been absorbed by the Dutch, and the Dutch empire in the New World had fallen to the English Crown. Yet late in the eighteenth century Albany was to all intents and purposes a Dutch village, and so cosmopolitan a seaport was New York that in 1700 eighteen languages were spoken by its inhabitants, who included French Canadians, Portuguese Jews, Norwegians, Danes, Bohemians, Poles, Germans, Italians, Irish, and Scotch, as well as English. The Virginia Company had imported Dutchmen, Frenchmen, Italians, Germans, and Poles—even a Persian, if an early record is correct. The Germans in Pennsylvania, lower New York and New Jersey were numerous and wealthy, supporting their own printing plants and publishing their own books. There were little islands of French Huguenots all the way from South Carolina to New England. Ulstermen, Highlanders and Scotch Lowlanders were struggling to subdue the great valley of Virginia and the back parts of North and South Carolina. There were colonies of Swiss and other Germanic groups including the Moravians, Schwenckfelders, Mennonites, and Inspirationists, who founded communities in Pennsylvania, Maryland, the Carolinas, and Georgia. There was an unknown number of Catholic Irish in the colonies; there were Jews in towns as far apart as Newport and Charleston; there were Negroes, slave and free, all along the Atlantic

seaboard; there were traces of Walloons, Portuguese, Spaniards, Armenians, and other human stock in the seaport
towns; there were Welsh miners and other Welshmen in
Pennsylvania, Virginia, and the Jerseys; and in sum, America
in 1775 was already a picturesquely variegated nation, as
Crèvecoeur was to recognize when he wrote his *Letters of
an American Farmer*. Out of these two centuries the American nation was born; out of them also American literature
was born, but you will find in colonial literature few traces of
inhabitants of the New World other than Indians and Englishmen. I do not say there is absolutely no reference to any
non-English stock by American writers before 1775; I do say
that, so far as any insight into the minds and culture of non-
English colonists is concerned, American colonial literature
might as well not exist. To be sure, the Dutch, the Germans,
and the French wrote and published a small body of material
in their native tongues, but by colonial literature we mean
of course colonial literature in English. This literature is
written as if it were to be read mainly by cultivated Lon-
doners, and as if the Englishman were the only person worth
writing for in the future United States. Of course, colonial
writers discussed the designs of the French king, which, since
he was French, were presumed to be hostile; they discussed
the designs of the Spanish king, who, since he was Catholic,
was assumed to be hostile; and they discussed the designs of
the Indians, who, since they were savages, were certainly
hostile. But this is not the same sort of thing as inquiring
sympathetically into the way of life of a Pennsylvania Dutch
farmer trying to turn a forest into a wheatfield. It is also
true, I know, that colonial literature seldom or never inquires
into the state of mind of an Englishman trying to turn a
forest into a wheatfield, but that is not now the point; the
point is that an English cultural tradition, an English literary
tradition, the tradition of London and Oxford and Cambridge and Trinity College, Dublin, became in all good faith

the tradition in which American writing was to express itself. Colonials of other stock and other tongues didn't have a chance.

Let us drop down to the seventy-five years which separate the Declaration of Independence from the Compromise of 1850. It is a blossoming period. Almost all of our standard authors were active in this period or were born within its magic confines. It is the period of Irving, Cooper and Bryant; of Emerson and Thoreau; of Longfellow and Lowell; of Whittier and Poe and Simms and Webster and Calhoun; it is, in short, the American Golden Day. It is also the period when the American novel passed beyond infantile imitations of second-rate English fiction into the maturity of Irving, Cooper, Hawthorne, Simms, and Mrs. Stowe.

All literary generalizations are open to exception, and it is true that in the writings of these great men you find here and there an attempt to look at life through the eyes of Americans not of English stock. In *Tales of a Wayside Inn,* for example, Longfellow deals sympathetically with the Jewish point of view, the Spanish point of view, and the French point of view; and other instances could be cited. But in the literature of the Golden Day, and particularly in the fiction of that period, you will find two interesting principles at work to condition literary treatment of non-English Americans. The first is that the "alien" is not sympathetically treated on an equal plane unless he is good and dead; the second is that, if he is living or if he is studied from a living model, he is reduced to a subordinate role and expected to furnish comic relief. Thus the Dutch are sympathetically pictured by Irving and Cooper, but the Dutch are all dead Dutchmen. The events pictured in the *Knickerbocker History of New York* and "The Legend of Sleepy Hollow" all happened a long while ago. When the American of non-English stock is studied from life—for example, by Cooper—he is promptly put in his place. The heroes and heroines of Cooper and Simms, Haw-

thorne and Poe are of English descent or bear English names
—not always, but usually; and the dialogue put into their
mouths is of the most correct and incorruptible English after
the fashion of London. For instance, in Cooper's *The Spy*
the principal figures talk like this:

"He who criticises ought to be able to perform," said Dunwoodie with a smile. "I call on Dr. Sitgreaves for a specimen of
the style he admires."

But during the story Cooper wants to picture an Irishwoman
named Betty Flanagan, and into her mouth he puts language
like this:

"Pooh!" said Betty, with infinite composure, "what a bothera-
tion yee make about a little whiskey; there was but a gallon be-
twixt a good two dozen of them, and I gave it to the boys to make
them sleep asy; sure, just as slumbering-drops."

And, a little later:

"Try a drop of the gift," said Betty soothingly, pouring a large
allowance of the wine into a bowl, and drinking it off as a taster
to the corps. "Faith, 'tis but a wishy-washy sort of stuff after all!"

I do not deny that Betty Flanagan is more amusing than
Colonel Dunwoodie and I do not deny that Cooper has endowed her with considerable vivacity, but the facts remain
that this is stage Irish, that Betty is useful mainly for comic
relief, and that an American of Irish descent might reasonably ask whether a whiskey-drinking woman of the camp
is to be considered an ideal incarnation of the cultural tradition of his people.

The seventy-five years I am speaking of is a period of wonderful achievements in American literature, but I cannot recall
a single masterpiece during those years which does not look
on American life through the eyes of an Anglo-American.
Certainly I can think of none which interprets American life
through the eyes of a Jew or a Catholic, a Latin or a Slav, a

German or a Dane. Yet, according to Marcus Hansen's authoritative study, *The Atlantic Migration,* there was a rush of people into the United States after the close of the Napoleonic wars. And in the decade from 1850 to 1860 over 2,500,000 aliens poured into the United States, he tells us. The number of foreign-born inhabitants doubled. The Irish increased by about 80 per cent, the French by 100 per cent, the Germans by about 110 per cent, the Swiss by almost 400 per cent, the Scandinavians by over 400 per cent. But it occurred to no writer during the Golden Day, save for occasional moments privately recorded in the notebooks of Hawthorne, Thoreau and Emerson, to study America through the eyes of an Irishman, a German, a Frenchman, a Swiss, or a Scandinavian. The dominant literary tradition was still the tradition of English gentility. I do not say this is a bad tradition, I do not say anybody was to blame for the omission I have noted; I am merely considering the implications of a national literature which had no place for the varying cultural traditions of four million new Americans not of English stock.

Let us pass to American literature during the last half of the nineteenth century. The situation is naturally more complex. On the one hand it is especially the period of Whitman, who made a complete break with the genteel tradition, who ushered in modern American literature, and who wrote in 1865:

I see men marching and countermarching by swift millions,
I see the frontiers and boundaries of the old aristocracies broken,
I see the landmarks of European kings removed,
I see this day the People beginning their landmarks, (all others give away;) . . .
Are all nations communing? is there going to be but one heart to the globe?
Is humanity forming en-masse? . . .

On the other hand, the tradition that American literature is simply an outlying and somewhat altered province of English literature receives some quite unpredictable support. There is a new emphasis on culture, for which we are indebted to Matthew Arnold, and there is a re-examination of Germanic origins, inspired by the Romantic Movement. We can illustrate both ideas, however, from Arnold.

At first glance, it seems as if the famous doctrine of culture promulgated by Arnold would work for a cosmopolitan outlook rather than for the support of the English cultural tradition in the United States. Culture, according to Arnold, means an acquaintance with the best that has been said and thought in the world; culture, he thought, was based upon a sound classical education; culture, he reminded us, was a proper fusion of the Hebraic and the Hellenic traditions. Nobody was more severe on the deficiencies of nineteenth-century England than was Arnold; nobody strove more heartily to break down the insularity of the Anglo-Saxon mind and to let in light and air. But in 1883 Arnold set out on an American tour, during which he delivered three lectures, later published as *Discourses in America*. Although nobody could understand him when he delivered these addresses, owing to the indistinctness of his British speech, he was nevertheless received by all the right people, President Eliot of Harvard condescended to help him with elocution lessons, and university circles, especially in the East, were notably impressed. And what were the *Discourses in America?* I shall confine myself to the first lecture he gave.

Entitled "Numbers," this was originally delivered in New York City, and is as pretty a little piece of antidemocratic propaganda as you can possibly find, even today. In this lecture American audiences were suavely informed that the majority is always bad and usually wrong; that a state can survive only if it has in it a saving remnant to guide and govern it; that the remnant must know righteousness when they see it; and that the most moral people in the world are the people of Germanic stock—that is, the English! Arnold proves this remarkable fact two ways. Modern France, he roundly says, is given over to the worship of the goddess Lubricity; whereas the English, including the English in America, are—saving a few faults, such as lack of amiability—the most serious, the most righteous, the most moral people the world has ever seen. And as some may think I am misrepresenting that great writer, let me quote his own words from the conclusion of the address:

You are fifty millions mainly sprung, as we in England are mainly sprung, from that German stock which has faults indeed, —faults which have diminished the extent of its influence, diminished its power of attraction and the interest of its history . . . Yet of the German stock it is, I think, true, as my father said more than fifty years ago, that it has been a stock 'of the most moral races of men that the world has yet seen, with the soundest laws, the least violent passions, the fairest domestic and civil virtues.' You come, therefore, of about the best parentage which a modern nation can have. Then you have had, as we in England have also had, but more entirely than we and more exclusively, the Puritan discipline. Certainly I am not blind to the faults of that discipline. . . . But as a stage and a discipline, and as means for enabling that poor inattentive and immoral creature, man, to love and appropriate and make part of his being divine ideas, on which he could not otherwise have laid or kept hold, the discipline of Puritanism has been invaluable. . . .

I have omitted one or two phrases, but nothing that affects the sense of this remarkable conclusion to Arnold's first lecture in America.

I do not know where Arnold got his figures. The census of 1890, however, covers the decade of his lectures. In 1890 the population was something over fifty-five millions, of whom about 24,500,000 were what we call "immigrants." In 1900, out of a population of sixty millions, 32,500,000 were immigrants. In 1920, out of a population of ninety-four millions, over 53,500,000 were immigrants, an increase of almost 120 per cent in thirty years. That is to say, there were thirteen million first-generation immigrants, nineteen million second-generation immigrants, and twenty million third-generation immigrants in the country. In 1790 Americans of British stock had numbered 77 per cent of the population; in 1920 they made up about 41 per cent. From 1820 to 1933 approximately thirty-eight million immigrants entered the country, and the majority of them did not come from Great Britain. But Matthew Arnold never troubled to find out the facts.

Now even if culture has to do with the best that has been said and thought in the world, culture for Arnold and his audiences was somehow in the special charge of the Anglo-Saxons—"the most moral races of men that the world has yet seen, with the soundest laws, the least violent passions, the fairest domestic and civil virtues," he says. Certainly culture cannot be put in charge of the Latin peoples, the chief of whom, according to Arnold, is given over to the worship of the goddess Lubricity. Certainly likewise, culture cannot be put in charge of the Catholic peoples, since, in Arnold's opinion, the discipline of Puritanism is invaluable. Certainly also it cannot be put in charge of Oriental peoples, since he thinks of Hebraism as one-sided. Accordingly, it must be left in charge of the upper-class Englishman; and it is not surprising to discover that American literary men obediently wrote in what Arnold assured them was the right tradition. Our poets during the period, as the late Amy Lowell once acidly remarked, were phonographs to greater English poets dead and gone. Our essayists—men like Stedman and Gilder and Henry Van Dyke—kept up the English tradition of the polite and harmless literary essay. Our novelists—at least our leading novelists like Howells and Henry James—confined their observations to New England and to New York City, and in the main did not discover that either New England or New York was populous with all sorts of persons not of Puritan descent. Yet at the turn of the century over half the schoolchildren in thirty leading American cities had foreign-born fathers. In the 1890's over half the immigrants who entered the country came from eastern and southeastern Europe. In the next decade this same vast region furnished four-fifths of the entering aliens. The Arnoldian doctrine of culture had not, however, prepared the American literary mind to deal sympathetically with this great human problem.

Americans of non-English stock were, however, too numerous to be disregarded, even by writers in the genteel tradition; and a formula was presently worked out which took care of them. I have remarked in the case of Cooper's *The Spy* how the Irish woman is used for purposes of comic relief and compelled to sit below the literary salt. In the fiction of the last half of the nineteenth century the American of non-English stock was similarly dealt with under the formula of local color. And the formula of local color fiction is that people are "quaint." Local color fiction was written about the Yankees of New England, and they were quaint; about California miners, and they were quaint. Local color fiction was also written about the Louisiana French, the Pennsylvania Dutch, the Scotch-Irish of the Allegheny Mountains, the Russian Jews in New York, the Negroes of the upper South, and a great many other groups—and they were all quaint. Notice that I include the Yankees in this list: the only difference is that the Yankee was sometimes promoted to be the chief character of a full-length novel, as in the case of Howells' *Silas Lapham* or Winston Churchill's *Mr. Crewe's Career,* whereas the alien seldom or never rose to that distinction. He kept on being quaint. And when you say that anybody is quaint you imply, of course, whether you mean to or not, that *you* are a person of superior culture and intelligence. You know the best that has been said and thought in the world, whereas all he knows is the life of his little village community. That is why he is quaint.

What, then, was the principal problem confronting American literature at the opening of the twentieth century? It was nothing less than the recapture of American literature by the American people. And here please do not misunderstand me. I have every reverence for the greatness of Franklin and Emerson and Melville and Henry James. They did their work according to the necessities which were laid upon them, and one cannot complain that it was thus and not otherwise. But it is also clear that a nation of 90,000,000 persons, of whom only a fraction were descended from the Mayflower and Jamestown generations, could not go on forever being satisfied by a literature which essentially served the cultural interests of a minority only. Either the literature would have to give way, or American culture would have to be remade in the spirit of English culture. Fortunately, at this point, what anybody might have predicted, occurred and saved the day: Americans of non-English stock, American authors whose ancestors landed in the United States at a date nearer to the sinking of the "Maine" than to the French and Indian Wars, became articulate. They poured into the publishing houses and they remade American letters.

The names of our standard authors—Franklin, Emerson, Hawthorne, Longfellow, Thoreau, Melville, Poe, and the rest —are, we somehow feel, standard English names, even though some of them are provably of French origin. What now are the names of some of the authors principally before the public in the last few decades? Here are a few: Theodore Dreiser, of German extraction; Eugene O'Neill, of Irish ancestry; Fannie Hurst, of Jewish blood; Carl Sandburg, a Swede; John Dos Passos—the name is Portuguese; James T. Farrell, an Irishman; O. E. Rolvaag, another Scandinavian; Archibald MacLeish, and that looks Scotch; Paul de Kruif— I suppose that to be Dutch; Carl Van Doren—another Dutch name; Saroyan, an Armenian—and so on indefinitely. Of course, names of British origin are not lacking—Mrs. Wharton, Sinclair Lewis, Margaret Mitchell, Ernest Hemingway, William Faulkner—but all I am trying to say is that in the twentieth century American literature is reflecting more faith-fully than ever before in its history the cultural and ethnic make-up of the American people. And in place of regretting, as overrefined and timid people do, the passing of the spirit of culture according to Matthew Arnold, I for one rejoice in the triumph of the spirit of democratic literature according to Walt Whitman. We do not have, except in the college en-trance requirements, an official literature. We do not have a literature expressing the belief of some particular race or creed that it is the divine privilege of that particular group to lord it over the rest of us. If literature ever reflects life directly, modern America—after this long history of trial and error—has at length learned to reflect directly the rich, variegated and contradictory character of the American people. It is a litera-ture of very great defects and of very great virtues, but it is a literature which, as I read it, seems to me to support the funda-mental doctrine of American life: namely, that human beings share a common quality of humanity. That, among other rea-sons, is why it is a literature of protest rather than a literature of complacence. No longer content with the genteel formula of knowing the best that has been thought and said in the world, the contemporary American author is trying to make the best that has been said and thought about a theory of life in the United States, prevail. He is carrying on a crusade against cruelty and injustice; he is carrying forward a move-ment for broader sympathy and more profound understanding among the elements in our polyglot population.

At this point objection may be raised that if it is a weakness in writers of the genteel Anglo-Saxon tradition to think that their cultural values are the only enduring values, there must be a similar error among writers rising out of the other racial and religious groups of which I speak. But as I have dwelt hitherto on the more unfavorable aspects of the standard literary tradition among us, let me point also to its strength. That strength lies in the truth that it has not been dominated by the spirit of Arnold. On the contrary, its great moments have been Jeffersonian. You will recall that on his tombstone Jefferson caused but three of his achievements to be inscribed: that he was the author of the Declaration of Independence, the author of the Virginia statute of religious freedom, and the founder of the University of Virginia. He was, in other words, a liberator—one who sought to establish the dignity of the individual as part of our cultural tradition. This, I need not remark, is what Emerson and Thoreau and Whitman and even Howells and James sought to establish and to maintain; this is what Hitler and Mussolini seek to overthrow. And it does not take much reading in the novels of Willa Cather about the Bohemians, or the novels of James T. Farrell about the Irish, or the essays of Louis Adamic about the Slavs, or the poems in which Carl Sandburg blends the traditions of Scandinavia with the traditions of the United States, to discover that a central fact about twentieth-century American literature is its concern for the dignity of individual life. When that dignity is outraged, whether by a lynching or by starvation, by snobbism or by contempt, by insufficient wages or by a refusal of human fellowship, these authors cry out against the injustice that has been done the American spirit. I think they are right to do so.

Patriotism, said Dr. Johnson in a celebrated phrase, is the last refuge of a scoundrel; and it sometimes seems as if our more perfervid patriots fall under the jurisdiction of Johnson's dictionary. If now I call the indefatigable Americanism of contemporary literature one of its most significant aspects, I refer, not to flag-waving, but to a spiritual affirmation of American life. It would have been easy for authors rising from the ranks of the new American stocks and only too conscious that the old American stock had not been gracious in its attitude toward later comers—it would have been easy, I say, for these authors to turn their backs on the United States and to create a literature of the sort the Nazis, the Fascists, and various other groups would have been only too delighted to encourage. It would have been possible to create an atmosphere, a climate of opinion in which the attention of the newer groups was turned away from America to the motherland; and we might have had a literature seeking to build a little Germany, another Italy, an imitation Sweden, a renovated Armenia, a new Jerusalem, or a second Greece in the United States. Such a literary tendency has, as a matter of fact, exhibited itself in Brazil and has had to be suppressed by the Brazilian government. But the novels and poems, the essays and plays originating in the newer American stocks have wellnigh unanimously rejected the Old World and have accepted the New. The writers have concerned themselves with the ways by which the newer races have been, or are being, assimilated into the life of the United States; and if they have painted pictures of injustice, if their pages have occasionally been cruel pages, it is not because their people are being turned away from an old folk tradition: it is because the old tradition in American life—what Mr. Granville Hicks has called the Great Tradition—has not assimilated the newcomer as graciously and as swiftly as these writers want him to be assimilated. They do not complain, these authors, except when the promise of American life has not been fulfilled; and they are, in fact, among those who have most readily caught up the torch, carried forward the idea, had their imaginations enkindled by what Mr. Michael Foster calls the American Dream.

So long as publishers are free to print what authors are free to write, I do not think we need fear that either fascism or communism will conquer the American mind. There were times when Hawthorne and Lowell, Poe and Lanier conceived too narrowly of the republic. Contemporary American literature, particularly American fiction, has its weaknesses—among them lack of direction and control, a readiness to accept the second-best thing rather than to await what is best and wisest; but if the question of fusing this polyglot republic into a spiritual unity were left in the hands of our writers only, there would be no fear of the result. They are unanimous in their support of the idea that in the United States, at least, humanity is more important than race, the dignity of the individual human being more precious than any doctrine of a *Herrenvolk,* economic autarchy, or any other of the ideas which make up the dictator state. It seems to me clear that we may look with confidence upon contemporary American letters as one of our chief instruments for the support of the republic, finding even in novelists of the second rank, if they are read aright, friends and aiders of those who would live in the spirit. And if I have seemed to deal harshly with the American classics, let me make amends by quoting from an old poem, and yet, I think, a very good one, the lines in which William Cullen Bryant prophesied that American liberty would always be a battle and a march:

> Oh! not yet
> Mayst thou unbrace thy corslet, nor lay by
> Thy sword; nor yet, O Freedom! close thy lids
> In slumber; for thine enemy never sleeps,
> And thou must watch and combat till the day
> Of the new earth and heaven.

To many, the earth seems to have achieved, not a new heaven and earth, but a new hell. American literature, however, is still struggling toward a new birth of freedom and of democratic humanity upon the earth.

12

NEW ENGLAND DILEMMA *

THE first annual report of James Bryant Conant to the Board of Overseers of Harvard College may in retrospect prove as significant as Turner's famous essay on the closing of the frontier. The report is dated January 8, 1934. It said:—

"Our Puritan ancestors thought of education and theology as inseparably connected. It is hard for us to recapture their point of view. . . . For a long period . . . Cambridge was located more nearly in the center of the population of the United States than it is at present. The problem of the immediate future is to devise ways and means to insure that we shall continue to obtain men of the greatest promise." "If we have," wrote Mr. Conant, "in each department of the University the most distinguished faculty which it is possible to obtain, we need have little worry about the future. If we fail in this regard, there are no educational panaceas which will restore Harvard to its position of leadership." "In the future even more than in the past," he remarked, "we should attract to our student body the most promising young men throughout the whole nation. To accomplish its mission. Harvard must be a truly national university . . . we should be able to say that any man with remarkable talents may obtain his education at Harvard, whether he be rich or penniless, whether he come from Boston or San Francisco."

I call this report significant because it marks the close of an epoch. Our oldest collegiate institution, an institution which had been a New England university enjoying national repute, declared through its president that henceforward it was to be

* 1940.

a national university which happens to be located in New England. Had Mr. Conant been president of Yale or Brown or Dartmouth, however, he might have said exactly the same thing.

Although Harvard has never drawn its staff exclusively from New England, the implication of the report is that it is now idle to think New England alone can supply the brains for a national university. Until the World War, New England exported scholars and scientists to the hinterland—an example is the arrival of William Vaughn Moody, Robert Morss Lovett, Robert Herrick, and John Matthews Manly on the campus of the young University of Chicago in the '90s. But in 1934 the president of Harvard expressed his anxiety lest scholars and scientists should fail to come from the hinterland to New England. "There are no educational panaceas which will restore Harvard to its position of leadership." The stream has reversed its flow.

When President Conant wrote, "Our Puritan ancestors thought of education and theology as inseparably connected," when he said, "It is hard for us to recapture their point of view," the implication was that an intellectual tradition has been exhausted. When he declared that "to accomplish its mission Harvard must be a truly national university," he turned from Cambridge to the United States. President Conant did not kill a three-hundred-year-old tradition. He merely recognized its extinction, and like a good administrator proposed the creation of a new intellectual order.

It is appropriate that the funeral oration should be pronounced by the president of Harvard College. The last stronghold of the New England intellect was not literature but the college; and New Englanders, though they saw their farmlands idle, their financial supremacy gone, their culture brushed aside by newer and more vigorous racial stocks, had comforted themselves with scenery and education. Scenery remains one of the most profitable New England industries, but it is difficult to say what intellectual outlook differentiates a New England college from a college located west of the Hudson. Formerly the New England colleges shared a philosophy compounded out of Congregationalism, Unitarianism, and Transcendentalism; formerly they shared a belief in culture exemplified by James Russell Lowell. But culture is a word without meaning in the modern world, and the philosophy is bankrupt. There remain a pleasant social tradition, a pleasant tradition of liberalism. But neither the social tradition nor the liberal tradition is any longer specific or unique. Colleges elsewhere have equally pleasant social traditions. Universities elsewhere have equal traditions of liberalism. The intellectual liberalism of Yale and the intellectual liberalism of the University of Chicago are now for practical purposes one. Contrast with this the difference between the intellectual outlook of Yale and the intellectual outlook of the University of Virginia in, let us say, 1850.

The fact that no New England college stands for a specific New England philosophy does not necessarily mean that New England colleges are for that reason inferior. Quite the contrary. But the development of a point of view in these institutions has been in large measure a development away from a representative philosophy and sectional values. President Conant's proclamation that Harvard is a national university has, for example, taken practical form in national scholarships, a program of reading in American history for undergraduates, and a program for graduate students leading to the Ph. D. in the history of American civilization. The most prominent member of the Harvard faculty recently in the public eye has been Felix Frankfurter, and the elevation of Mr. Frankfurter to the Supreme Court was not due to anything specifically Yankee in Mr. Frankfurter's philosophy of the law.

Yale has nourished Mr. Thurman Arnold, but Mr. Arnold's attack on the folklore of capitalism is, to put it mildly, not a defense of State Street. Yale has also published the admirable *Chronicles of America* series and nourished the excellent historical work of Seymour, Gabriel, Monaghan, and others, but these interpretations of history do not represent a New England interpretation of history in the sense that Mr. Douglas Freeman's *The South to Posterity* represents a Southern interpretation of history.

Again, the liveliest college faculty in the region seems to be at the moment at Williams, but the essays of Max Lerner do not discuss democracy in the brahmin spirit of Lowell's famous address. Professor Hans Kohn of Smith would, I surmise, write exactly as he does if he were at Washington University, St. Louis. No group of philosophers continues the traditions of Emerson and Alcott, or, for that matter, the traditions of Royce and James. Dartmouth, Amherst, Wellesley, Bowdoin, Wheaton, Bennington, the University of Maine, the University of Vermont, are good schools, but they do not seem to be militantly New England schools.

Nobody goes from a college post east of the Hudson to a college post west of the Mississippi with that sense of Ovidian exile among the Goths which led George Edward Woodberry, teaching at Nebraska in 1877, to write pathetic letters to Charles Eliot Norton; Norton responding, "What a chance it affords to study Primitive Institutions!" The University of Nebraska is not a primitive institution, and Westerners find it superior to the effete East. As Mr. Conant dryly observed, Cambridge was once located more nearly in the centre of the population of the United States than it is at present.

II

What is a New England point of view? What is a New England philosophy? What is the New England way of life?

The fact that nobody can answer these questions is, of course, precisely the point. In the nineteenth century the questions would have been answerable. They included what Poe

208

acidly summed up as Frogpondism. They meant a Protestant outlook, even if one were a member of no particular church. They meant a placid consciousness of intellectual superiority to barbarians in Broadway and the West. They meant all that is apparent in Thomas Bailey Aldrich's claim that, though he was not genuine Boston, he was Boston-plated.

Writing Bayard Taylor in 1866, Aldrich said:—

I miss my few dear friends in New York—but that is all. There is a finer intellectual atmosphere here [in Boston] than in our city. It is true, a poor literary man could not earn his salt, or more than that, out of pure literary labor in Boston: but then he couldn't do it in New York, unless he turned *journalist.* The people of Boston are full-blooded *readers,* appreciative, trained. The humblest man of letters has a position here which he doesn't have in New York. To be known as an able writer is to have the choicest society opened to you . . . here [he] is supposed necessarily to be a gentleman. In New York—he's a Bohemian! outside of his personal friends he has no standing.

This is the unadulterated snobbery of the genteel tradition, but it is snobbery concerning something real. A provincial is merely a man who is proud of belonging to a cultural tradition which he believes to be *per se* superior to any other cultural tradition. When a writer stands outside such a tradition and looks at it without believing in it, the result is *The Late George Apley.* When he stands inside of it and believes in it, the result is the creation of the *Atlantic Monthly* with Lowell as editor and Holmes as chief contributor. *The Late George Apley* has its chuckling excellence, but its excellence is not that of *The Autocrat of the Breakfast Table.* Contemporary New Englandism is an inheritance, not a belief; a mode of behavior, not an idea.

The difference is made clear by a glance at the South. It is commonly said that in the twentieth century the South enjoys an intellectual renaissance. Though the intellectual life of the South, like the middle class, is always rising, the production of books and magazines about that region has undeniably increased. Good work has come out of various parts of that region, but a fructifying influence has poured especially from two centres—Chapel Hill, North Carolina, and Nashville, Tennessee. At the University of North Carolina, though it is possible that no one could give a definition of the Southern way of life, a group of men arose determined not merely that the Southern way of life should be improved, but also that it should be preserved. A second group arose at Vanderbilt.

In the one university, men like Howard W. Odum, Frederick H. Koch, Rupert B. Vance, Paul Green, Edgar W. Knight, E. C. Branson, L. R. Wilson, and others decided to focus the best brains they could assemble upon the problem of Southern values. The result was not only a rich historical and sociological literature; their activities also had important repercussions in imaginative writing from the Carolina folk plays to the novels of Thomas Wolfe. In the other university a group of young poets, weary of Southern sentimentalism, determined that the South was entitled to an intelligent literature. They were presently forced by the logic of their philosophy to consider the question of Southern values, and the result was the agrarian pronouncement, *I'll Take My Stand*. One may debate endlessly the question whether the Tarheels or the Tennesseans advanced the right solution, but the point is that a solution was looked for. And that solution focuses upon the assumption that the Southern way of life is both valuable and defensible. There is no similar focus for a philosophy of value, so far as I can see, in all New England. New England is centrifugal, not centripetal.

To be sure, literature in New England now resembles the multitudinous laughter of the waves. In the summer not a country lane in Connecticut, New Hampshire, or Vermont but resounds with the click of typewriters; not a village on the coast of Rhode Island, Massachusetts, or Maine but in it novelists, poets, dramatists, critics, artists, college professors, and musicians outnumber the local population which they support. New England advertised itself as the vacation land, and all the muses moved in—from New York. But there is a difference between writing books in New England and writing New England books, and there is an even more crucial difference between describing New England and believing in it. When local color peers in at the door, regional philosophy flies out at the window. In July and August, New England is a vast antique shop rummaged for ancient articles. Admiring grandfather's clock, however, is not synonymous with that deep, unconscious act of faith which led Hawthorne to produce *Grandfather's Chair*.

III

New England literature has always tended to fall into two broad categories—the historical and the argumentative. The golden days of New England have always been in the past. Bradford and Winthrop lamented the degeneration which time soon wrought at Plymouth and Boston; Cotton Mather's *Magnalia* is as much a picture of the good old times as the histories of Samuel Eliot Morison; and the solemn purpose of the Connecticut Wits embalmed the Revolution in the cold coffin of epic poetry. Bryant, Longfellow, Whittier, Lowell, Holmes, Henry Adams, were all more or less reminiscent. The standard textbook phrase for the fictions of Sarah Orne Jewett, Mary E. Wilkins Freeman, and others of that generation is "chroniclers of New England decline." Tilbury Town had already been painted and analyzed by Nathaniel Hawthorne, and *Mourning Becomes Electra* was no revelation to anybody who had read *The House of the Seven Gables*.

The notion that the New England way of life has decayed is perhaps the liveliest tradition in the literary history of three centuries. But, though the complaint that New England is not what she was is perennial, the habit of looking backward engenders the habit of looking away from the present. The concept of New England as the Old Curiosity Shop comes in time to negate everything that Concord once stood for. Antiques are not culture.

It is curious how much of the organized intellectual energy of New England goes into a past which almost nobody attacks and ignores a present which almost nobody defends. The Colonial Society of Massachusetts, the Essex Historical Institute, the *New England Historical and Genealogical Register,* the American Antiquarian Society—one could add indefinitely to such a roll call. Doubtless these venerable institutions are flavorsome and valuable, but they march resolutely away from the twentieth century. I observe with interest that the Trustees of Public Reservations have just purchased the Old Manse. I am glad they will preserve the Old Manse, but who will preserve Emerson—him who wrote, "The mind of this country, taught to aim at low objects, eats upon itself. There is no work for any but the decorous and the complaisant." He also wrote, "We will speak our own minds." I think he referred to more than academic freedom.

The other side of New England letters is argumentative. Up to the World War, New England had something or other to defend. It might be Calvinism or the colonial charters, the Hartford Convention or Daniel Webster, transcendentalism or the Union, civil service reform or the Republican Party. It might even be culture. I suppose the last New Englander who really fought for culture was Charles Eliot Norton, who, though he was capable of disliking *Alice in Wonderland,* had in his quiet way a fighting philosophy. "The concern for beauty, as the highest end of work, and as the noblest expression of life, hardly exists among us," he wrote in an essay, "and forms no part of our character as a nation." This is at least perfectly definite, and he labored for twenty-three years to reform the national character by culture. We still believe in education, but who, even in New England, militantly believes in culture? The polemical strength of New England letters has vanished for the sufficient reason that New England has nothing to defend.

I suppose the two events of recent years that have most deeply stirred emotion in this region have been the Sacco-Vanzetti case and the hate-Roosevelt ground swell. In the Sacco-Vanzetti case my sympathies were with the opposition. I believe these men were innocent, and I am therefore prejudiced. But what seems to me the most disheartening thing about that tragedy is not that the men were executed, but that nobody defended the state. They died because justice and the commonwealth demanded it. No one, however, ringingly demonstrated what concept of justice and the state made this inexorable demand.

If strong conservative convictions existed, they were not adequately expressed. Conservatism usually takes refuge in silence, but Massachusetts was under attack, and who effectively defended Massachusetts?

Characteristic of certain classes and communities in New England is the strong, stubborn, covert opposition to the New Deal. But it does not take intellectual form. If President Roosevelt's policies really threaten the New England way of life, who explains or trenchantly defends what is threatened? What public man now stands for this region as Daniel Webster once stood for this region? What Congressman is essentially Yankee as John Quincy Adams was Yankee? I do not refer to his accent but to his stubborn belief in the right of petition.

Who presents a program or a policy? Is there any economic theory concerning these states which is even as articulate or as vocal as the Townsend plan? We have half a dozen governors, twelve senators, a regiment of representatives, and local leaders by the gross. Can any one of them say what he stands for and why he stands for it in terms that cut through the blurred phraseology of politics?

Of course brains are rare and statesmen do not grow on

every blackberry bush, but it is felt that a whole way of life is threatened, and it would seem that six commonwealths, scores of colleges, innumerable newspapers, and a battery of magazines could produce something beyond emotionalism and platitudes. Clay and Calhoun had no doubt what New England stood for; they ran into it.

I suppose a typical problem before New England at the moment is whether existing shoe factories shall be injured by the setting up of a shoe factory in Maryland imported from Czechoslovakia. Fears for the extinction of New England industries lead their bond-holders to denounce Secretary Hull and vote the Republican ticket. It is true that world trade is choked up and must be unchoked, but not until every dividend is paid. Industry and commerce will presumably continue to exist, but is that the height of our great argument? The same low practicality is common and universal. The tariff has always been a local issue, but it is a local issue in Wisconsin no less than in Rhode Island. I do not recall what stand Emerson and Alcott took on the tariff. When New England calls the roll of its great men, it has not hitherto rated them by the money they earned or kept. I am told the tariff is basic in history, and there are those who say it lies at the bottom of the Civil War. Despite the economic historians, however, New England has assumed that the men who got themselves killed at Bunker Hill or Gettysburg died, not for their pocketbooks, but for their convictions. If New England is synonymous with the interest rate, President Conant's remarks are superfluous.

IV

The New England way of life has been a Yankee way of life, and of course the Yankee has traditionally looked after his savings. Let us, however, broaden the perspective to include the late George Apley. The New England way was also the "Old American" way, and the "Old Americans" are now an out-numbered clan, grimly holding on to financial and social power where they can, yielding only to death and superior taxes. The social cleavage they have thus created is of course the New England tragedy. Such heroism may be magnificent, as the holding of Thermopylæ was magnificent, but the Spartans yielded in the end. It took a more active strategist to rout the Persian host.

It is disheartening to trace the blindness of "Old Americans" from the mild bewilderment of Emerson and Thoreau, confronted by Irish laborers on the Fitchburg railroad, to its climactic expression in Aldrich's "Unguarded Gates," a poem which is pure snobbery in classic verse. Lovely as it is to be conscious of superior rectitude, by refusing to reinvigorate virtue from the common people the New England intellect has run thin and bloodless; and so long as it persists in regarding Irishmen, Italians, Jews, Portuguese, French Canadians, and other late arrivals as interlopers, it cannot fully renew itself on its own soil. For these are precisely the groups which are rich in the qualities the New England intellectual tradition gravely needs—earthiness, emotion, a deep sense of life, a belief that intellect is not all. Finding they are not wanted, the "immigrants" have struck back by two characteristically American attacks: they have conquered at the polls, and they are trying to conquer in the countinghouse. New England is therefore a house divided against itself. In contrast, the superior flexibility of the New Yorker has made his city, despite transient racial strains, the metropolis of the future, rich in the arts and the sciences. Mr. Apley, however, refuses to admit that a profitable amalgam of cultures can take place. After him, the deluge.

The rising culture in New England is a Catholic culture, the traditional culture of New England is a Protestant culture, but it does not follow that the twain shall never meet. A large and influential section of the Catholic Church in New England is Irish, and if anything is characteristic of Irish Catholicism it is that it constitutes the Puritan branch of the church universal. Like the Puritan faith, it has been a persecuted faith, and, like the Pilgrims, Irish Catholics sought refuge in a foreign land. Irish Catholic morality is, moreover, singularly like Puritan morality: it stresses the domestic virtues; it demands thrift and sobriety of its parishioners and, to an astonishing degree, succeeds in obtaining them; and its censorship is precisely the Puritan censorship. I have heard a college professor, descended from a long line of New England aristocrats, and an Irish priest express identical (and, as I thought, mistaken) opinions of James Joyce's *Ulysses*. On the other hand, Charles Francis Adams and Father Ahern, speaking at a dinner held to check racial antagonism, uttered similar sentiments and did not seem incongruous. The Charitable Irish Society points with pride to a history older than that of the Daughters of the American Revolution. Though the mayor of Boston is named Tobin and the governor of Massachusetts is called Saltonstall, neither has proposed to tear down Faneuil Hall. To be sure, there are difficulties, and it is likeness rather than difference which holds men apart—witness Massachusetts and South Carolina in the Civil War. A low order of political morality may justly be charged against certain Irish wards and certain Irish politicians; but, having recently reread Mr. Winston Churchill's *Coniston* and *Mr. Crew's Career,* I learned that a low order of political morality could once be justly charged against the sovereign state of New Hampshire. The political boss in *Coniston* is named Jethro Bass. The present governor of that reformed commonwealth is named Murphy. He is a vast improvement on Jethro.

But though the parallel is as striking as the difference between these two traditions, George Apley still clings to the inviolable shade. Hibernia for him is embodied in that low fellow, the ward boss, who is so singularly uninterested in the taxes imposed on the ancestral Apley home. Of course, even an Irishman in Mr. Apley's opinion is entitled to courtesy and political rights. So likewise is the Jew, concerning whom

Mr. Apley has forgotten that Puritanism has been defined as Old Testament religion. There is likewise the Italian. In Norton's day some knowledge of Italy, even if it was no more than engravings of Italian masterpieces hung on the library wall, was a part of culture, but Mr. Apley fails to comprehend that the race which produced the Sistine Madonna might eventually create its American counterpart. As for the French Canadians, forgetting that in the seventeenth and eighteenth centuries Canada was a nearer neighbor than New York, Mr. Apley remembers only that they work in mills, the bonds of which have regrettably depreciated since the advent of that man Roosevelt. Besides, there are yet dimmer races—Portuguese and Poles, Swedes and Finns, the Negro, in whose cause Mr. Apley's ancestor lost an arm at Antietam. Are there not social workers? Is there not a Community Fund? Mr. Apley subscribes to it. Accredited agencies do this sort of thing so well.

Yet Mr. Apley cannot stand forever, a Yankee Marius surveying, not the ruins of Carthage, but the ghost of Rome. The province of New England long since disappeared; it has been replaced by a Federal Reserve District. Six states occupy the kingdom which formerly gave laws to the barbarians, and Mr. Apley, who voted for Calvin Coolidge, has done all he could in his own political tradition to federalize his native state. Regrettably, when Vermont and Massachusetts joined hands to manufacture silent Cal for the export trade, the result was not the conquest of the barbarians, but the rout of economic royalty under F. D. R.

I wonder what Emerson, who found even Webster inadequate, would have said about the last New England President? He declared that the god who made New Hampshire taunted the land with little men. When a little man became consul, New England, which had fought to force South Carolina back into the Union, was herself forced to rejoin the republic. Now, through various federal agencies, the republic is trying to preserve New England, and only Vermont and Maine are coy.

I heard some days since of two decaying towns. In one, a young Polish girl is writing verses. I thought of Emily Dickinson. In the other, young Yankees graduating from high school find nothing more to do than play games in the house of a benevolent member of the community. Does not even the sin of having "nothing to do" awaken reverberations? All over New England young men and women stand idle, looking for leadership. *It Can't Happen Here* may yet happen here. They are not, I think, afraid of poverty,—their ancestors were not,—but they are afraid of the poverty of the spirit. We have tinkered with the situation at Ware or in the case of the Amoskeag mills or elsewhere, but who has told us whether these efforts are panaceas or remedies?

Meanwhile, great minds in these states concentrate on international affairs. What shall we do about Finland? Russia? Germany? The Allies? Japan? What shall we do in the forthcoming presidential campaign? What shall we do about the interest rate? A more pertinent question is: What shall we do about New England? It is just possible that if New England began to set its house in order the country would beat a path to its door. If the moral leadership in Jonathan Edwards's country mounts no higher than the Christian Front and the fantastic red-shirt group recently ejected from the Harvard Yard, New England has indeed rejoined the rest of the country.

Young men are sick and weary waiting for a moral leadership that nowhere appears. Men who read Robert Frost strangely say that moral idealism is no longer possible. The same persons who are daily outraged by events in China, Finland, Germany, and Spain deny the possibility that morality exists, and do not see they are inconsistent. The world is very evil, the times are waxing late. But the world has always been evil, sometimes more and sometimes less, and it is always too late. Men of conviction, however, also come too early and are therefore misunderstood and martyrized, but I am not interested in the precise position of the hour hand on the clock. I observe rather that refugees are still arriving in Boston harbor because, with all its clouds and darkness over it, they believe in the promise of American life. One of them said to me tonight, "Oh, it is good to be in a free country." Having Czechoslovakia in mind, we despair too easily. The New England village stands white and clean like other mortuary monuments, but at any rate it stands, and the steeple on the empty church points unwaveringly upward. All that is lacking is a speaker, a congregation, and a burning word. I call for a statement of human integrity.

v

There used to be an annual conference at Williams College on international affairs. Why not an annual conference on New England affairs? We cannot reform the nation wholesale, but only piece by piece. Men who contribute money to fight injustice in California do not even contribute brain power to fight poverty in Vermont. What is done in New York and Colorado affects New England, but what is done in New England also affects Colorado and New York. We hear so much about the shrinking sides of the world that there are those who regard Connecticut as a borough of New York City. In New York, however, Boston is more remote than Hollywood. I have not heard Mayor La Guardia discuss rural slums or the decay of New England mills. I have not even read in the *Saturday Review of Literature* the pertinent question: Who are the heirs of Alcott, Emerson, Thoreau? I hear much talk of *Moby Dick,* which was written in Lenox almost a hundred years ago, and that book is supposed to prove that the universe is evil. I had thought it had something to do with the dauntless spirit of man.

Catholic or Protestant does not matter; Old American or

219

New American does not matter; communist or economic royalist does not matter; even George Apley does not matter. What matters is the sense of deadness and the desire of life. We have two needs in what was formerly a theocracy: conviction and application.

What is to be done for the Merrimac Valley, the abandoned farms, the silent villages, the metropolitan slums, the broken windows of the mills? I am not economist enough to say, but I suppose there must be economists who can take their eyes off Washington. All machinery is ridiculous, and committees and conferences abound with stupidity, like the Chardon Street Convention, that byword for the ridiculousness of the come-outers and the vegetarians. But cannot we do better than an annual governors' conference? Is Harvard, is Yale, is Brown, are the colleges forever to centre their attention on what is sublime and historical? Shall our debates concern only the world? If rugged individualism is a failure in the economic sphere, rugged determination is not therefore to be abandoned. We cannot be passive and silent forever. I have read of a balanced economy, but I never saw it in New England, and I do not think that State Street and welfare workers between them will attain it. One's ancestors are, conceivably, dead. A Cambridge poet of some renown and orthodox ancestry once wrote, "Act,—act in the living Present!" I am told the poem is old-fashioned, and begin to believe it.

The next line is "Heart within, and God o'erhead!" I assume that Catholic, Protestant, and Jew equally admit His existence, but they seem, some of them, dubious about His power. Very well. Let us know the worst. Let us welcome skeptic and atheist if necessary, remembering that Heaven helps those who help themselves. As for heart, a thousand testimonies declare its existence. Read the ads for charitable associations in the *Boston Evening Transcript*. A heart beats in the Irish, the Italian, the Polish breast. I read in a Quaker poet, not unknown to the anthologies:—

Yet here at least an earnest sense
Of human right and weal is shown;
    A hate of tyranny intense,
    And hearty in its vehemence,
As if my brother's pain and sorrow were my own.

This is dated from Amesbury, eleventh month, 1847. I heard similar sentiments more rhetorically expressed at a St. Patrick's Day dinner in 1939.

The cry is for a program. Programs are born, not made, is apparently the assumption, as if the Pilgrims knew precisely where they were going and what they were going to do. As a matter of history, they were tricked and deceived. Having only the pragmatic belief that they could create an economy in the wilderness, they merely began New England. We, too, live in a wilderness equally threatening, but nothing less than a declaration of bankruptcy and a total reorganization of society will satisfy us. Softly, softly. Let us take one step at a time, being, indeed, unable to walk otherwise. The calm belief that Yankee ingenuity is not confined to bolts and screws is enough for the moment. Dilemmas are not susceptible of logical resolution. An old and battered program concerns the rights of man. If we cannot agree about church and ancestry, let us at least agree that we stand where we stand. By common consent certain things are evil and remain so, among them being starvation, idleness, and disbelief.

If we must have a platform, I suggest we reinstitute the Concord school of philosophy, though there be not a transcendentalist on the faculty. Our books are disparate, atomic, descriptive. Save for Robert Frost, there is none who stands for the New England way. I read the social history of Virginia in the novels of Ellen Glasgow, but where shall I turn to read the social history of Maine, Connecticut, Rhode Island? Moving pictures in costumed prose are not what most we need. Once the Saturday Club expressed something, but what do these admirable historical novels express except an artistic arrangement of the past? Even Sam Slick and Shore Acres have vanished from the theatre. Fishermen still put out of Gloucester, but it is now some decades since Kipling, a transient Englishman, wrote *Captains Courageous*. I have read no short stories about the Portuguese since Wilbur Daniel Steele. The *Yale Review* discusses everything except Connecticut, the *Atlantic Monthly* is now a national magazine.

And yet it is not magazines and reviews we need, nor yet fishermen or Portuguese or comic Yankees or farmers, but a passionate belief in values and in a way of life some centuries old. There are times when *Little Women* seems more masterly than *The Last Puritan*. Miss Alcott did what she did, and not something else. We tire of fine skepticism, and long for an affirmation, even if it concern only simple things. What shall it profit an author if he gain royalties and lose his own soul? What contract did Longfellow make, and did he bargain for the movie rights of *Hiawatha*?

To be sure, it is easy to drop into a scolding tone. To be sure, also, New England—there she stands. But how long she shall stand, or rather how long she shall stand as New England, once the home of men who believed there were eternal verities, or whether she shall stand simply as a territory belonging to the United States—this is the New England Dilemma.

13

TRIBALISM *

I RECENTLY received a questionnaire designed to elicit my opinions about the war. Of the nine questions it contained, only two were of a general nature; the rest concerned the British Empire. One offered me six policies of which three involved our relations with Great Britain. Another question asked me to choose between policing the world by myself and dividing the job with Great Britain, China, Russia, or the Netherlands. In a third, I was asked to vote as between free trade with the British Empire, and a tariff barrier; and between admitting Canada and Australia as states in our Union, and maintaining friendly relations with them as dominions. I was then offered four statements, three of which assumed as a matter of course that the British Empire must rule the world with the aid of the United States. The document concluded with a battery of generalizations, of which these are specimens: "The British are naturally a more law-abiding people than Americans." "The British have a right to expect more help in this war from South Ireland than they are getting."

Now I have the same sort of respect for the British Empire that Mark Twain had for the equator. It is a fact in nature. The British, moreover, are our gallant allies and are quite as brave as our gallant allies the Chinese, the Russians, the Greeks, the Yugoslavs, the Dutch, and the Fighting French. I respect the British for what they have endured at Dunkirk

* The Phi Beta Kappa Address, Wellesley College, 1942.

223

and Malta, Coventry and Plymouth. I am not, and I have never been, an Anglophobe. I make my living by teaching the literature of England, and I know something of what Great Britain has contributed to the wealth, the culture, the stability, and the happiness of the world.

Nevertheless, this questionnaire seemed to me wholly bad. I did not answer it both because I do not know who was responsible for it and because its language was misleading. Take, for example, the last sentence I quoted: "The British have a right to expect more help in this war from South Ireland than they are getting"—a sentence which cleverly conceals a leading question. Of course the British have a right to any expectation they think they have a right to. Yet the real question is not the rightness of their expectations, but the probability that the De Valera government will act. If a sufficient number of Americans check this sentence affirmatively, we shall be told, however, that the United States "expects" Eire to enter the war. Observe how the word "expect" has changed its meaning. It is thus that propaganda is made.

This, however, is not the chief reason for my refusal to reply. My chief reason arises from my hope that this questionnaire does not fall into the hands of a patriotic Chinaman or a patriotic Dutchman or a patriotic Russian or a patriotic Yugoslav or a patriotic Greek. I can imagine the emotions with which a cultivated Hindu may read this document, with its calm obliteration of three-fourths of mankind. Indeed, I hope the questionnaire has not fallen into the hands of the Germans, since it will be cited by them as proof of their righteousness in fighting to free the world from the hypocritical supremacy of the Anglo-Saxons.

This document is a perfect example of tribalism. When the tribe thinks it is superior to the human family, the result is tribalism. There is a vague feeling among us that only the enemy suffers from tribalism. We have to thank the Nazis for the most outrageous form of this fallacy, to be sure. The monstrous Nordic myth, a myth without basis in history, in anthropology, in philology, or in natural science, reveals by its colossal crudity all that is fallacious in the idea of tribalism. If we are ever to have enduring peace, we must destroy Nazi tribalism and all the so-called philosophy which supports it. The Aryan fairy-tale can impose only upon the sort of mind that believes there is something tainted in Negro blood, some genetic tendency in Jews towards money-getting, or some hereditary cowardice in Italians which prevents them from being good soldiers. But we cannot win the war only to substitute for Nazi tribalism a more genteel tribalism of our own. Have we cleansed our hands of this guilt? Let us see.

II

Before the Japanese started the southward drive towards Australia and just after the creation of a military alliance in the Pacific among the British Empire, the United States, China, and the Dutch, a high Australian official made what I can only call an unfortunate statement. He said that Australia is a white man's country and that the Australians mean to keep it so. I do not know how this pronouncement was received by General Chiang Kai-shek and his wife, but I trust they read it with smiles that were childlike and bland. Is it not asking a good deal of the hard-pressed Chinese to fight on our side in order that Australia may remain a white man's country? I had thought the objects of the war were of a less tribal nature than this.

I have since read, as everyone has read, of the arrival of American Negro troops down under; and I find that American correspondents report with relief that the Australians are being nice to them—nicer, one gathers, than are we at home. But why we should ask colored men to die in order that Australia shall remain a white man's country remains a military mystery. Substitute "free" for "white" in the statement, and it will make sense. Put "white" back in again, and you have tribalism.

I do not know how many people listened to the speeches made and broadcast at the East-West dinner in New York over which Mr. Willkie presided some weeks ago. I stumbled upon it while trying to avoid some of the more distressing forms of radio advertising. The dial suddenly brought me the voice of an eloquent Hindu whose name I never learned, but whose words should be studied in our schools. He and his people, he said, were willing to die in order to destroy fascism, but they were not willing to die in order to preserve Western democracy, or the British Empire, or Christian civilization. He intimated that he was not impressed by Christian civilization. He said with quiet irony that the culture of India is older by some thousands of years than the culture of the British Isles. He remarked that Western democracy was so feeble it could not prevent the rise of Mussolini or of Hitler. These are not pleasant sayings. Unfortunately they contain much truth. The old shibboleths have lost their magic in the ancient East.

Two or three nights later I happened to be reading that precious example of romantic egotism, Trelawny's *Adventures of a Younger Son*. It was published a little more than a century ago. Here is a passage: "In India Europeans lord it over the conquered natives with a high hand. Every outrage may be committed almost with impunity, and their ready flexibility of temperament has acquired a servile subordination. Resistance, or even complaint, they scarcely urge; and the greatest kindness from Europeans, for long and faithful services, never exceeds what is shewn to dogs—they are patted when their masters are in good humour, and beaten when they are vexed—at least it was so when I was there." This was written, I repeat, a little more than a hundred years ago. The manners of Europeans in the Far East have, I trust, improved, and the manners of the Japanese have certainly degenerated. Doubtless both China and Japan suffer from tribalisms of

226

their own. But the elephant, you recall, has a long memory, and the elephant is not an Occidental animal. Small wonder that my eloquent and anonymous Hindu warned his unseen audience that words like "Western democracy," "Christian civilization," "white supremacy," and the like are not going to win the allegiance of Asia—and without the aid of the Orient we cannot, in many people's opinion, win the war.

In the year 1849 John Mitchell Kemble, editor of Beowulf, published *The Saxons in England*. He had studied at Göttingen under Jakob Grimm, the gentlest and noblest of men, but a genius whose teachings were, ironically enough, to lead to the most ignoble and ferocious of theories. *The Saxons in England* is an important book because it is the first English example, however harmless, of the tribalism of the nineteenth century. "Written at a time when the foundations of existing European governments seemed falling to ruin," says an historian of literature, it "declared that England owed her preeminence among nations, her stability and her security, to the principles and institutions bequeathed by the Teutonic invaders." The work of Kemble was continued by E. A. Freeman, William Stubbs, and John Richard Green, whose *Short History of the English People* has probably taught more people English history than any other single volume. Yet it is a volume which, at bottom, rests upon the concept of tribalism. E. A. Freeman was asked to lecture at the Johns Hopkins University and the Lowell Institute in 1881. "The institutions of Massachusetts or Maryland," he said, "are not simply the institutions of Massachusetts and Maryland. They are part of the institutions of the Teutonic race, and those are again part of the general institutions of the whole Aryan family." There were, he taught, "three Englands"—Germany, England, and the United States, and he had come here to lecture, with, in Professor Cargill's phrase, "a mighty resolve to knit up the racial consciousness." American Anglo-Saxons naturally applauded, but neo-Teutonism aroused less enthusiasm among

Americans not born—and I quote the conditions for a college scholarship I know—"of that old Anglo-Saxon stock which has gone forth from New England into all parts of the United States and has been the means of giving strength and stability and character to our government." In Wisconsin, where I grew up, the postmaster was named Skaar, the Congressman was named Esch, the Senator was named La Follette, the president of the university was named Van Hise, and the creator of the so-called "Wisconsin idea" was named McCarthy. We thought we had a pretty stable government, but there wasn't an Anglo-Saxon in the lot.

III

We sometimes act as if the growth among us of organizations like the Christian Front, the Ku Klux Klan, the Anglo-Saxon League, the Silver Shirts, and other virulent tribal clubs is mysteriously due to enemy propaganda. The inference is unwarranted. Like seed in the parable, propaganda falls upon rocky ground and upon fruitful soil alike, but it flourishes only where the earth is ready to receive it. Unfortunately, the ground has been prepared among us by very respectable gardeners. Back in 1848 I find an article in the *American Whig Review* about the future destiny of the Anglo-Saxons, which makes interesting reading. The author lays down the premiss that the present age is developing, with startling rapidity, the national characteristics of races which must be ultimately subordinated to one race, and that race the Anglo-Saxon. Why? I quote: "At present it might appear as singular as it will be found true, that the Anglo-Saxon race has ever been distinguished from all others, by moral elevation, by religious fervor. How much of this should be attributed to a direct interposition of the Deity in their behalf, and how much, on the other hand, belongs to their own silent efforts, we need not determine." The author, however, did determine. He reached the conclusion that "Providence has raised up, and sustained, and qualified the Anglo-Saxon race, to perform a great work in reclaiming the world; has guided and protected them from temptation, or brought them from it *purified,* and ennobled by every scene of trial; and has given to them—to *us*—the destinies of the world."

I have sought vainly, since I first read this article, for some phrase that would characterize the peculiar complacency of the idea that God has favored any one race over any other, or purified or ennobled any one race in preference to the rest. The only satisfactory comment I have been able to find upon the majesty of this self-laudation is in an essay of Mark Twain's. A Jew had observed to him that there was no uncourteous reference to his people in Twain's books and asked how it happened. Clemens replied it was "because the disposition was lacking. I am quite sure," he said, "that (bar one) I have no race prejudices, and I think I have no color prejudices nor caste prejudices nor creed prejudices. Indeed, I know it. I can stand any society. All that I care to know is that a man is a human being—that is enough for me; he can't be any worse."

Let us drop down to the year 1877 and to an American magazine, the *Galaxy,* important and influential in its day. Here is an article, "A Dream of Anglo-Saxondom." The author dwells with pride upon the fact that the Anglo-Saxons miraculously escape from ordinary natural laws. The Anglo-Saxon stands apart from all other races. "The Anglo-Saxon," he writes, "establishes himself in distant corners of the world, where the climate and conditions of life are totally diverse; but his character is apparently not subject to the changes which external influences have wrought on other races." In fifty years, he said, the Anglo-Saxons will possess "almost a monopoly of the undeveloped resources of the globe." "The United States," he averred, "is destined to be the chief seat and breeding ground of the race for many generations to come. . . ."

Some people nowadays are talking very glibly about the "American century." I quote this vision of the American century recorded in 1877.

With what a gorgeous pageant the Anglo-Saxon peoples will celebrate their confederation! What a triumphal procession of subject races: Indians of the East by thousands, their rajahs, richly apparelled, mounted upon elephants; tribes of red Indians from the Western plains, tamed for the nonce; Nubians, Egyptians, picturesque Arabs from the Barbary deserts; dark masses of Ethiopians, piratical Malays, dragon-bearing Chinese from Hong Kong and San Francisco; haughty and oleaginous descendants of the Aztecs; Esquimeaux in their quaint envelopes of skins; lithe and hungry-eyed Fijians; proud and war-like Moors, marching with their more docile kinsmen, the Kanakas; hairy and half-made Australian savages, who look indeed as though the 'prentice hand of Nature had experimented with them before it essayed nobler humanity—men, in short, of well-nigh every barbarous kind, from every quarter of the globe, will grace this crowning triumph of the Anglo-Saxon race!

The only possible comment on this circus procession was uttered by Mr. Dooley in 1898. "I'm wan," he said,

iv th' hottest Anglo-Saxons that iver come out iv Anglo-Saxony. . . . I tell ye, whin th' Clan an' the Sons iv Sweden an' th' Banana Club an' th' Circle Françaize an' th' Pollacky Benivolent Society an' th' Rooshian Sons of Dinnymite an' th' Benny Brith an' th' Coffee Clutch that Schwartzmeister r-runs an' th' Turnd'yemind an' th' Holland society an' th' Afro-Americans an' th' other Anglo-Saxons begin f'r to raise their Anglo-Saxon battle cry, it'll be all day with th' eight or nine people in th' wurruld that has th' misfortune iv not bein' brought up Anglo-Saxons.

IV

Global warfare requires global thinking, and global thinking cannot be tribal, as even the Nazis are clever enough to know, since in Arabia they picture themselves as protecting the Semites and in the Far East they ally themselves with the Japanese. The inconsistencies of the enemy do not, however,

230

justify us in being inconsistent ourselves. And as I may have hitherto seemed hostile to the British, let me heartily and sincerely affirm that the *Pax Britannica* has worked in the past as the *furor Teutonicus* will never work in the future. But it has worked, as in French Canada or Dutch South Africa, only in proportion as it has avoided tribalism; and it has failed, as in Ireland and Burma, mainly in proportion as the Anglo-Saxons have insisted that they were the people chosen of God. They are not the chosen people. The oppressed of the earth, fighting to rid themselves of the tyranny of the Nazis, are not fighting to retain, restore, or increase some other form of tribalism; and phrases like "the American century" do not appeal in Africa and Asia, Russia and South America. Let us have done with the notion that because in self-defense we have lent our arms to a dozen nations over the earth, these nations are meekly going to submit to our influence when peace is restored. It is not thus we shall ever found the parliament of man, the federation of the world.

No, global warfare demands global thinking, and global thinking requires global education. Are we intelligently preparing ourselves not merely to support the war but also to support the peace? To ask the question is to answer it. We are not preparing ourselves, and I fear our education is becoming more, rather than less, tribal. Particularly that part of a college education which deals with human history and human values is currently under two contradictory pressures. Each of these pressures is away from global thinking, the supposition being, apparently, that by supporting two errors we shall create at least one truth. Both movements result from well-meant desires to aid and strengthen the democratic state against fascism, but both suffer from the same radical defect. One is a drive to require of all college students a course in American culture, American history, American institutions, or the like; and the other is the instituting of "broad" courses in the humanities, survey courses in the history of Western man, great authors, or something of that order. There is merit in each of these ideas; but I may be pardoned for saying that amid the inevitable and appalling anarchy of the post-war world, we shall need to rely upon something broader than American culture or European history. The first is, I fear, open to the charge of tribalism in a small way, and the second to the charge of tribalism on a larger scale.

The threat of provincialism, the threat of chauvinism in the proposed requirement of courses in American history or literature has been felt by thoughtful men, who propose to correct error, if it arises, by requiring, in addition, general courses in the humane tradition. Characteristically these courses are to begin with the thought of Greece and Rome, sweep through the Middle Ages and the Renaissance, and descend to the modern world of Europe and the United States. If the course in American institutions shall prove narrow, the course in great authors or in general literature or in the intellectual history of Europe will, it is thought, broaden the outlook of our students.

To be sure, it will. But will it broaden that outlook in the right way? Do we need to know more of Europe merely, or do we need to alter the whole basis of our thought about mankind?

v

Have you ever looked at a map drawn to show the land-masses of the earth as they really are and not as the Western world fondly imagines them as being? Our maps customarily show Europe, or the Atlantic Ocean, or the North American continent, or the New World as the center of the known universe. But if you will look at a map which places the great land-mass of Asia-Africa-Russia in the center of the page, the East Indies and Australia being but the southeastern extension of that mass, you will discover that Western Europe is a rather minor peninsula extending along the Atlantic Ocean;

and by consulting almost any table of world population you will also discover that of the nineteen hundred million human beings in the world, something like thirteen hundred million do not live in Western Europe or the New World, and have very little interest in its cultural history. It is a sobering thought that there are more Chinese in the world than there are people in Western Europe; that the Hindu population of India about equals the total population of North and South America; that the population of Africa is about the size of the population of Russia and that we of the so-called "civilized tradition" know almost nothing about either. There are, I find, about fifty-five major political divisions in Africa, a continent of immense importance to the future of freedom, but I suspect that if I were to ask any one of us to draw a freehand map of that enormous area, he would end in the condition described by Dean Swift: —

> So geographers, in Afric maps,
> With savage pictures fill their gaps,
> And o'er unhabitable downs
> Place elephants for want of towns.

I do not pretend that the tribes of Uganda are as important to us as the tribes of Hellas, but total warfare involves the total history of mankind, and how and where Asia and Africa, China and India, the empire of the Mongols and the empire of the Saracens are to be studied in the ordinary curriculum of the American college is a problem we have never, never faced.

With his customary eloquence Mr. Walter Lippmann has recently called us to return to the traditions which begin with Greece and Rome. Likewise President Hutchins of Chicago has insisted that we shall return to the traditions which begin with Aristotle and Aquinas. Incidentally, I am not aware that the medieval university reduced the B.A. degree to the junior-college level, but apparently we are to modernize our medievalism. Neither of these reformers seems to me really to re-form. If our return to scholasticism is merely to strengthen our belief that we are the people and wisdom will die with us; if our return to the classics is to be merely a modern version of the Renaissance; if we are to be so absorbed by Europe that we continue to turn our backs upon the rest of the globe, we shall continue to rest complacently in a larger sort of tribalism. That can lead only to disaster.

About a quarter of a century ago H. G. Wells published a book which everybody read and nobody paid any attention to. The book is almost a book of prophecy. I refer to his *Outline of History*. I quote from it two passages. Here is the first one: —

Western writers are apt, through their patriotic predispositions, to overestimate the organization, civilizing work, and security of the absolute monarchy that established itself in Rome after the accession of Augustus Caesar. From it we derive the political traditions of Britain, France, Spain, Germany, and Italy, and these countries loom big in the perspectives of European writers. . . . By the scale of a world history the Roman Empire ceases to seem so overwhelmingly important. . . . Compared with the quiet steady expansion, the security, and the civilizing task of the contemporary Chinese Empire, or with Egypt between 4000 and 1000 B.C., or with Sumer before the Semitic conquest, this amounts to a mere incident in history.

Here is my second quotation:

It is difficult to believe that any large number of people really accepted this . . . painting of the map of Africa in European colors as a permanent new settlement of the world's affairs, but . . . there was but a shallow historical background to the European mind in the nineteenth century. . . . They had no sense of the transferability of science and its fruits. . . . They do not realize that in Asia the average brain is not one whit inferior in quality to the average European brain; that history shows Asiatics to be as bold, as vigorous, as generous, as self-sacrificing, and as capable of strong collective action as Europeans; and that there are and must continue to be a great many more Asiatics than Europeans in the world.

I am not wise enough, singlehanded and alone, to rewrite the college curriculum, but I am profoundly convinced that our absorption with the culture of Western Europe must go. We need to learn in all humility how small a part we and Europe have played in the total history of mankind. We must immensely expand our mental horizon. We must alter our whole concept of cultural education on both practical and theoretical grounds. Anything short of global thinking in higher education will be inadequate so long as the world is dominated by the airplane and the bomb. We must get out from under the shadow of Occidental tribalism and move into the broader realm of responsibility for the human race.

I have said the arguments for this change are both practical and theoretical. The practical arguments arise from the success of our enemies and the practice of our friends. If we had learned half as much about Japanese mentality and Japanese culture as the Japanese have learned about European culture and American mentality, we should not now be frantically hunting for Americans possessing even an elementary knowledge of Japanese geography, Japanese history, or the Japanese language. If we knew half as much about the traditions of the East as the Germans know about the traditions of, let us say, Arabia, the East would not now be as suspicious of us as it probably is. If the Chinese, clinging to their immemorial culture, can yet profit from the traditions of the West, cannot we, clinging to the traditions of the Occident, learn profitable things from the culture of the East? Until we can learn to take the point of view that Plato has no monopoly of wisdom nor Aristotle of intellect; that, however influential the ideas of Mr. T. S. Eliot may be, they cannot compare in importance or influence with the ideas of Siddhartha Gautama known as Buddha; until we can humble ourselves to learn that there are cultures and traditions, literature and wisdom, art and morality older and richer, perhaps even wiser, than our own —until we can remake our thought about history and humanity in some such terms as these, we cannot reach the height of our great opportunity.

As I see it, the problem before Western education is how, while we cling to what is sound in national traditions, we can begin to think and act not merely as Americans, not merely as Europeans, but as members of the human race. I might remark of the requirement of courses in American history that if they return to the wisdom of the founding fathers they will help us, but only then; and I might remark of the requirement of a general course in the humanities that everything depends upon the points of reference we select. We can be crippled by these requirements or we can be enriched. We can be enriched, however, only if we return to the great eighteenth century concept, important for the last time in that century, of universal humanity. It is significant that the word "race" does not appear in the Declaration of Independence or the Constitution of the United States.

I have spoken, however imperfectly, of global thinking and global education, but I find, as I constantly do find in this connection, that the wise men of the Enlightenment have anticipated us. They did not propose to confine education or the benefits of humane society to the United States or the Anglo-Saxons or Western Europe or even the countries of Christendom. They saw, as we must see if we are to survive the war and construct a durable order of peace in the world, that this order must be based upon comprehension, not withdrawal; upon the concept of the human race, not of tribalism; upon the adjustment under sympathetic leadership of the conflicts of many cultures, many traditions, many nations, many men. Nothing short of this universality will serve.

AMERICAN SCHOLARSHIP AND AMERICAN LITERATURE

1. V. L. Parrington, *The Colonial Mind* (*Main Currents in American Thought,* vol. I, New York, 1927), "Introduction," p. iii.
2. *American Literature,* III, 321–323 (November, 1931).
3. Ludwig Lewisohn, *Expression in America* (New York, 1932), p. 244.
4. Walter Millis, *The Road to War* (Boston, 1935), pp. 41–42.
5. Burton J. Hendrick, *The Training of an American: The Earlier Life and Letters of Walter H. Page, 1855–1913* (Boston, 1928), pp. 60–67.
6. H. M. Jones and T. E. Casady, *The Life of Moses Coit Tyler* (Ann Arbor, 1933), pp. 157, 218–220.
7. Professor Krapp's *The English Language in America,* published by the association, is a linguistic, and not a literary, study.
8. *PMLA,* III, 238–244; lii.
9. *PMLA,* XXXVI, xlvi–lx. For the original committee report see the unnumbered pages bound in the front of this volume.
10. I make the total forty-five by a strict count. However, there are four other articles which in a larger sense have something to do with American literature in the sense that they have something to do with American English, giving a total of forty-nine articles of all kinds.
11. "Leaves from My Journal in Italy," *Works,* Riverside ed. (Boston, 1890), I, 113.

ORIGINS OF THE COLONIAL IDEA

1. Classical example is not cited in the literature until late. At first antiquity is used to sanction expansionism rather than as a model of technique. See for example the prefatory matter to Hakluyt's *Divers Voyages* (London: Hakluyt Society, 1850), p. 9, and the glancing reference by John Smith to the example of Rome in *A Description of New England* (1616) in *Travels and Works of Captain John Smith,* ed. Arber-Bradley (Edinburgh, 1910), I, 209–211. By 1630, however, more detailed references appear. Thus in Sir William Alexander's *The Mapp and Description of New-England* one finds such a passage as this: "The

Romanes comming to command a well peopled World, had no vse of Colonies, but only thereby to reward such old deseruing Souldiers as (age and merit pleading an immunitie from any further constrained trauell) had brauely exceeded the ordinary course of time appointed for military seruice. . . ." And again: "The *Romanes* did build some Townes which they did plant with their owne people by all rigour to curbe the Natiues next adjacent thereunto. . . ." (In *Royal Letters, Charters, and Tracts, relating to the Colonization of New Scotland,* ed. David Laing, Edinburgh: Bannatyne Club Publications, 1867, pp. 3–4). And in John White's *The Planters Plea* (Force, *Tracts,* vol. II, no. 3) one reads that "the *Romans* use was to proclaime that they intended to plant a Colony of such a number in such a place, and as many as would give in their names should receive so many acres of Ground, and enjoy such other priviledges as they thought fit to grant them. . . ." (p. 24). But by 1630 English practice had been more or less stabilized and these fuller references to classical practice lacked the influence they might have had earlier.

2. Cf. *Politics,* Bk. VII, chap. iv.

3. Egerton points out that Cromwell's military settlements in Ireland were the closest English parallel to Roman colonization. Hugh Edward Egerton, *A Short History of British Colonial Policy* (London, 1897), p. 8.

4. For example, the study of classical practice might have had important effects upon race relationships in North America. Given the prestige which surrounded the figure of Alexander in Renaissance Europe, his rejection of Aristotelian racism and his official encouragement of intermarriage between the Graeco-Macedonian conquerors and their Persian subjects might possibly have encouraged greater intermixture between the English and the Indians than that represented by John Rolfe and Pocahontas. Roman theory was divided. The Romans could not think of kinship with the Carthaginians, and practiced extermination against the Belgians and the Jews. Juvenal complains of the influx of Greeks and Hellenized Orientals into Rome. On the other hand, both Cicero and Seneca insisted that Romans, Africans, Spaniards, and Gauls were all alike members of the human family. See the illuminating discussion in A. D. A. De Kat Angelino, *Colonial Policy,* trans. G. J. Renier (The Hague, 1931), I, 224–239.

5. *The Libelle of Englyshe Polycye,* ed. Sir George Warner (Oxford, 1926), p. 39.

6. *The Interlude of the Four Elements,* ed. J. O. Halliwell (London: The Percy Society, 1848), p. 29.

7. These instances are in the NED. Examination of the slips assembled at the University of Michigan for the *Early Modern English Dictionary* reveals no earlier example. This search, and that for instances of "plantation," were made through the kindness of the staff of that enterprise.

8. Thus in 1572, when Sir Thomas Smith was trying to settle Ulster with Englishmen, his pamphlet refers to "the peopling and inhabiting the Cuntrie," but speaks neither of colony nor of plantation. George Hill, *An Historical Account of the MacDonnells of Antrim* (Belfast, 1873), pp. 405–415. "Plantation" came into general use *after* American enterprises had been launched.

9. In addition, there is some indication that the Roman and Scandinavian conquests of Britain, not to speak of the Norman conquest, vaguely colored the idea of settlement with the idea of military invasion and of "progress" concomitant with it. It is notable that both Virginia and New England employed the warrior-settler type of occupier as Pennsylvania did not. Thus Crashaw appeals in his sermon to the rigor of ancient virtue: "Stately houses, costly apparell, rich furniture, soft beds, daintie fare, dalliance and pleasures . . . are not the meanes whereby *our forefathers* conquered kingdomes, subdued their enemies, conuerted heathen, ciuilized the Barbarians, and setled their commonwealths. . . ." (W. Crashaw, *A Sermon Preached in London before . . . his Maiesties Counsell for . . . Virginea, Febr. 21. 1609,* London, 1610, sig. F4.) And William Strachey was even more explicit: "Had not this violence and this injury bene offred to us by the Romans (as the warlike Scots did the same, likewise, in Caledonia, unto the Picts), even by Julius Caesar himself, then by the emperour Claudius, who was therefore called Britannicus, and his captains, Aulus Plautius and Vespatian (who tooke in the Isle of Wight); and lastly, by the first lieutenant sent hither, Ostorious Scapula (as writes Tacitus in the lief of Agricola), who reduced the conquered partes of our barbarous iland into provinces, and established in them colonies of old souldiers; building castells and townes, and in every corner teaching us even to knowe the powerfull discourse of divine reason (which makes us only men, and distinguisheth us from beasts, amongst whome we lived as naked and as beastly as they). We might yet have lyved overgrowen satyrs, rude and untutred, wandring in the woodes, dwelling in caves, and hunting for our dynners, as the wild beasts in the forrests for their praye, prostetuting our daughters to straungers, sacrificing our childrene to idolls, nay, eating our owne childrene, as did the Scots in those daies. . . ." (William Strachey, "Praemonition to the Reader," *The*

Historie of Travaile into Virginia Britannia, ed. R. H. Major, London: Hakluyt Society, 1849, p. 18).

10. Sombart flatly declares that all modern colony-making is military, and traces its origins to the crusades. *Der Moderne Kapitalismus,* 2d ed., Bd. I (Munich, 1916), pp. 434–439.

11. There are various accounts, but that in Albert G. Keller, *Colonization* (Boston, 1908), pp. 60–74, is brief and clear. The closest analogue in British history is of course the "factory" in India.

12. Although Anglo-Venetian trade declined in the sixteenth century, it was not until 1587, when the last argosy was wrecked off the Needles, that formal relations between the two powers ended. See W. Cunningham, *The Growth of English Industry and Commerce in Modern Times: The Mercantile System* (Cambridge, 1925), p. 74.

13. Patents issued by the crown of course varied among themselves, but the general principle is evident. Because the "adventurers" expected immediate profit, colonial enterprise was often hamstrung; and as late as 1625 Bacon was still warning the state that the "base and hasty drawing of profit in the first years" ruined a plantation. See "Of Plantations" in *The Essays or Counsels, Civil and Moral, of Francis Bacon* (Oxford, 1890).

14. The literature includes many passages illustrative of this conflict. A representative instance occurs in Ralph Hamor's account of Virginia under Dale and Gates. The distress of the colony Hamor explains as being due to the fact that "formerly, when our people were fed out of the common store, and laboured joyntly in the manuring of the ground, and planting Corne, glad was that man that could slip from his labour; nay, the most honest of them in a generall businesse, would not take so much faithfull and true paines, in a weeke, as now hee will doe in a day, neither cared they for the increase, presuming that howsoever their harvest prospered, the generall store must maintayne them. . . . To prevent which mischiefe hereafter Sir Thomas Dale hath taken a new course, throughout the whole Colonie, by which meanes, the generall store (apparell only excepted) shall not bee charged with any thing: and thus it is, hee hath allotted to every man in the Colonie, three English Acres of cleere Corne ground, which every man is to ma[n]ure and tend. . . ." *Hakluytus Posthumus or Purchas His Pilgrimes* (Glasgow: James MacLehose and Sons, 1906), XIX, 95.

15. Of course no English city could stand legally in relation to a plantation as Venice, an independent state, stood in relation to its *fondachi,* but "plantations" were financially associated with particular cities nevertheless. Thus the present county of Londonderry in Ireland

was handed over to twelve London companies for a plantation. See the proposals entitled "Motives and Reasons to induce the City of London to undertake plantation in the north of Ireland," issued by the Privy Council in 1609, printed in George Hill, *An Historical Account of the Plantation in Ulster at the Commencement of the Seventeenth Century, 1608–1620* (Belfast, 1877), pp. 360–363. In the same year the Virginia Company made a similar appeal to London for support. See the documents extracted in Alexander Brown, *The Genesis of the United States* (Boston, 1891), I, 250 ff. The second charter of the Virginia Company included fifty-six of the city companies of London among the incorporators, and the fact that the two great companies to whom patents were originally issued were known as the London Company and the Plymouth Company is significant. Among other instances of appeals made by a colonizing company to a municipality for support see the curious document addressed to the "Mayor and Jurats" of Sandwich printed in Edward D. Neill, *Virginia Vetusta* (Albany, 1885), pp. 66–74.

16. Ethical casuistry is repeatedly exercised to create a juridical defence for the invasion. Thus Sir George Peckham in his "true Report" writes that because "the lawfulnesse to plant in those Countreyes in some mens judgements seemeth very doubtfull, I will beginne the proofe of the lawfulnesse of trade, traffique, and planting," which he does by arguing that if the savages are peaceful, the law of nations (which he identifies with the law of nature) requires that strangers [*i.e.,* the English] should not be driven away; and if they are hostile, "I holde it no breach of equitie for the Christians to defend themselves, to pursue revenge with force, and to doe whatsoever is necessarie for the atteining of their safetie. . . ." Hakluyt, *Principal Navigations* (London: Hakluyt Society, Extra Series, 1903–05), VIII, 97–100. An amusing variant of this extraordinary argument is the evident relief of Sir Ferdinando Gorges in being able to assert clear title to his New England grants because the Indians had disappeared: ". . . for want of an head, the rest of his great *Sagamores* fell at variance among themselves, spoiled and destroyed each others people and provision, and famine took hould of many, which was seconded by a great and generall plague, which so violently rained for three yeares together, that in a manner the greater part of that Land was left desert without any to disturb or appease our free and peaceable possession thereof, from whence we may justly conclude, that *GOD* made the way to effect his work according to the time he had assigned for laying the foundation thereof." See "A Briefe Narration of the Originall Under-

takings of the Advancement of Plantations Into the parts of America" (London, 1658) in *Sir Ferdinando Gorges and His Province of Maine,* ed. James Phinney Baxter (Boston: The Prince Society, 1890), II, 76–77.

17. The relation of Irish precedent to America is shown in a remark of Sir George Peckham on the possibility of subduing the Indians. Let the English remember, he said, that Strongbow "by himselfe and his allies and assistants, at their owne proper charges passed over into Ireland, and there made conquest of the now countrey, and then kingdome of Lynester, at which time it was very populous and strong." "A true Report of the late discoveries, and possession taken in the right of the Crowne of England of the Newfound Lands, By that valiant and worthy Gentleman, Sir Humfrey Gilbert Knight . . ." (1583) in *Principal Navigations,* edition cited, VIII, 123.

18. The tract issued on behalf of Sir Thomas Smith's proposed colony of Ards in County Down, for example, is emphatic in declaring that a few hundred footmen and horsemen could keep the Irish in subjection. See Hill, *The MacDonnells of Antrim,* p. 407; and also Spenser's *View of the Present State of Ireland,* ed. W. L. Renwick (London, 1934), pp. 157–158; Richard Bagwell, *Ireland under the Tudors* (London, 1885–1890), II, 211; and various passages in Constantia Maxwell, *Irish History from Contemporary Sources, 1509–1610* (London, 1923). Had Ireland never existed, the English in America would probably have refused to sell firearms to the Indians, who were "naked and unarmed, destitute of edged tools or weapons" in the words of one explorer; but the immediacy with which the English colonists were instructed to keep the natives unarmed suggests that Irish experience was pertinent.

19. Ireland, wrote the Venetian ambassador at the close of the century, "may well be called the Englishman's grave." Maxwell, pp. 45; 213, quoting the *Calendar of State Papers, Ireland,* and *Cal. Carew MSS.*

20. Maxwell, p. 219.

21. Maxwell, pp. 234; 212; 220; 198–199.

22. Maxwell, p. 117.

23. Bagwell, II, 113.

24. Spenser, *op. cit.,* pp. 72; 73–75; 81.

25. Second edition, re-titled *The Discovery and Conquest of Terra Florida* (1611), ed. William B. Rye (London: Hakluyt Society, 1851), pp. 27–28.

26. *Op. cit.,* pp. 6–7.

27. Smith, *Travels and Works,* edition cited, I, 64–73.

28. Edward Arber, *The Story of the Pilgrim Fathers* (London, 1897), p. 453; Thomas Morton, *New English Canaan,* ed. C. F. Adams, Jr. (Boston: Prince Society, 1883), p. 134.

29. Smith, p. 72.

30. *Coll. Mass. Hist. Soc.,* 1 Ser. I, 125 ff.

31. "I vnderstand it would be very gratefull to our neighbours that such Pequts as fall to them be not enslaved, like those which are taken in warr: but (as they say is their generall custome) be vsed kindly, haue howses, & goods, & fields given them: because they voluntarily choose to come in to them, & if not receaved will [go] to the enemie or turne wild Irish themselues. . . ." *Coll. Mass. Hist. Soc.,* 4 ser. VI, 194–195; *Publications of the Narragansett Club,* VI, 32–34. I owe this reference to the kindness of Mr. Allyn B. Forbes. For other parallels see Strachey's *Historie of Travaile into Virginia Britannia,* edition cited, pp. 65, 66, 72, 76, 112.

32. So Gilbert reported to Cecil, "being for my part constantly of this opinion that no conquered nation will ever yeild willingly their obedience for love but rather for fear." Churchyard praised him for it: "Also it gave him such expedition in his services as that thereby he recovered more Fortes in one daie then by strong hand would have been wonne in a yere, respectyng the smalness of his Companie, and the gayning of time was one of his chiefest cares, bothe because he had no provision for victuales for his people, but pulled it as it were out of the enemies mouth perforce." The parallel to much American practice is close. Sir Henry Sydney said that after Gilbert's work was done in Ireland, "the name of an Englishman is more terrible now to them than the sight of a hundred was before." W. G. Gosling, *The Life of Sir Humfrey Gilbert* (London, 1911), pp. 46–47; 48; 49.

33. From "A Trewe Relacyon of the p'cedeinges and ocurentes of momente wch have hapened in Virginia," in Neill, *Virginia Vetusta,* p. viii.

34. Hakluyt, *Principal Navigations,* edition cited, VIII, 349; 351.

35. About this year Sir James Croft proposed that a colony of married English soldiers and their families be settled at Baltimore in West Munster to hold the land, on the analogy of the English garrison at Calais. Bagwell, *op. cit.,* I, 360. The scheme proved abortive. After the death of Henry VIII the native Irish were either shot down or driven out from Leix and Offaly, when it was proposed to re-settle these territories with English soldiers and colonists, leases to be granted by the crown for twenty-one years. The Shane O'Neill hostilities of 1559–60 ended the attempt. In 1567–8 Sir Peter Carew pressed vague claims

upon Munster, and a company of "gentlemen" from the west of England, including Gilbert and Sir Richard Grenville, was formed for settling, but though Gilbert harried the land with fire and sword, the enterprise collapsed. In 1572 Sir Thomas Smith made an offer to the crown to take possession of Ards in Ulster, establish a permanent garrison and colony, and so create a plantation. He was murdered in 1573, and the settlement, too weak from the beginning, dwindled under the ineffectual leadership of his son. Some time later Robert Devereux, Earl of Essex, sought to retrieve Ulster, but being harassed by both Shane O'Neill and the Scots, after some highly successful massacres, he abandoned his plantation after two years. The first really successful plantation was the colonization of Derry (Londonderry) by twelve London companies in 1608. On this see George Hill, *op. cit.* The most thorough treatise on the whole subject is Moritz Julius Bonn, *Die Englische Kolonisation in Irland,* 2 vols. (Stuttgart and Berlin, 1906).

36. Once replenished with Englishmen and "polliced with Englishe lawes," Ireland will be "as great commoditie to the Prince as the realme of England," says the author. A few hundred men only are needed, and for them the proprietor proposed to construct fortified posts on the seashore and the frontier, to build a common storehouse, and to lodge his men. The parallel of Jamestown will occur to everyone. Hill, *An Historical Account of the MacDonnells of Antrim,* pp. 405–415.

37. "A Brife description of Ireland: Made in this yeere. 1589. by Robert Payne vnto xxv. of his partners for whom he is vndertaker there. Truely published verbatim, according to his letters, by Nich, Gorsan one of the said partners, for that he would his countrymen should be partakers of the many good Notes therein conteined. With diuers Notes taken out of others the Authoures letters written to his said partners, sithenes the first Impression, well worth the reading" (London, 1590), in *Tracts Relating to Ireland printed for the Irish Archaeological Society,* vol. I, ed. Aquilla Smith (Dublin, 1841). This pamphlet springs from a scheme to divide the forfeited lands of Desmond and his followers into seignories of from four to twelve thousand acres, these to be allotted to younger sons and settled by English farmers, hop-planters, gardeners, wheelwrights, smiths, carpenters, and so on. As in the case of the Smith plantation, an inconsiderable number migrated, only to be harassed and spoiled by the wild Irish.

38. Reprinted in Hill, *An Historical Account of the Plantation in Ulster,* pp. 360–363.

39. "If multitudes of men were employed proportionally to these commodities, many thousands would be set at work, to the great

service of the King, the strength of his realm, and the advancement of several trades. It might ease the city of an insupportable burthen of persons, which it might conveniently spare, all parts of the city being so surcharged that one tradesman is scarce able to live by another; and it would also be a means to free and preserve the city from infection."

40. Hill, *ibid.*, pp. 441, 443.

41. Hill, *op. cit.*, p. 590. On the other hand it is possible to paint too dark a picture of Irish failure. In 1630 in his *The Planters Plea* John White found it necessary to combat the notion that Ireland was a better place than New England for surplus population. The arguments which he is compelled to meet are that Ireland is closer home, belongs to the crown, is empty of people in many parts, is fruitful, is an important part of the English defence system, and needs help to recover from its superstition. See chapter iv, "That New-England is a fit Country for the seating of an English Colonie, for the propagation of Religion" in Force, *Tracts*, vol. II, no. 3. And in the same year Sir William Alexander, in his *The Mapp and Description of New-England*, remarked of Ireland that he found "a Plantation there inferiour to none that hath beene heretofore." ". . . our King hath onely diuided the most seditious families of the *Irish* by dispersing them in sundry parts within the Countrey, not to extinguish, but to dissipate their power. . . . And our King hath incorporated some of his best *Brittaines* with the *Irish,* planted in sundry places without power to oppresse, but onely to ciuilize them by their example. Thus *Ireland* which heretofore was scarcely discouered, and only irritated by others, prouing to the *English* as the *Lowe-Countries* did to *Spaine,* a meanes whereby to waste their men, and their money, is now really conquered . . ." Laing, *op. cit.,* p. 4.

42. Quoted in Maxwell, p. 248, note. See the passage from the *Calendar of State Papers, Ireland,* to the effect that, though there are some wise and virtuous settlers, there are too many "traitors, murderers, thieves, coseners, cony-catchers, shifting mates, runners away with other men's wives, some having two or three wives, persons divorced living loosely, bankrupts, carnall gospellers, Papists, Puritans and Brownists." This was written in 1598.

43. Gilbert's "Discourse on Ireland" of 1572 reads much like a colonization project for the New World, but was never published. It points out the dangers of Ireland remaining "vncyvyll," since, if rebellion continues, "the contry [is] apt to haue ayde of Spanyardes or scottes or bothe and also of other Contries." The benefits of making Ireland

"cyvill and vnder Subiection of good lawes" include quietness and decrease of expense, the preservation of the island from conquest, "great proffit that in short tyme would growe vnto England by the revenues of landes," customs fees, the sale of English merchandise, and the income from fishing, minerals, and metals. In order to divert the trade to England, he urges government to "haue vpon eche haven of Ireland fortresses to be made to be kept wth a garrison of English souldiors and the like in euery notable porte towne," and suggests that as tenures-in-chief in Ireland fall in, they be brought under English control. Quoted in *Sir Humfrey Gylberte and his Enterprise of Colonization in America* (Boston: Publications of the Prince Society, 1903), pp. 223–26. The original is among the Carew Manuscripts in the Lambeth Library.

44. See J. P. Baxter, *Sir Ferdinando Gorges, op. cit.,* I, 37–58.

45. During the session of parliament held February–May, 1624, Southampton appeared as an authority on Irish affairs and was a member of the committee to consider the defence of that island.

46. According to the *Dictionary of National Biography* there are forty-two manuscript volumes by Carew on Irish affairs in the Lambeth Library, and four more in the Bodleian.

47. Dated, according to his editors, January 1, 1608/9. See the *Life of Bacon,* Vol. XI of *The Works of Francis Bacon,* ed. Spedding, Ellis and Heath (London, 1868), pp. 110–116.

48. *CSP, Dom., 1591–4,* p. 181; and see *Archaeologia Americana: Transactions and Collections of the Am. Ant. Soc.,* IV, 27–28.

49. Brown, *Genesis of the United States,* II, 845.

50. See *CSP, Colonial,* I, 50.

51. *Proc. Am. Phil. Soc.,* September, 1942, pp. 463 ff. In the *Winthrop Papers,* I (1929), 281, an interesting letter from John Winthrop Sr. to his son, then at Trinity College, Dublin, dated April 20, 1623, adds in a postscript: "I wish oft God would open a waye to settle me in Ireland, if it might be for his glorye."

52. "If we consider the nature of these Irish customs [*i.e.,* the Brehon laws], we shall find that the people that doth use them must of necessity be enemies to all good government." Sir John Davies, *A Discovery of the True Causes why Ireland was never entirely Subdued* (1612), quoted in Maxwell, pp. 351–52. And see Bonn, *op. cit.,* Bd. I, pp. 169 ff.

53. Spenser proposed a system of military garrisons in Ireland, for "this was the Course which the Romaines obserued in the Conquest of England" (one of the few references to classical example to be found

in the Tudor colonizing material), and proposed to divide the land into seignories. Lords of the manor were to avoid "the worst and most decayed men," and settlers were "to bee chosen out of all partes of this Realme, eyther by discression of wise men there vnto appointed or by lott, or by the drum, as was the ould vse in sending forthe of Collonies, or such other good meanes as shall in theire wisdome bee thought metest. . . ." He would permit the renting of lands to the natives only provided that "in noe place vnder any landlorde there shall be manie of them planted togeather." *Op. cit.,* pp. 161 ff.

54. As early as 1521 the Earl of Surrey wrote Henry VIII: "And after my poor opinion, unless your Grace send inhabitants, of your own natural subjects, to inhabit such countries [regions] as shall be won, all your charges should be but wastefully spent. For if this country's people, if the Irish, should inhabit, undoubtedly they would return to their old ill-rooted customs, whensoever they might see any time to take their advantage, according as they have ever yet done, and daily do. And if all the people of this land should be compelled to fall to labour (which they will never do, as long as they may find any country in the land to go unto), yet, after my opinion, there should not be found number sufficient to inhabit well the third part of the land." Maxwell, pp. 90–91.

55. "First, when men come into a country vast and void of all things necessary for the use of man's life, if they set up together in a place, one of them will the better supply the wants of another: work-folks of all sorts will be the more continually set a-work without loss of time." "Secondly, it will draw out of the inhabited country of Ireland provisions and victuals and many necessaries, because they shall be sure of utterance [*i.e.,* circulation]. . . ." And lastly "by a slight fortification of no great charge," the danger of revolt may be prevented. The parallels to American practice are too obvious for comment. *Works,* edition cited, XI, 124–125.

56. The classic case which illustrates the feudal implications of the Ireland-Nova Scotia-America triangle is, of course, that of George Calvert, who owned 2300 acres of land in County Longford, became Lord Baltimore on the Irish establishment, was a member of the Virginia Company, acquired "Avalon" in Newfoundland, and asked for and received Maryland as a county palatine on terms which his settlers later denounced as giving him more autocratic powers than were possessed even by the crown. See Bernard C. Steiner, "The First Lord Baltimore and His Colonial Projects," *Annual Report of the American Historical Association* (Washington, 1906), 2 vols., vol. I.

57. See the documents cumulated in Laing, *op. cit.*

58. Almost the sole writer to have seen the significance of the Irish colonial experiment for American history is Edward P. Cheyney, "Some English Conditions Surrounding the Settlement of Virginia," *Am. Hist. Rev.*, XII, 507–528.

59. *Short History of British Expansion* (London, 1927), p. 287.

60. J. A. Williamson, *The Age of Drake* (London, 1938), pp. 3 ff.

61. From 1523 to 1542, as part of the conflict between Francis I and Spain, French privateers had attacked the Spanish treasure fleet, many of the French being Huguenots who assailed the Spaniards because the latter were Catholics. Villegagnon's unfortunate attempt to found a Huguenot colony in Brazil, begun in 1555, was dead by 1558. The fate of the Ribaut colony in Florida (1562) is among the horrors of colonial history. See for an interesting discussion of this phase of international rivalry J. A. Williamson, *Sir John Hawkins: The Time and the Man* (Oxford, 1927), chapter i.

62. Williamson, *Sir John Hawkins,* pp. 72–73. Williamson notes that the treacherous attack on Hawkins at San Juan de Ulloa, coming on top of the merciless extermination by the Spaniards of the French in Florida, ended the friendship hitherto formally maintained by Spain and England.

63. By Hakluyt; see *Principal Navigations,* edition cited, VII, 158–203.

64. *Ibid.,* VII, 244–250.

65. The "certain Gentlemen" are to choose a "first Seate" on a bay so that the enemy "shalbe forced to lie in open rode abroade without." It is expected that they shall live by sea-traffic, since, "if they shall live without sea traffique, at the first they become naked by want of linnen and woollen, and very miserable by infinite wants . . . and so will they be forced . . . to depart, or else easely they will be consumed by the Spanyards, by the Frenchmen, or by the naturall inhabitants of the countrey, and so the enterprize becomes reprochfull to our Nation. . . ." Space for "the scope of a citie" is all that the project demands. Contrast this program with the grant of huge areas of land to the London and Plymouth companies later.

66. The petition is printed in *Sir Humfrey Gylberte and his Enterprise of Colonization in America* (Boston: Prince Society, 1903), pp. 228–237.

67. "A Discourse of the Commoditie of the Taking of the Straight of Magellan" in *Tudor Economic Documents,* ed. R. H. Tawney and Eileen Powers, III, 224–232. It is interesting to note that the Spaniards

sent 400 men to hold the straits in 1582, one survivor being picked up in 1589.

68. In his *The Voyagers and Elizabethan Drama* (Boston, 1938), pp. 285–287, Robert R. Cawley points out that there are ten allusions to Drake in the plays of the time for one to any other voyager. On the true significance of Drake's circumnavigation of the globe see Henry R. Wagner, *Sir Francis Drake's Voyage Around the World* (San Francisco, 1926).

69. "Making war with Spain and not the planting of colonies was the driving force that determined the direction of Elizabethan activities, at least in the waters of the northern Atlantic, and for seventy years after the Armada this was relentlessly pursued, not by kings but by valiant captains, merchants, and trading companies, as an accepted part of the parliamentary and Puritan programme, until the menace of Spanish domination was removed and England had obtained a permanent hold upon some of the richest parts of the declining Spanish empire." C. M. Andrews, *The Colonial Period of American History* (New Haven and London, 1934), I, 25. One cannot agree with Alexander Brown (*The Genesis of the United States,* I, 43) who, though he says flatly that Spain "was really the chief obstacle which had to be met and overcome," argues that "our founders managed the affair with such diplomacy, they accomplished their object so quietly, that 'the generality' in England and Virginia were probably never fully aware of the great and real danger which at first threatened the enterprise." If anything is clear from the material, it is that the generality were perfectly well informed of what the nation, with or without the connivance of government, was doing.

70. Charles Leigh tried to colonize Guiana in 1604–6; Robert Harcourt tried again in 1609; and in 1613 Harcourt received a grant from James I for this purpose. In 1617 Raleigh sailed for the Orinoco, but paused to assault San Tomé on the way, to the ruin of the enterprise. In 1610–11 Sir Thomas Roe explored the Amazon and left colonists at the mouth of the river, whose fate remains obscure. In 1620 Captain Roger North planted a colony in the same region, which lasted to 1623, and which was reëstablished in 1627. And there were later attempts.

71. Williamson, *Short History of British Expansion,* p. 209.

72. *Ibid.,* p. 269. In 1629–30 Providence Island [Santa Catilina] was colonized, in 1640 Belize and in 1646 the Bahamas.

73. See Arthur Percival Newton, *The Colonizing Activities of the English Puritans: The Last Phase of the Elizabethan Struggle with*

Spain (New Haven, 1914). From 1631 to 1635 continued efforts were made by the more worldly minded English puritans to create a puritan community on Providence Island. There was an intimate connection between the Massachusetts Bay enterprise and the Gulf of Mexico one, but the Providence company found it "almost impossible to secure emigrants of decent standing," the population, with the exception of a few planters and a minister, being mainly bond servants. After 1635 the island became principally a base for privateering. Nevertheless Pym wrote about that year: "Although we cannot procure so many religious persons as we desire, yet, when the place is safe, godly persons and families will be encouraged to transport themselves; and though God succour not our endeavors in that, yet we may make a civil commodity of it, upholding the profession of religion, moral duty, and justice, till God shall please to plant amongst us a more settled Church" (p. 200).

74. Williamson, *Short History*, p. 189. The Hudson River was also suggested.

AMERICAN PROSE STYLE: 1700–1770

1. See Kenneth B. Murdock, *Selections from Cotton Mather* (New York, 1926), Introduction, pp. xli–xlii.

2. I have followed Murdock's text, *ibid.*, pp. 18–19.

3. *The Complete Works of Benjamin Franklin* (New York, 1887–88), I, 47–49.

4. This collection is briefly described in *The Huntington Library Bulletin*, No. 1 (May, 1931), p. 75. In addition to the Eames collection this article draws upon other relevant material in the Huntington Library and in the William L. Clements Library, Ann Arbor.

5. W. Fraser Mitchell, *English Pulpit Oratory from Andrewes to Tillotson: A Study of its Literary Aspects* (London and New York, 1932); Caroline Francis Richardson, *English Preachers and Preaching, 1640–1670: A Secular Study* (London, 1928).

6. Among the many passages quoted by these authorities, I cite the following from Richard Baxter as typical: "Ministers, therefore, must be observant of the Case of their Flocks, that they may know what is most necessary for them, both for Matter and for Manner. And usually Matter is first to be regarded, as being of more Concernment than the Manner. . . . It is commonly Empty Ignorant Men that want the Matter and Substance of True Learning, that are over Curious and Sollicitous about Words and Ornaments, when the Ancient, Experienced, most Learned Men, abound in Substantial Verities, usually deliv-

ered in the plainest Dress. . . . All our Teaching must be as Plain and Evident as we can make it. . . . He that would be understood must speak to the Capacity of his Hearers, and make it his Business to make himself understood. Truth loves the Light, and is most Beautiful when most naked. It's a Sign of an envious Enemy to hide the Truth; and a Sign of an Hypocrite to do this under pretence of Revealing it: And therefore painted obscure Sermons (like the Painted Glass in the Windows that keep out the Light) are two [sic] oft the Marks of painted Hypocrites. If you would not teach Men, what do you in the Pulpit? If you would, why do you not speak so as to be understood?" This was written about 1655. See Mitchell, *op. cit.*, pp. 103–104.

7. London, 1674. This book I consulted in the private library of Mr. William G. Mather, of Cleveland, Ohio, who kindly gave me permission to use his remarkable collection of Matheriana.

8. *Parentator* (Boston, 1724), p. 215.

9. From "To the Reader" in that pamphlet.

10. Samuel Mather, *The Life of the Very Reverend and Learned Cotton Mather, D.D. & F.R.S. Late Pastor of the North Church in Boston. Who Died, Feb. 13. 1727, 8* (Boston, 1729), p. 72.

11. *The A, B, C. of Religion. Lessons Relating to the Fear of God, Fitted unto the Youngest & Lowest Capacities. And Children Suitably instructed in the Maxims of Religion* (Boston, 1713), p. 4.

12. *Duodecennium Luctuosum. The History of a Long War With Indian Salvages, . . . From the Year, 1702. To the Year, 1714* (Boston, 1714), p. 12.

13. *Bonifacius. An Essay Upon the Good, that is to be Devised and Designed, by those Who Desire to Answer the Great End of Life, and to Do Good While they Live* (Boston, 1710), p. xv.

14. *Just Commemorations. The Death of Good Men, Considered; and The Characters of Some who have lately Died in the Service of the Churches, Exhibited* (Boston [1715]), p. 34.

15. *Ibid.*, p. ii.

16. Samuel Mather, *op. cit.*, pp. 68–69.

17. *Ibid.* The Rev. Samuel Mather was not without the family failing. Note the "quaintness" in this passage from his sermon on the deceased: "*First;* I shall give some Account *of his Departure.* Indeed it was not as ELIJAH's, who, instead of a *cold Sweat,* was fill'd with inexpressible *Warmth* and immortal *Vigour;* instead of a *Ratling in the Throat* was *singing* with Transport; and instead of the pale *Image of Death* had a never-fading *Bloom* on his Countenance." (*The Departure and Character of Elijah Considered and Improved. A Sermon*

After the Decease of the very Reverend and Learned Cotton Mather [Boston, 1728], p. 13.)

18. This was the *Elementa Rhetorices* of William Dugard.

19. *Manuductio ad Ministerium* (Boston, 1726), pp. 32, 34, 35, 42. When writing verse, "let not the *Circaean* Cup intoxicate you" (p. 42). The need of a learned ministry is to be met by a sound knowledge of Latin, enough Greek for theological study, and Hebrew—to be learned in the time the young candidate might otherwise spend smoking! After Hebrew, Syriac will be easy (pp. 28–29, 30). Much time is to be spent in the study of natural philosophy, which displays God in his works: "Be sure, The *Experimental Philosophy* is that, in which alone your Mind can be at all established" (p. 50). History and music (in which you are to "Do as you please"), and the formation of a small learned society, or sodality, are other important items (pp. 57, 72 ff.).

20. *Ibid.*, p. 44. Cf. the passage (quoted above) in which Samuel Mather describes Cotton Mather's style as "*stuck with Jewels.*"

21. *Ibid.*, pp. 44–47. The latter part of this passage contains Mather's discussion of Senecan and Ciceronian styles.

22. *Op. cit.*, p. 33.

23. *The Departure of Elijah lamented. A Sermon Occasioned By the Great & Publick Loss In the Decease Of the very Reverend & Learned Cotton Mather* (Boston, 1728), p. 24.

24. *The Example of Christ, as a Guide to Ministers & People, considered and inforced. In A Sermon Preach'd at the Ordination Of the Reverend Mr. Edmund Noyes* (Boston, 1751). The minister is to base himself on Scripture expressions. "This will give a solemn Elegance to his Language, and divine Truths will ever appear better in this Dress, than in all the *studied* Pomp of *Greek* or *Roman* Eloquence.—And having set the Truth in an easy and clear Light, let him press the same upon the Mind and Conscience, with every rational & divine Argument the Subject *naturally* admits of." (The quotations are from pp. 22–23.) Note the contrast between Tucker's turning away from Greek and Roman eloquence, and Cotton Mather. It is perhaps significant that the sermon also contains a severe denunciation of religious enthusiasm.

25. *Preaching Peace by Jesus Christ describ'd and urg'd, as the principal Design of the Gospel-Ministry* (Boston, 1753), pp. 9–10.

26. *Sermons Upon the following Subjects, Viz. On Hearing the Word . . .* (Boston, 1755), pp. ii–iii.

27. *The Work of a Gospel-Minister, and the Importance of approving himself to GOD in it* (New-Haven, 1755), p. 15.

28. *A Sermon Preach'd In the first Parish, in Kellingley, At the*

Ordination Of the Reverend Mr. Aaron Brown (New-London, 1754). See pp. 6–8.

29. *Christ the grand Subject of Gospel-Preaching; the Power of God, manifested in the Work of Faith; and Unbelief under the Gospel, lamented* (New-York, 1755), p. 24. Note, amid this plea for lucidity, the vestigial remnant of "quaintness" in the play on the word "crucified." Buell repeated and reinforced this doctrine at the ordination of the Rev. Samson Occum, the Mohegan Indian. However much fine language "may please the vitiated Taste and Humours of some, the two distant Poles are not more remote from each other, than such Manner of Pulpit Work from a genuine Aptitude and Tendency to pierce the Heart, to awaken the Conscience, and to do good to the Souls of Men." The best preachers "communicate their Thoughts in a correct, masculine, nervous, striking and charming Stile and Diction." It is "unnatural and disagreeable" when "the Preacher who has not a natural spontaneous flow of ready and elegant Expressions, has labour'd hard to polish his little Composition, by the constant Glitter of shining Phrases, by arranging his Words, beautifying his Language, rounding his Periods, so as really to stiffen his Discourse: When by minding little Things over much, he has betray'd the Want of a Heart deeply aw'd and impress'd with a Sense of what he is about." (*The Excellence and Importance of the saving Knowledge of the Lord Jesus Christ in the Gospel-Preacher, plainly and seriously represented and enforced* [New-York, 1861], pp. 34–35. He has other remarks on the same subject; see pp. 36–37.)

30. *Discourses on Public Occasions in America* (London, 1762; 2d ed.), p. 135. Note, however, that he says he has revised a sermon by the Rev. Mr. Barton, which had certain faults: "in composition" there is "a certain incommunicable art of making one part rise gracefully out of another" which Barton lacks. ("Appendix" to *Discourses*, p. 4.)

31. *Of the Pastoral Care: A Sermon Preached to the Reverend Ministers of the Province of the Massachusetts-Bay in New-England, at Their Annual Convention in Boston, On May 27. 1762* (Boston, 1762), p. 20.

32. *Christ the grand Subject of the Gospel Ministry. A Sermon Preached at the Ordination Of the Reverend Mr. Samuel West* [son of the preacher], . . . *in Needham* (Boston, 1764), pp. 4, 5, 6, 7, 8. There is much else of value in this sermon that I have not quoted. Here, as elsewhere in the citations made, I have silently corrected obvious typographical errors in the text.

33. *A Sermon Preached July 4, 1764. At the Ordination of the Rev-*

erend Mr. Edward Brooks, to the Pastoral Care of the Church in North-Yarmouth (Boston, 1764), pp. 24–25, 27. See also pp. 28–30.

34. *A Sermon Preached at the Ordination of the Rev. Mr. Gyles Merrill, To the Pastoral Care of the Church and Congregation In Plastow, and the North Part of Haverhill* (Boston, 1765), p. 16.

35. *A Sermon Preached September 17. 1766. At the Ordination Of the Reverend Mr. Ebenezer Thayer, To the Pastoral Care of the first Church in Hampton* (Boston, 1766), pp. 16–17. Ministers "lean too much to their own understanding, and are wise above what is written. They lay much greater stress on their own curious refinements and subtile reasonings, than on the express declarations of the holy scriptures" (p. 15).

36. Joseph Perry, *The Character and Reward of the Faithful and Wise Minister of Jesus Christ: A Sermon, Occasioned by the Much Lamented Death of the Reverend Nathanael Hooker, Pastor of the fourth Church of Christ in Hartford* (Hartford, 1770), p. 19.

37. Cf. the quotation from Baxter, note 6, *supra.*

38. *A Sermon Preached September 25th 1771. By John Hunt, M.A. At his Ordination* (Boston, 1772), pp. 19, 20.

39. *A Sermon Preached before the Ministers Of the Province of the Massachusetts-Bay, in New-England, at their Annual Convention in Boston* (Boston, 1772), pp. 44–45.

40. *Novum Organum* (tr. Ellis and Spedding), I, xliii.

41. From this point of view it is perhaps not without significance that Nathaniel Ward, the most intolerant of the earlier Massachusetts Puritans, wrote the most fantastic American prose of the seventeenth century—*The Simple Cobler of Aggawam* (London, 1647).

42. *Malachi. Or, The Everlasting Gospel, Preached unto the Nations* (Boston, 1717), pp. 73–74.

43. *Brethren dwelling together in Unity. The True Basis for an Union Among the People of God, Offered and Asserted* (Boston, 1718), pp. 21, 23. Papists are exempted from toleration, but Mather laments that "NEW-ENGLAND also has in some Former Times, done some Things of this Aspect [religious persecution], which would not now be so well approved of" (p. 39). Increase Mather contributed a preface of four pages, in which he expressed pleasure in the situation, and added, speaking of the Baptists: "Suppose their particular Opinion to be an Error, our holding Communion with them, does not intimate any approbation of it. If it did, we must renounce Communion with all the men in the World" (p. ii). The following sentence is not without pathos: "May I now I am going out of the World, leave a dying Example to

those that shall survive me, of a Catholick and Christian Spirit, and of Charitableness to those that may in controversal and extrafundamental Opinions differ from us" (p. iv).

44. *The Pious cry to the Lord for Help when the Godly and Faithful fail among them* (Boston, 1746), p. 27. The passage on toleration is on p. 31. Cushing's "Genius" inclined him "either to unbyass'd Reasoning or agreable Observations" (p. 25).

45. *The Example of Christ, as a Guide to Ministers & People, considered and inforced* (Boston, 1751), pp. 22, 23. See p. 82, *supra,* for other passages from this sermon.

46. *A Continuation of the Calm and Dispassionate Vindication of the Professors of the Church of England, against the Abusive Misrepresentations and fallacious Argumentations of Mr. Noah Hobart* (Boston, 1751), pp. 5–6.

47. *A Sermon Preach'd in the Audience of His Excellency William Shirley, Esq; Captain General, Governour and Commander in Chief, The Honourable His Majesty's Council, and the Honourable House of Representatives, Of . . . Massachusetts-Bay* (Boston, 1754), p. 10.

48. *Sermons Upon the following Subjects* (Boston, 1755), pp. ii, iii.

49. *Ibid.,* p. 103.

50. *A Discourse On Rev. XV. 3ᵈ, 4ᵗʰ. Occasioned by the Earthquakes In November 1755* (Boston, 1755), p. 71.

51. *A Letter of Reproof to Mr. John Cleaveland of Ipswich* (Boston, 1764), p. 4.

52. *Remarks on an Anonymous Tract* (Boston, 1765), pp. 3, 78.

53. *The Supreme Deity Of our Lord Jesus Christ, maintained* (Boston, 1757), pp. 1–2.

54. *Discourses on Several Public Occasions* (London, 1759), p. vii. This is the first edition. Cf. note 30, *supra.*

55. Cf., in this respect, the injunctions laid by Jonathan Edwards upon himself in writing on natural science. See W. P. Upham, in *Proceedings of the Massachusetts Historical Society,* 2d Ser., XV (1902), pp. 514–21.

56. *A Sermon Preached at the Ordination of the Rev. William Whitwell, To the . . . Congregation in Marblehead* (Boston, 1762), pp. 10, 11, 16–17. The directions for preaching are like the description given of Cushing's oratory. Cf. p. 91, *supra.*

57. *The Church of Christ a firm and durable House. Shown in A Number of Sermons On Matth. XVI. 18* (New-London, 1767), pp. iv–v.

58. *A Candid Examination of Dr. Mayhew's Observations on the*

Charter and Conduct of the Society for the propagation of the Gospel in foreign parts (Boston, 1763), p. 1.

59. *A Friendly Expostulation, With all Persons concern'd in publishing A late Pamphlet* (New York, 1763), p. 3.

60. Chandler Robbins, *Some brief Remarks on A Piece published by John Cotton, Esq.;* (Boston, 1774), p. 1. "As much brevity as is consistent with clearness, is always most eligible in all writings, especially of this kind." (*Loc. cit.*)

61. I have again preferred to use the Murdock text, *op. cit.,* pp. 1, 13–14, 6.

62. *Ibid.,* pp. 26–27. The quotation from Cicero may be found on p. 9.

63. *The Present State of Virginia* (London, 1724), pp. vi, vii.

64. *Indian Converts: or, Some account of the Lives and Dying Speeches of a considerable Number of the Christianized Indians* (London, 1727), p. ix.

65. *A Chronological History of New-England In the Form of Annals* (Boston, 1736). The dedication to Belcher, which contains the passage cited, is printed in the first eight unnumbered pages.

66. *Ibid.,* pp. i–x.

67. Charles N. Davies, who once owned the Huntington Library copy, wrote in it that this "is perhaps the best written book extant on the subject of Congregational Churches."

68. *An Historical Discourse on the Civil and Religious Affairs of the Colony of Rhode-Island* (Boston, 1739), pp. 10–11 (of Dedication).

69. *The History of the First Discovery and Settlement of Virginia* (Williamsburg, 1747), pp. iii–viii.

70. *A Short Narrative Of Mischief done by the French and Indian Enemy, on the Western Frontiers Of the Province of the Massachusetts-Bay* (Boston, 1750), p. 1. The publication was posthumous.

71. The literature of hatred could be considerably enriched by extracts from colonial writings directed against the French, the extent and vituperation of which are scarcely suspected by those who have not toiled through the material. The difficulty is that a paper devoted to the subject would become tedious by the mere iteration of animosity. Of hundreds of examples, the following paragraph by Thomas Prince is a fair sample: "From their wicked Thirst of arbitrary Power, they [the French Bourbons] have by Wars, Blood and Treachery, abolished the ancient Liberties of *France,* and made their Subjects, both common People and Nobles Slaves. From their cruel Hatred of the reform'd Religion, they have destroy'd above *Two Thousand* Protestant Churches in that Kingdom; banished their Ministers; imprisoned, tortured,

butchered and ruined above a *Million* of their People. And from their restless Eagerness to gain the *Monarchy* of *Europe,* they have, by un-provoked Wars, Battles, Sieges and mortal Sicknesses occasioned thereby, sacrificed *Millions* of their own Subjects and of their Neighbours round about them. They never made a *Treaty* without perfidious Violation in the fittest Time for their Advantage: They never made a *War* without fallacious and unjust Pretences: and they never made a *Peace,* without Additions to their Power and Empire." This, by one of the calmer minds in New England. (*The Salvations of God in 1746. In Part set forth in a Sermon At the South Church in Boston, Nov. 27 1746* [Boston, 1746], pp. 11–12.) When Indian massacre is added to this amalgam, the colonial preacher uses language comparable to that of Swinburne's *Dirae.*

72. *Historical Memoirs, Relating to the Housatunnuk Indians: Or, An Account of the Methods used, and Pains taken, for the Propagation of the Gospel among that Heathenish-Tribe* (Boston, 1753), pp. i–iii.

73. *The History Of the Province of New-York* (London, 1757), pp. xi–xii. I take "my Profession" in the above quotation to be an ironical reference to the fact that Smith was a minister—or did he have his function as a school-teacher in mind?

74. Jared Eliot is ignored by Tyler, by the *Cambridge History of American Literature,* and by Parrington, who might be expected to dis-cuss him because of the economic implications of the *Essay.*

75. *An Essay on the Invention, or Art of making very good, if not the best Iron, from black Sea Sand* (New-York, 1762), p. 17.

76. Murdock, *Selections from Cotton Mather,* p. 262.

77. *A Review of the Military Operations in North-America* (London, 1757), pp. 30–31. There is more to this character sketch, but I have quoted enough to give its quality.

The Drift to Liberalism in the American Eighteenth Century

1. Perhaps the clearest single statement of the classical point of view is that of Professor Arthur O. Lovejoy in his article "Optimism and Romanticism," *Publications of the Modern Language Association,* XLII (1926), especially pp. 942–943: "For two centuries the thought of the Western world, and, above all, the efforts made during those centuries for improvement and correction in beliefs, in institutions, and in art, had been, in the main, dominated by the assumption that, in each phase of human activity, excellence consists in conforming as nearly as possible to a standard conceived as universal, static [,] uncomplicated, uniform

for every rational being. Rationality and uniformity were, indeed, commonly assumed to be inseparable notions. . . . 'Nature' was the word oftenest used to designate such a standard of excellence; and nature . . . 'is everywhere the same.' The norm . . . of truth or of beauty, was simple and invariant. . . . It was their supposed greater universality, both in content and in appeal, which constituted the essence of the superiority attributed to the classical models. In every domain . . . the program of improvement or reform was one of simplification, standardization, the avoidance of the particular, the elimination of local variations and individual diversities supposed to have arisen through some . . . aberration from the uniformity of the 'natural' order."

Thus deism sought to bring men back to the "simple creed . . . supposed to be literally catholic, *i.e.,* to have been understood and accepted *semper, ubique et ab omnibus.*" Ethics was summed up "in the law of nature, of which universality was the distinguishing mark." Political philosophy, conceived of as resting upon natural rights, was concerned with the generic in man. In the aesthetics of literature "the high neoclassical dogma demanded that the subject-matter and emotional content of a drama or epic should be limited to that which is universal in human experience and capable of appealing equally to all men in all times and all lands."

2. "On the Discrimination of Romanticisms," *PMLA,* XXXIX (1924), 229–253.

3. Thus Henry A. Beers, who might be presumed to know romanticism when he saw it, recognizes no "romantic period" in his *Outline Sketch of American Literature* (1887; revised as *Initial Studies in American Letters,* 1895) and says little more about the origins of transcendentalism than that the movement was a restatement of the idealistic philosophy (p. 121). F. L. Pattee's *History of American Literature* (1896) has no section on the "romantic period," does not recognize romanticism in the index, and speaks only generally of romantic poetry. E. P. Whipple's *American Literature and Other Papers* (1896) speaks in like terms of the influence of English romanticism on American writers. C. F. Richardson, *American Literature: 1607–1885* (popular edition, 1898), touches on romanticism in passing. Barrett Wendell, *A Literary History of America* (1900), which with all its crotchets, is penetrating, discusses English romanticism as a background to nineteenth-century American literature, but distinguishes no separate period. William P. Trent, *A History of American Literature: 1607–1865* (1908), has only brief references. John Macy, *The Spirit of American Literature* (1913), recognizes no "romantic period," though the author talks in

general terms of such a subject as Emerson's relation to European thought. Leon Kellner, *American Literature* (trans. by Julia Franklin, 1915), remarks that "spirits of a higher strain followed slavishly in the footsteps of the English [romantic] poets" (p. 57), and says that "an admiration of German philosophy" was common to the transcendentalists (p. 81), but makes no separate division. Though Stanley T. Williams, *The American Spirit in Letters* (1926), makes casual reference to obvious relations with Europe, "romanticism" does not appear in the index or the table of contents. It might be thought that romanticism would be a concept useful to the thesis of Ludwig Lewisohn (*Expression in America,* 1932), but he uses the term only generally. Romanticism appears only infrequently in V. F. Calverton, *The Liberation of American Literature* (1932). Percy H. Boynton's *Literature and American Life* (1936) does not discover a "romantic period" and stresses native elements.

4. V. L. Parrington, *Main Currents in American Thought,* vol. II (1927); Ernest E. Leisy, *American Literature: An Interpretative Survey* (1929); Russell Blankenship, *American Literature as an Expression of the National Mind* (1931), pp. 48–49, 199; Thomas H. Dickinson, *The Making of American Literature* (1932), subdividing the period into two phases: 1789–1830, 1830–1855; Tremaine McDowell, *The Romantic Triumph: American Literature from 1830 to 1860* (1933): see the introductory essay, pp. 1–8; James McDonald Miller, *An Outline of American Literature* (1934), which subdivides the period into two phases: 1800–1825, 1825–1850; Walter Fuller Taylor, *A History of American Letters* (1936), pt. iii.

5. *America in Literature* (1903), pp. 193, 222, 250.

6. These quotations are, in order, from Taylor, pp. 141–142; C. R. Fish, *The Rise of the Common Man* (1927), p. 255; Parrington, *The Romantic Revolution,* p. 322; Miller, p. 101; Whipple, p. 35; Frederic I. Carpenter, "The Vogue of Ossian in America: A Study in Taste," *American Literature,* II (1930–31), 405; Lewisohn, p. 153, who adds that "even the transcendentalist revolt did not forget what was due to birth and breeding. . . ." Bliss Perry, *The American Spirit in Literature: A Chronicle of Great Interpreters* (1918), remarks that the "Renascence of New England" was due to many causes, but that it "is a good illustration of that law of 'tension and release,' which the late Professor Shaler liked to demonstrate in all organic life" (p. 111).

7. The authors cited are, in order, Miller, p. 90; Woodberry, p. 125; Parrington, *The Romantic Revolution,* p. vi; Grace Warren Landrum, "Notes on the Reading of the Old South," *American Literature,* III

(1931-32), 60-71; Leisy, p. 67; Parrington, *op. cit.,* pp. 28 ff., 111; Taylor, p. 215. Landrum notes, however, that economics and politics absorbed a great deal of the intellectual energy of the South, and discovers a marked religious and theological interest among the middle classes. Parrington is especially confused. "French revolutionary theory" is for him "French romantic philosophy" (*The Colonial Mind,* pp. 342-357; *The Romantic Revolution,* pp. vi-vii), but in sections iv and v of pt. i of "The Mind of the South" in *The Romantic Revolution* note that the taste of Wirt was formed by the (older) eighteenth century (p. 31); that Tucker is essentially anti-romantic (p. 70); that Caruthers was a liberal who did not believe in emancipation, elsewhere credited to "French romanticism" (p. 43); and that Kennedy is a Federalist of whom "devout romantic" (p. 49) is used in a sense directly opposite to that in which Jefferson is elsewhere "romantic."

8. To John Macy, Irving as a representative Knickerbocker is no more eighteenth-century than his British contemporaries (pp. 27 ff.); whereas to Leisy, Irving is romantic when, "in conformity with foreign tradition, [the Knickerbocker writers] garbed the landscape of the Hudson in idyllic hue" (p. 67). To Wendell, Irving expresses "romantic sentiment" (p. 179); whereas Parrington, who emphasizes Irving's dislike of the "romantic revolution," cryptically tells us that this "most distinguished of our early romantics" was "immolated on the altar of romanticism"—*i.e.,* "lured . . . away into sterile wastes." He also says that New York had no intellectual revolution corresponding to that in New England (*The Romantic Revolution,* p. 200), and that Philadelphia "remained content with the ways of the eighteenth century, immersed in an old-fashioned culture" (p. 187), whereas Blankenship assures us that Philadelphia was the center of "French and English influence" (p. 206). Miller remarks that the Middle East was materialistic in temper, but "just as romantic as the territorial expansion in the West" (p. 140). Cooper is by a number of writers classed with the romantics because he wrote historical novels and displayed a "love of nature" and of the frontier; but Whipple remarks that "no Hamlets or Werthers or Renés or Childe Harolds" tenant his woods or walk his quarterdecks, and thinks a physician of the mind would recommend him to "weak and sentimental natures" (p. 47). Wendell remarks that "the old world was looking for some wild manifestation of this new, hardly apprehended, western democracy" and got only Bryant, Irving, and Cooper (p. 203); and Parrington, that Cooper's "romantic impulses are held in check by a growing tendency towards realism" (p. 234). [Had Parrington read *The Crater?*] Although each of these statements may

be justified, that fact does not help us to apprehend what is meant by the romantic movement in America.

9. "Two great romantic forces were shaping the economic progress of the country, the brilliant industrial expansion of the East with its attendant influx of new blood from Ireland and Germany, and the great migration to the valleys of the Mississippi and the Missouri." The literary expression of the period (1825–1850) was as a result "extravagantly romantic in temper" and "of course, the literature which such a temper [frontier optimism] produced was romantic" (Miller, pp. 98–99, 133). For Mrs. Hazard, however, frontier "romanticism" is not the result of optimism, but of defeat (*The Frontier in American Literature*, 1927, p. 70). To Dorothy Anne Dondore "this romantic literature . . . does not represent the most distinctive contribution of the prairie" (*The Prairie and the Making of Middle America*, 1926, p. 288), whereas Boynton (*Literature and American Life*) notes that the frontier goes romantic because of nostalgia (p. 600).

10. "The creative influence of the French Revolution upon the western world resulted from the enormous impetus which it gave to the movement to democratize American life and institutions" (Parrington, *The Colonial Mind*, p. 321). "The first stage in the romanticization of American thought resulted from the naturalization of French revolutionary theory" (*The Romantic Revolution*, p. vi). See also Blankenship, pp. 180, 186.

11. McDowell, p. 3.

12. According to Foerster, *The Reinterpretation of American Literature* (1928), the temporal background of American romanticism is Revolutionary idealism and Puritan idealism. According to Williams (p. 136) romanticism is the flowering of Puritan idealism.

13. Pattee, p. 197. This revolt later "drifted into intellectual and humanitarian channels."

14. Harry H. Clark, *Poems of Freneau* (1929), p. xlii; see also his article, "What Made Freneau the Father of American Poetry?" *Studies in Philology*, XXVI (1929), 1–22.

15. Whipple, p. 40, tells us that Dana's novels are romantic and that they deal with "the darker passions of our nature," and on the next page explains that this is due to Dana's "overpowering conception of the terrible reality of sin." The same is true of Washington Allston (p. 42).

16. Macy, chapter on Emerson; and others.

17. Woodberry, p. 222.

18. "In Europe man had to flee from society and seek nature; in

America nature came to a man's door and demanded admittance" (Blankenship, p. 202).

19. Richardson, I, 263.

20. Taylor, p. 86.

21. Miller, p. 98.

22. Taylor, p. 87.

23. Miller, p. 74; and others.

24. Whipple, pp. 57, 61.

25. Kellner, p. 57.

26. Dickinson, pp. 259 ff.; and others.

27. Miller, pp. 83, 133; and others; and see note 9.

28. Wendell, p. 177. He finds Irving an inciting force.

29. Parrington, *The Romantic Revolution,* p. 331, who is followed by Blankenship, p. 205. The stress laid by these authors on Channing's twenty-one months in Richmond is remarkable. Because Channing's influence on transcendentalism was important, Parrington seeks to unite him with Jeffersonianism and "French romantic philosophy." He writes that Channing read "French revolutionary thought" in Virginia and that "one can scarcely over-emphasize the influence of his Virginia experience." He also informs us that "French romantic philosophy was a commonplace in Virginia libraries." Aside from the fact that "French romantic philosophy" is left persistently undefined, not a shadow of proof is offered that it was a "commonplace in Virginia libraries." Although it is true that Channing read Mary Wollstonecraft, Godwin, and Rousseau in Richmond (see *Memoir of William Ellery Channing,* 6th ed., 1854, I, 101, 102), none of these represents "French romantic philosophy" in the sense in which Parrington seems elsewhere to use the term; and the only other French authors mentioned by Channing in his Virginia period are Voltaire, Sully (p. 99), and Fénelon (p. 107)!

In fact, the more one studies the very full *Memoir,* the more one is convinced that Parrington did not read it. In revulsion from the enthusiam at Harvard for the French Revolution at its beginning, Channing was led to Hutcheson and Ferguson, "the two authors who most served to guide his thought at this period." "It was while reading one day, in the former, some of the various passages in which he asserts man's capacity for disinterested affection, and considers virtue as the sacrifice of private interests and the bearing of private evils for the public good . . . that there suddenly burst upon [Channing's] mind that view of the dignity of human nature, which was ever after to 'uphold and cherish' him. . . . He was, at the time, walking as he read beneath a clump of willows . . . in the meadow a little north of Judge

Dana's. . . . It seemed to him, that he then passed through a new spiritual birth, and entered upon the day of eternal peace and joy" (p. 63; and see the confirmation in a letter written in later years, p. 64). The biographer further states: "As Hutcheson was the medium of awakening within him the consciousness of an exhaustless tendency in the human soul to moral perfection, so Ferguson on Civil Society was the means of concentrating his energies upon the thought of social progress. Years afterwards, his remembrance of the enthusiasm in the cause of humanity, first called out in him by this book, was so strong, that he recommended it in terms which would certainly be thought . . . greatly to exaggerate its merits" (pp. 64–65). A third influence was Price, who "saved me from Locke's Philosophy. He gave me the doctrine of ideas, and during my life I have written the words Love, Right, etc., with a capital. That book probably moulded my philosophy into the form it has always retained" (p. 66; see the confirmatory letter from Newport, October 1798, pp. 76–78).

As for Channing's Virginia experiences, he may have dreamed of "a *perfect society,*" but the supposed spread of "French romantic philosophy" among the Virginians had little enough to do with it. "Could I," he wrote, "only take from the Virginians their *sensuality* and their *slaves,* I should think them the greatest people in the world. As it is . . . with a few great virtues, they have innumerable vices" (p. 83; and see also p. 85). He was at the time a strong Federalist (p. 85) and therefore opposed to Jeffersonianism; and though he wrote that "my political opinions have varied a little" (p. 86) in Virginia, they did not veer to the French, for his denunciation of France (pp. 86–95) could hardly be stronger, and he says that he relies "implicitly on the firmness and independence of [President John Adams]" to curb the French, he thought John Marshall "one of the greatest men in the country," and he is "happy to hear that the same odium is everywhere attached to the name of Jacobin." Note his denunciation of French revolutionary thought ("founded in infidelity, impiety and atheism") in 1810 (p. 333).

30. Trent, p. 302.

31. Clark, p. xlii.

32. Listing the qualities of American romanticism, Kaufman says that "primitivism is omitted because of its conspicuous absence in American literature" (in Foerster, p. 120). Contrast Clark, who argues at some length (pp. xl–xliii) that Freneau's primitivistic theories underlie his radicalism and his romanticism.

33. Thus Walter Just, who seems to have been the first to discover

a romantic movement as such in American literature (*Die Romantische Bewegung in der Amerikanischen Literatur: Brown, Poe, Hawthorne,* 1910), confines his exemplars to those who develop aimlessness in life! "Zu einem der wesentlichen Punkte, die sich in den Lebensläufen aller Romantiker finden, rechnet Ricarda Huch die Beruflosigkeit" (p. 8), and following this guide he discusses only Brown, Poe, and Hawthorne. "In der Beziehung waren alle drei . . . echte Romantiker, sie lebten ausser in der realen Welt in einer Welt der Phantasie, die sie in sich aufbauten" (p. 13), cultivated the inner life, and were impractical in the outer. Taylor, however, says that "in America, the romantic movement was both held in check and outfitted with new materials by a number of distinctly American factors," which he lists as the prior achievement of democracy, the frontier, evangelical religion, American rather than European, nature, the American rather than the European, past, the national ideals, an agrarian economic structure, an immature, oversentimental, and self-conscious society, certain sectional divergencies, and certain conditions of publication (p. 91). For Leisy the qualities of American romanticism are the cultivation of the sense of wonder, the grotesque, and the ego, an interest in the Middle Ages, the discipline of nature, enthusiasm for social reform, interest in the national past, humanitarianism, etc. (pp. 67–68). Even if all three writers are correct, one's knowledge of the American romantic movement as such is not clarified.

34. Parrington, *The Romantic Revolution,* p. iii.

35. Blankenship, p. 195.

36. Clark, *Poems of Freneau,* p. xxxv.

37. Gilbert Chinard, *Thomas Jefferson: The Apostle of Americanism* (1929), p. 87. For Chinard, Jefferson was a Christian stoic, whose attitude slowly changed while he was still a young man in Virginia. "What brought a change . . . is certainly not the influence of the 'infidel French philosophers.' The volume of extracts which I published under the title of 'The Literary Bible of Thomas Jefferson' [i.e., Jefferson's commonplace book] does not contain a single quotation from Voltaire, Diderot, or Rousseau, and French literature is represented only by a few insignificant lines from Racine. It is more likely that the first doubts were injected into his mind by the reading of Bolingbroke" (p. 21). Jefferson's political philosophy rested primarily on Hooker and Locke. "Can any one imagine anything farther from the universal humanitarianism of the French philosophers?" (pp. 52–53). "Jefferson proposed a definition of liberty entirely different from the French conception as found in Rousseau and reproduced in the 'Déclaration des

droits de l'homme' of May 29, 1793" (p. 84). Jefferson's "great am-
bition at that time was to promote a renaissance of Anglo-Saxon primitive institutions on the new continent" (p. 86). See also pp. 121; 122–
123; 127; 130; 173 ff.; 204–205; 215 ff.; 328 ff.; 471; 493; 495; 496;
498–499; 522–524 for further explicit denials by this writer that Jefferson was importantly indebted to "French romantic philosophy."

38. But see in this connection the striking article by Chester E. Jor-
genson, "Emerson's Paradise under the Shadow of Swords," *Philological
Quarterly*, XI (1932), 274–292, especially section iii.

39. By Clark especially. See, in addition to his *Poems of Freneau*,
such an article as his "Toward a Reinterpretation of Thomas Paine,"
American Literature, V (1934–35), 133–145.

40. Clark, *Poems of Freneau*, pp. xxxvi–xxxvii. "Nature is herself
rational. Lands, seas, flowers, trees, beasts, and man are

> But thoughts on Reason's scale combin'd,
> Ideas of the Almighty mind.

Since the Creator—who is 'the First Spring of Reason,' an 'Intellectual
Flame'—has revealed His Reason in nature and natural laws, the study
of these laws in science, which 'stands firm on Reason,' enables man
(in Paine's words) to 'see God, as it were, face to face.'" See also his
article, "What Made Freneau the Father of American Poetry?" already
cited.

41. Clark, *loc. cit.*

42. The general acceptance of the theory that the universe is in Calvinist doctrine "bad" seems to be due to the prestige of I. W. Riley,
who in his *American Thought from Puritanism to Pragmatism and
Beyond* (2d ed., 1923) rather unfortunately remarks that "as a theory
of the cosmos, Calvinism teaches that the world is under the curse
of the divine displeasure; that it conceals rather than displays its
creator; that it is created from nothing and is destined to return to
nothing; that the evil in it is a permissive act of God." If the universe
was thus cursed, and if it conceals rather than reveals its creator, Jonathan Edwards fell into dreadful heresy when he wrote that "all beauty
consists in similarness or identity of relation," and that "the Equalities
in a beauty . . . are so numerous, that it would be a most tedious piece
of work to enumerate them. There are millions of these Equalities. Of
these consist the beautiful shape of flowers, the beauty of the body of
man, and of the bodies of other animals. That sort of beauty which is
called Natural, as of vines, plants, trees, etc., consists of a very complicated harmony; and all the natural motions, and tendencies, and

figures of bodies in the Universe are done according to proportion, and therein is their beauty." "For Being, if we examine narrowly, is nothing else but Proportion. When one being is inconsistent with another being, then Being is contradicted." ("Notes on the Mind," pp. 34 ff., in Clarence H. Faust and Thomas H. Johnson, *Jonathan Edwards,* 1935.) And cf. "Dissertation concerning the End for which God Created the World" (*op. cit.,* p. 343), in which the student will learn that God created the world for his glory, that "light is the external expression, exhibition and manifestation of the excellency of the luminary, of the sun, for instance," and "by a participation of this communication from the sun . . . surrounding objects receive all their lustre, beauty and brightness. It is by this that *all nature is quickened and receives life, comfort and joy"* (my italics).

43. *Institutes of the Christian Religion* (trans. by John Allen, 2 vols. in one, 1841, 3d Am. ed.), II, i, 5, p. 225.

44. *Op. cit.,* pp. 58–59 (I, v, 2).

45. Benjamin B. Warfield, *Calvin and Calvinism* (1931), p. 44; and see chap. V.

46. Cf. the "deistic" Franklin: ". . . I imagine it great Vanity in me to suppose, that the *Supremely Perfect* does in the least regard such an inconsiderable Nothing as Man. More especially, since it is impossible for me to have any positive clear idea of that which is infinite and incomprehensible. I cannot conceive otherwise than that He, the *Infinite Father,* expects or requires no Worship or Praise from us, but that he is even infinitely above it."—"Articles of Belief and Acts of Religion" (1728).

47. Cf. Franklin, *loc. cit:* "Also when I stretch my imagination through and beyond our system of planets, beyond the visible fixed stars themselves, into that space which is every way infinite, and conceive it filled with suns liks ours, each with a chorus of worlds for ever moving round him; then this little ball on which we move, seems, even in my narrow imagination, to be almost nothing, and myself less than nothing, and of no sort of consequence."

48. Benjamin Colman, *A Humble Discourse of the Incomprehensibleness of God, In Four Sermons* (Boston, 1715), pp. 17, 27 ff., 32, 34, 47.

49. C. A. Moore, "The Return to Nature in English Poetry of the Eighteenth Century," *Studies in Philology,* XIV (1917), 243–291. Moore says that "there is ample evidence to confirm Biese's remark that 'to Judaism and Christianity, Nature was a fallen angel, separated as far as possible from her God'" (p. 290). This may, indeed, be true

of early Christian literature and of medieval theology in part, but I am unable to see that it is true of Calvinism.

50. Clark, "What Made Freneau the Father of American Poetry?" *op. cit.*, p. 3.

51. Walter C. Bronson, *American Poems* (1912), pp. 1, 4–19, 37. Nathaniel Evans, *Poems on Several Occasions* (Philadelphia, 1722), p. 33; Bronson, pp. 45–46.

52. Francis Higginson reports on his voyage to New England in 1629: "Fourthly, our passage was both pleasurable and profitable. For we received instruction and delight in beholding the wonders of the Lord in deep waters, and sometimes seeing the sea round us appearing with a terrible countenance, and, as it were, full of high hills and deep valleys; and sometimes it appeared as a most plain and even meadow. And ever and anon we saw divers kinds of fishes sporting in the great waters, great grampuses and huge whales, going by companies, and puffing up water streams. Those that love their own chimney-corner, and dare not go far beyond their own town's end, shall never have the honor to see these wonderful works of Almighty God" (Stedman and Hutchinson, *A Library of American Literature,* I, 1887, p. 141). I am unable to see why this is less "concrete" than Freneau's ocean poetry; e.g., "Hatteras," in which the poet writes:

> In fathoms five the anchor gone;
> While here we furl the sail,
> No longer vainly labouring on
> Against the western gale:
> While here thy bare and barren cliffs,
> O HATTERAS, I survey,
> And shallow grounds and broken reefs—
> What shall console my stay!

> The dangerous shoal, that breaks the wave
> In columns to the sky;
> The tempests black, that hourly rave,
> Portend all danger nigh:
> Sad are my dreams on ocean's verge!
> The Atlantic round me flows,
> Upon whose ancient angry surge
> No traveller finds repose!

The poem goes on to refer to a pilot who, "with busy hands, Employs both oar and sail" (a phrase that would have drawn a smile from

Cooper), and who has "in depths of woods his hut" where lives "a wedded nymph"; the pilot's hopes are, in the best manner of eighteenth-century diction, "in yonder flock, Or some few hives of bees"; in the sixth stanza he has become a "commodore" who "spreads his tottering sails," while the "fond nymph" is adjured to "restrain those idle fears" in the seventh stanza. I may add that Hatteras, a low sandy island, has no cliffs, and that tempests black do not hourly rave around it. And if I seem to have chosen a peculiarly apt poem for this comparison, reminding the reader that Freneau spent many years on the sea, I refer him to the diction of "St. Catherine's," "Neversink," "On Arriving in South Carolina, 1798," "The Hurricane," and other poetical expressions of a maritime existence.

53. Cotton Mather, *Coheleth: A Soul Upon Reflection* (Boston, 1720), p. 5; Jonathan Edwards, "Notes on the Mind," in Faust and Johnson, *op. cit.,* pp. 29-30; Ralph Waldo Emerson, chap. VII ("Spirit") of *Nature,* fifth and eighth paragraphs.

54. "Our first literary period . . . fills the larger part of that century in which American civilization had its planting; even as its training into some maturity and power has been the business of the eighteenth and nineteenth centuries. . . . [The colonial writers] founded that literature; they are its Fathers; they stamped their spiritual lineaments upon it; and we shall never deeply enter into the meanings of American literature in its later forms without tracing it back, affectionately, to its beginnings with them" (*A History of American Literature during the Colonial Period,* student ed., 2 vols. in one, 1909, pp. 6-7). "The entire body of American writings, from 1763 to 1783 . . . is here delineated in its most characteristic examples, for the purpose of exhibiting the several stages of thought and emotion through which the American people passed during the two decades of the struggle which resulted in our national Independence" (*The Literary History of the American Revolution,* student ed., 2 vols. in one, n.d., p. vi). It is improbable that these two great works will ever be wholly superseded. When Tyler wrote, however, he necessarily lacked the richer interpretation which subsequent scholarship has brought to the movement of thought in the seventeenth and eighteenth centuries.

55. The anti-Catholic literature of the colonial period (and later) is enormous; and the fear and hatred of Catholicism, from the beginnings through the defeat of Al Smith, though politely ignored by literary and philosophic historians, is one of the dominant facts in American intellectual development.

56. Thus, until late in the nineteenth century, the United States has

been on the whole relatively poor in abstract speculation, in metaphysical thought for its own sake, in aesthetic theory, in pure science, and other branches of thought which do not appeal directly to conscience; and relatively rich in didactic literature, in moral reform movements, in ethical speculation, and in the ethical interpretation of religious experience.

57. William Charvat, *The Origins of American Critical Thought: 1810–1835* (1936). This excellent study should be carefully read by all students of American romantic literature. In these years the American mind winnowed out romantic elements not acceptable to the national temperament. Thus Byron was banished before the period closed; Keats and Shelley were neglected; Wordsworth and Coleridge accepted with reservations; Hazlitt was attacked; and Scott welcomed. Freneau was ignored largely because of the general disgust with his politics. Criticism was "preoccupied with the social implications of literature, and . . . questions of art and technique were too often neglected" (p. 6).

58. Charvat, p. 7. On the general teleology of the American view see "Influence of European Ideas in Nineteenth-Century America," below.

59. G. Adolf Koch, *Republican Religion: The American Revolution and the Cult of Reason* (1933). "Our story is thus of the rise, the short-lived triumph, and the collapse of an intellectual movement reflected on this side of the Atlantic in the last three decades of the eighteenth century" (p. 292).

60. I here find myself in sharp contrast to Norman Foerster, who writes that "what we lacked in this country was not, certainly, a Romantic Movement, but a Victorian era at all comparable with England's. Our Victorianism was both brief and undistinguished" (*op. cit.*, p. 34). On the contrary, I should say that in the field of ideas the most striking parallel to the development of American thought in the nineteenth century is that in Victorian England.

61. Allen Porterfield, in his *Outline of German Romanticism* (1914), has conveniently assembled (pp. 177 ff.) some characteristic "definitions" of German romanticism. Some of these naturally approximate to a statement of the American movement in sense four (above), but I believe the candid student will be impressed by the total inapplicability of most of these statements to the aims and accomplishments of American romantic writers. Even when the words apply, the whole tone and feeling of these statements belong in a world alien to America.

62. I suppose that Thoreau's "Civil Disobedience" comes the closest to philosophic anarchy of all of the important "romantic" documents in the movement. But though Thoreau desires to refuse taxes to a

government which upholds slavery, note that his appeal is to the "higher law": "For eighteen hundred years, though perchance I have no right to say it, the New Testament has been written; yet where is the legislator who has wisdom and practical talent enough to avail himself of the light which it sheds on the science of legislation? The authority of government, even such as I am willing to submit to,—for I will cheerfully obey those who know and can do better than I, and in many things even those who neither know nor can do so well,—is still an impure one: to be strictly just, it must have the sanction and consent of the governed. . . . I please myself with imagining a State at last which can afford to be just to all men, and to treat the individual with respect as a neighbor; which even would not think it inconsistent with its own repose if a few were to live aloof from it, not meddling with it, nor embraced by it, who fulfilled all the duties of neighbors and fellow-men" (last paragraph). The ethical "tone" here is that of Robert Frost, and not, shall I say, of Hart Crane. And in this connection it is well to remember the scepticism with which Emerson, Thoreau, Hawthorne, Melville, and Poe regarded most of the reformers of their time—scepticism springing from a distrust of the capacity of average human nature released from customary ethical sanctions. Because of the weakness of human nature, moral law is necessary for control; they did not share Shelley's flaming enthusiasm for philosophical anarchy, and consequently did not, like him, throw themselves enthusiastically into practical reform movements.

63. Attacks on the study of Latin and Greek are among the standard themes of American educational theory in the eighteenth century. Cotton Mather, though he wanted *"Castalio* for the Latin Tongue, and *Posselius* for the Greek," wanted also to substitute "profitable sentences" for the "Vain Fictions and Filthy Stories" of antiquity—scarcely a classical ideal! (See *Bonifacius,* 1710, pp. 109 ff.; and cf. the eulogy of Cheever, in *Corderius Americanus,* 1708, as a grammar-master.) In *The Present State of Virginia* (1724) Hugh Jones says that Virginia children found *"Grammar* Learning taught after the common roundabout Way . . . not much beneficial nor delightful," and thought that "without going directly to *Rome* and *Athens,*" "all the Arts, Sciences, and learned Accomplishments of the Antients and Moderns" can be "conveyed" in English "without the Fatigue and Expence of another Language for which few of them have little Use or Necessity" (p. 46). In 1751 Richard Peters in a *Sermon on Education,* though he paid lip service to the classical languages, thought them but "a small Part of Education" and chiefly useful "to correct, refine and beautify" English,

on the study of which he lays much stress (pp. 22–24). Franklin's plea for an English academy is, of course, well known. *The Independent Reflector* of Livingston and Smith declared the study of Greek and Latin in the main "perfectly idle and insignificant." Classical learning, though it may "perhaps procure its Possessor the Name of a Scholar . . . is in Reality no more than a specious Kind of Ignorance" (no. XVII, March 22, 1753). Though William Smith in *A General Idea of the College of Mirania* (1753) sets up a "Latin School" as part of his ideal curriculum, he satirizes classical scholarship and condemns "the Practice of neglecting the Mother-Tongue, and embarrassing a young Student, by obliging him to speak or compose in a dead Language" (pp. 36–37). To omit much else, note the attack on classical learning and the plea for a study of English in Trumbull's *The Progress of Dulness* (1772), especially in the opening pages.

64. I follow Lovejoy in referring deism to the classical world-order. See his "Parallel of Deism and Classicism," *Modern Philology, XXIX* (1931–32), 281–299, in which he points out that deism shares with the Enlightenment the doctrines of uniformitarianism, rationalistic individualism, the appeal to the *consensus gentium,* cosmopolitanism (*natura* as opposed to *natio*), an antipathy to "enthusiasm" and "originality," intellectual equalitarianism, etc. See also his "Optimism and Romanticism," pp. 921–945.

65. A great deal of evidence could be assembled to show that for European romantics the new nation represented the ideal to which they were striving as a political concept. See, for example, Walter Graham, "Politics of the Greater Romantic Poets," *PMLA, XXXVI* (1921), 60–78, in which he notes that for Byron America is the home of true political freedom ("Ode to Venice"; "Ode to Napoleon"; *Childe Harold,* IV: xcvi; etc.). Shelley hailed the republic as the "Eagle" among nations (*Revolt of Islam,* XI: xii ff.). The Americans were conscious of their romantic destiny, as appears in patriotic poetry from the days of the Hartford Wits.

THE INFLUENCE OF EUROPEAN IDEAS IN NINETEENTH-CENTURY AMERICA

1. André Siegfried, *America Comes of Age* (New York, 1927), concludes by contrasting European and American civilization (chap. xxvii), but the true climax of the book is its theory of a working alliance between the British Empire and the United States. See, e.g., pp. 313, 334–343. F. Schönemann, *Die Vereinigten Staaten von Amerika,* 2 vols. (Stuttgart and Berlin, 1932), devotes most of volume one to examining the place of the United States in international affairs and the contribu-

tions made by foreign immigration to the country. Part iii of volume two discusses American culture, and attempts to define its relationship to European culture. This relationship, Schönemann says, is a "more or less conscious eclecticism" (II, 379). The important thing, however, is to discover how the eclecticism operates.

2. Even in the celebrated instance of the frontier, the concept, as it has been worked out by American historians, is open to the constant correction implied in the truth that America is the European frontier through long periods—something Emerson was shrewd enough to observe when he said that Europe extends to the Alleghanies. The host of European travelers in America during the nineteenth century were examining the results of the transplantation of European culture to the frontier. The development of Canada, Australia, and New Zealand, or of the French empire in Africa offers analogous cases. Nor is the question merely one of a form of words. One may, for example, rightly attribute part of the vogue of individualism in this country to the influence of the physical frontier, but to ignore the constant re-enforcement of an individualistic philosophy of life from the effects of European revolutionary movements in 1830 and 1848, from social philosophies like Fourierism, theological systems like Lutheranism, or politico-economic ideologies like Benthamism, is to mis-read history. Thus, the *Life, Letters and Journals of George Ticknor,* 2 vols. (Boston, 1909), shows how an American cosmopolitan is re-enforced in his political liberalism by his experiences abroad. See, e.g., Ticknor's talk with Metternich (II, 12–20), a conversation which helped to confirm Ticknor's "Americanism."

3. Donald McConnell, *Economic Virtues in the United States* (New York, 1930), especially chap. iii. The justification of Siegfried's statement that "America is not only Protestant in her religious and social development, but essentially Calvinistic" lies partially in the transformation noted by McConnell. Of course, this is not the whole story of the Know Nothing party.

4. For example, the long line of anti-French and anti-Catholic pronouncements from colonial pulpits is the ancestor of such recent exhibits of American prejudice as the present suspicion of French motives or the defeat of Al Smith. No one who has not explored this literature can realize either its extent or its venom. Seventeenth-century hatred of the Pope and Jesuit, once common in Great Britain, still lives in the United States.

5. An illuminating example of the ways in which a European idea may be adopted is furnished by the imitation of German university

publican Religion (New York, 1933), chap. viii, cites a great many intellectual attacks on deism and infidelity. The Methodists and Baptists forwarded an emotional revival of religion (in which they were followed by the Presbyterians) which swept the country at the opening of the century. The excesses of the movement are studied in O. W. Elsbree, *The Rise of the Missionary Spirit in America, 1790–1815* (New York, 1928), especially chap. vi. See also P. G. Mode, *The Frontier Spirit in American Christianity* (New York, 1923).

12. Among the distressing lapses of American literary criticism is the failure properly to estimate the intellectual evolution of the Connecticut Wits, who are usually dismissed as conservatives in art and Federalists in politics. Thus the only available modern reprint of any of their works, *The Connecticut Wits* (New York, 1926), edited by the late V. L. Parrington, opens with an introduction which describes them as "the literary old guard of eighteenth century Toryism," who "would hold no commerce with 'French infidel philosophy'" because they were "such stalwart exemplars" of Federalism; yet the very selections thus introduced exhibit radical theories of education, an eager interest in the latest poetical practice of Great Britain, a considerable interest in the rights-of-man attitude, and various other "liberal" or "radical" ideas. Indeed, one has to read long in the book before one comes to much expression of Federalism. The significant point is not the final point of view of the Connecticut Wits, but the roads which led them to that point of view. [Since this was written Leon Howard has brought out his magisterial volume, *The Connecticut Wits*.]

13. The political and social expression of this nationalism has often been remarked by the historians. In literature, a succession of addresses and essays precedes Emerson's *The American Scholar* (1837), the best known being, of course, W. E. Channing's "Remarks on National Literature" (1830), which was in turn a review of C. J. Ingersoll's *Discourse concerning the Influence of America on the Mind*, an oration before the American Philosophical Society delivered in 1823, pleading for a national literature. The creation of a truly national literature was the main purpose of the Connecticut Wits.

14. Of course the distrust of Europe is an old American trait of mind, appearing in colonial sermons from a very early period in proportion as it is the hope of a community to build up a better society uncontaminated by the vices of the Continent. Even so cosmopolitan a mind as Jefferson's thought that the less the United States knew of Europe, the better off the country would be, as numerous passages in his writings show.

ideals in Virginia, Michigan, Maryland, and Missouri. Jefferson's plan of the University of Virginia, influenced by Dupont de Nemours and Destutt de Tracy, also includes the German idea of rotation in office; yet Jefferson had no direct connection with German universities, and the question of influence through immigration does not arise. Tappan's plans for the University of Michigan, however, were the result of a trip to Germany, during which he reached the conclusion that the Prussian educational system was "a glorious achievement" (Charles M. Perry, *Henry Philip Tappan*, Ann Arbor, 1933, p. 152). At the same time Cousin's report on the Prussian educational system was already known in Michigan through the efforts of J. D. Pierce and I. E. Crary (B. A. Hinsdale and I. N. Demmon, *History of the University of Michigan*, Ann Arbor, 1906, pp. 15–17). Tappan expressly modeled the University after German institutions, and brought the German astronomer, Brünnow, to Ann Arbor. Brünnow (who became Tappan's son-in-law) undoubtedly influenced Tappan's ideas, for his resignation was forced at the same time as Tappan's. Here, then, one has an instance of both direct influence and indirect influence. In the case of the Johns Hopkins University, however, one sees the adoption of the German notion of graduate work directly from a European model by Gilman, whereas the creation of Washington University in St. Louis in its modern form undoubtedly owes much to the sympathetic interest of the German element in Missouri. In other words, the general idea of German university training is influential upon the United States (a) indirectly through French mediation; (b) directly through the visits of American observers to Germany; (c) directly through the importation of German professors; and (d) more or less directly through the influence of a German-American population. Similar tangles confront the inquirer in almost any field.

6. Of course the *Concordat*, by restoring the church, tended to delimit French rationalism. Napoleon's own dislike of "idéologues" probably helped to turn French opinion against the *philosophes*. His continuing enmity towards Mme. de Staël, whose point of view was that of cosmopolitanism, illustrates the antagonism of the new order towards the old.

7. An illustration from each of two literatures will exemplify this change in opinion. The thesis of Lessing's *Nathan der Weise* is that tolerance and cosmopolitanism are desirable. His last work was on "The Education of the Human Race," and his great critical masterpiece, the *Laokoon*, was concerned with a general aesthetic problem. Just twenty-five years after the death of Lessing appeared Körner's *Leyer*

und Schwert, which is a practical denial of the premises of Lessing, celebrating a German God and the glories of the Fatherland. See, for example, "Mein Vaterland," with its nationalistic conception of the poet's function:

> Wie heiszt des Sängers Vaterland?—
> Jetzt über seiner Söhne Leichen,
> Jetzt weint es unter fremden Streichen;
> Sonst hiesz es nur das Land der Eichen,
> Das freie Land, das deutsche Land.
> So hiesz mein Vaterland!

And consider such a poem as "Was uns bleibt," with this characteristic stanza:

> Was uns bleibt?—*Rühmt nicht des Wissens Bronnen,*
> *Nicht der Künste friedensreichen Strand!*
> Für die Knechte giebt es keine Sonnen,
> *Und die Kunst verlangt ein Vaterland.*
> Aller Götter Stimmen sind verklungen
> Vor dem Jammerton der Sklaverei,
> Und Homer, er hätte nie gesungen:
> Doch sein Griechenland war frei!

In English literature, contrast such a familiar passage as this, from Goldsmith's *The Traveller:*

> In every government, though terrors reign,
> Though tyrant kings or tyrant laws restrain,
> How small, of all that human hearts endure,
> That part which laws or kings can cause or cure!

with Coleridge's "France: An Ode" or with Wordsworth's war poems; e.g., the sonnet beginning "Great men have been among us," with its calm assumption that all the sound thinkers are British:

> These moralists could act and comprehend:
> They knew how genuine glory was put on;
> Taught us how rightfully a nation shone
> In splendour. . . .

whereas

> France, 'tis strange,
> Hath brought forth no such souls as we had then.
> Perpetual emptiness! unceasing change!
> No single volume paramount, no code,
> No master spirit, no determined road;
> But equally a want of books and men!

The Traveller appeared one year after the conclusion of the Se[v]... War; the sonnet was composed in 1802 or thereabouts.

8. The literature of the Catholic Reaction is well known, and [...] Chateaubriand, Bonald, De Maistre, *et al.* In Germany the [...] Görres is representative, as are the later careers of the Schle[...] England Southey's *Book of the Church,* Coleridge's *Lay Sermo*[...] Wordsworth's *Ecclesiastical Sonnets* are representative of an equ[...] movement.

9. I owe a representative example to Professor J. H. Randall[...] *Making of the Modern Mind* (Boston, 1926), in which he cites [...] sage from Goethe's *Dichtung und Wahrheit* concerning Goethe's [...] ing of Holbach's *Système de la Nature* when the poet was a y[...] man in Strassburg. He found the book unsatisfactory: "Matter wa[...] posed to have existed and to have been in motion from all eternity[...] to this motion, to right and to left and in every direction, were a[...] uted the infinite phenomena of existence. We might have allowed [...] so much to pass, if the author, out of his matter in motion, had r[...] built up the world before our eyes. But he seemed to know as l[...] about nature as we did; for, after simply propounding some gen[...] ideas, he forthwith disregards them in order to change what se[...] above nature, or a higher nature within nature, into matter with weig[...] and motion, but without aim or shape—and by this he fancies he h[...] gained much" (*Poetry and Truth,* translated by M. S. Smith, 2 vol[...] London, 1913, II, 39–40). Yet this unflattering dismissal of one of th[...] great figures of eighteenth-century rationalism is preceded by a para[...] graph in which Goethe and his friends are pictured as desirous "o[...] becoming more and more rational, of making ourselves more and mor[...] independent of external things, and even of ourselves" (II, 39). Spinoz[...] proved more satisfactory; Goethe agrees with him that "Nature works [...] after such eternal necessary, divine laws, that the Deity Himself could [...] alter nothing in them" (II, 206). A mind which has rejected Holbach [...] and welcomed Spinoza illustrates the re-direction of rationalism of [...] which I speak.

10. See C. D. Hazen, "American Opinion of the French Revolution," *The Johns Hopkins University Studies in Historical and Political Science,* Extra Vol. XVI; E. R. White, *American Opinion of France* (New York, 1927), chap. i; and my *America and French Culture* (Chapel Hill, 1927), especially chaps. xi, xiii, xv.

11. Thus at Yale Timothy Dwight delivered regularly a series of 173 sermons designed to meet every argument of infidelity. See his *Theology Explained and Defended,* 5 vols., London, 1824. G. A. Koch, *Re-*

15. One curious proof is the rapidity with which the influence of the men of the eighteenth century diminishes in American public life. Europe of the Restoration was guided by such essentially eighteenth-century intellects as Metternich, Talleyrand, Palmerston, Polignac, the rulers of the petty Italian states, and so on. In the United States, though Madison and Monroe succeed Jefferson, and though the egregious John Randolph lingers long in Congress, the whole tone of public discussion by 1815, one feels, is quite different from what it had been under Washington and John Adams. Cf. the final chapter of Henry Adams's *History of the United States during the Administrations of Jefferson and Madison.*

16. The slowness with which the teaching of modern foreign languages spread through the school systems may be seen in C. R. Handschin, *The Teaching of Modern Languages in the United States,* U. S. Bureau of Education, Bulletin, 1913, no. 3. Even when languages are taught, they are not always used, as witness the present inability of most American college graduates to read or speak the foreign languages they have studied. Moreover, difficulties of communication until late in the century made it practically impossible for European magazines, newspapers, and books to be widely distributed over the country.

17. See F. L. Mott, *A History of American Magazines, 1741–1850* (New York, 1930). The most obvious case is the modeling of the American quarterlies, like *The North American Review* or *The Southern Quarterly Review,* on the British quarterlies, but the whole tone and temper of American periodical publication in this period is clearly influenced by British example. The republication of articles from British periodicals, often without credit, profoundly influenced the tone of the magazines.

18. The standard studies are W. B. Cairns, *British Criticisms of American Writings, 1783–1815, University of Wisconsin Studies,* 1918, and *British Criticisms of American Writings, 1815–1833, University of Wisconsin Studies,* 1922.

19. There is no sound history of American criticism, and the influence of British periodical criticism has scarcely been studied. For example, is the following from *Graham's Magazine* for March, 1842, a reprint of Macaulay? "That Lord Brougham *was* an extraordinary man no one in his senses will deny. An intellect of unusual capacity, goaded into diseased actions by passions nearly ferocious, enabled him to astonish the world, and especially the 'hero-worshippers,' as the author of Sartor Resartus has it, by the combined extent and variety of his mental triumphs. Attempting many things, it may at least be said, that he

egregiously failed in none. But that he pre-eminently excelled in any cannot be affirmed with truth, and might well be denied *à priori*. We have no faith in admirable Crichtons, and this merely because we *have* implicit faith in Nature and her laws. . . . The Broughams of the human intellect are never its Newtons or its Bayles," etc. It happens to be by Edgar Allan Poe, usually labeled a "romantic" critic! The truth is, of course, that Poe's artistic ideals were romantic, his mode of criticism that of the judicial sort. Like Macaulay he summons writers before the bar of judgment, weighs the degree of their offences and their virtues, and delivers a court-room verdict. If the influence of British judicial criticism was strong even in his case, how much stronger was it in the case of less original men!

20. For example, the American criticism of French literature, especially of the romantic school, is strongly influenced by contemporary British prejudice. See, for some choice specimens, my article, "American Comments on George Sand, 1837–1848," *American Literature,* III, 389–407 (Jan., 1932); and the revealing article by Grace B. Sherrer, "French Culture as Presented to Middle-Class America by *Godey's Lady's Book,* 1830–1840," *ibid.,* III, 277–286 (Nov., 1931). Paradoxically, Americans displayed more independence in judging a British writer than they did in judging a continental one.

21. There is no history of American theological thought as such, most "church histories" being either of the denominational or the institutional sort, and most books on the subject emphasizing the "American" aspects of religion. I believe an investigation of such characteristic magazines as the Calvinistic *Panoplist* (1805–1820), the Unitarian *Christian Examiner* (1813–1869), the Presbyterian-Congregational *Christian Spectator* (1819–1838), *The Methodist Review* (1818———), the Presbyterian *Biblical Repertory* (1829–1888), and so on, would reveal an important phase of American intellectual development. I have given the most familiar names of these periodicals, the titles sometimes changing.— Chalmers and Paley were widely influential, and such questions as the orthodoxy of *Essays and Reviews* were widely debated in the United States.

22. Thus Channing's *The Moral Argument against Calvinism* (1820) is a thoroughly well-reasoned piece of argumentation. Parrington (*Main Currents in American Thought,* II, 328–338) notes that the famous ordination sermon which Channing preached in 1819 is "a reasoned attack upon Trinitarian Calvinism," but he seems to me to over-emphasize here as elsewhere the influence of "French romanticism" (whatever that means) upon Calvinism.

23. The list of professors is merely representative; more will be found in L. van Becelaere, *La Philosophie en Amérique* (New York, 1904), chap. iii. See also chap. v of I. W. Riley, *American Thought from Puritanism to Pragmatism and Beyond* (New York, 1923).

24. See E. R. A. Seligman, "Economics in the United States: An Historical Sketch," *Essays in Economics* (New York, 1925); C. F. Dunbar, "Economic Science in America, 1776–1876," *Economic Essays* (New York, 1904); A. D. H. Kaplin, *Henry Charles Carey: A Study in American Economic Thought* (Baltimore, 1931).

25. The following quotations from Francis Wayland's *The Elements of Political Economy* (4th ed., Boston, 1849), are characteristic: "Political Economy is the Science of Wealth. . . . By Science, as the word is here used, we mean a systematic arrangement of the laws which God has established, so far as they have been discovered, of any department of human knowledge. It is obvious, upon the slightest reflection, that the Creator has subjected the accumulation of the blessings of this life to some determinate laws" (p. 15). "The whole wealth of the world has been created by the union of human industry with the materials which God had originally spread around us. Hence, all that is necessary to the creation of wealth, is capital and industry" (p. 29). "If God have made labor necessary to our well being, in our present state; if he have set before us sufficient rewards to stimulate us to labor; and if he have attached to idleness correspondent punishments, it is manifest that the intention of this constitution will not be accomplished, unless both of these classes of motives are allowed to operate upon man. We shall, therefore, coöperate with Him, in just so far as we allow his designs to take effect in the manner he intended" (p. 118). Discussing the high mortality rate in certain portions of the globe, he writes: "Now, we can scarcely suppose that to be the condition of man which his Creator intended, in which so large a number perish in infancy, from suffering, from hardship, and from want. Hence, I suppose the natural cost of labor, or that cost which corresponds with the proper condition of man, would be that which allows of the rearing of such a number of children as naturally falls to the lot of the human race. This, however, presupposes the laborers to be industrious, virtuous, and frugal" (p. 294). Even as late as H. C. Carey's *The Unity of Law* (Philadelphia, 1872), one finds similar teleology; e.g., "Side by side with the forces thus converted travels always the first of the great laws above referred to, providing, as it does, that growth of force shall be accompanied by changes in the distribution of labor's products; present mental and moral force claiming a constantly increased proportion as compared with that ap-

propriated to the merely material force resulting from accumulations of the past; labor thus tending to an equality with capital, and man becoming from hour to hour more free. In the whole range of law there is nothing more beautiful than this; nothing furnishing more thorough proof that that High Intelligence to which man stands indebted for the wonderful mechanism of each and every part of his physical form, had not failed to provide for the societary body laws fully fitted to prepare him for becoming master of nature, master of himself, and prompt to unite with his fellow-men in all measures tending to thorough development of the highest faculties with which he and they had been endowed" (p. xvii).

26. It would be interesting to discover to what extent the great vogue of Macaulay in the United States helped to increase the American belief in progress in the mechanic arts coupled with decay in the fine arts. Macaulay's essays on Bacon and Mackintosh are, of course, the classical statements of his belief in this respect. See also his "Dryden."

27. The Sunday school begins in England with Robert Raikes in 1780, and seems to have been well established along the Atlantic seaboard at the opening of the nineteenth century. The infant school is especially associated with Robert Owen, who established one at New Lanark in 1816. Bell's *An Experiment in Education* was published in 1797; Lancaster began work a little later. Lancaster visited the United States about 1818 and organized schools. The Lancasterian schools seem to have died out by the Civil War. See E. P. Cubberley, *Public Education in the United States* (Boston, 1919), chap. iv; E. W. Knight, *Education in the United States* (Boston, 1929), chap. vi. E. E. Slosson, *The American Spirit in Education* (New Haven, 1921), is clear, but lacks details. See the bibliographies in Knight or Slosson.

28. Such as A. D. Murphey's report to the North Carolina legislature (1817), which displays familiarity with the French system; the reprinting of the English translation of Cousin's report to the French government (1831; the American edition appeared in 1834), which made the Prussian ideal known in other countries; Calvin Stowe's report (1837) to the Ohio legislature; A. D. Bache's *Education in Europe* (1839); Horace Mann's classical statement of 1843; Henry Barnard's *National Education in Europe* (1854), etc. Most of these find their ideal in the Prussian system; and most of them speak with admiration of Pestalozzi.

29. The pedagogical methods of Pestalozzi were of course non-rationalistic in their assumptions, in contrast to those of Bell and Lancaster.

30. Save in isolated instances the American adaptation of continental university ideals was delayed until after the Civil War.

31. See F. Cajori, *The Teaching and History of Mathematics in the United States,* Bureau of Education, Circular No. 3 (Washington, 1890); L. C. Karpinski, *The History of Arithmetic* (Chicago, 1925), especially chap. iii; D. E. Smith and J. Ginsburg, *A History of Mathematics in America before 1900* (Chicago, 1934).

32. The bitterness of the quarrel between Newton and Leibnitz "stopped almost completely all interchange of ideas on scientific subjects. The English adhered closely to Newton's methods and, until about 1820, remained, in most cases, ignorant of the brilliant mathematical discoveries that were being made on the Continent. The loss in point of scientific advantage was almost entirely on the side of Britain" (F. Cajori, *History of Mathematics,* 2nd ed., New York, 1919, p. 217). Cajori, who has examined a number of the earlier American mathematical texts, finds them appealing to the memory rather than to (purely) logical demonstration. They are founded on British commercial arithmetics and surveyors' books (Cajori, *The Teaching and History of Mathematics,* the section entitled "Influx of English Mathematics, 1776–1820"). Karpinski, *op. cit.,* lists a number of these (pp. 78–99). The need of keeping accounts and of surveying helped to keep mathematics "practical."

33. Cajori, *op. cit.,* the section entitled "Influx of French Mathematics."

34. Smith and Ginsburg, *op. cit.,* p. 91. In addition to Bowditch and Adrian these authors cite only Patterson, Rogers, Farrar, Strong, Gill, Bache, and Hassler as worth discussing, and find their contributions minor.

35. Both Franklin and Jefferson helped along a tendency towards useful invention and the creation of "gadgets." Note the ideology implicit in this passage from Ramsay, *History of South Carolina* (1809), II, 216: "Two ingenious artists, Miller and Whitney of Connecticut, invented a saw-gin for the separation of the wool from the seed [of cotton] which has facilitated that operation in the highest degree. The legislature of South-Carolina purchased their patent right for 50,000 dollars, and then munificently threw open its use and benefits to all its citizens." Or this from Tudor, *Letters on the Eastern States* (1819), p. 266: "There are no people more ingenious in the use and invention of machinery, no country more prolific in patents, than the one under consideration. Good mechanics are to be found in every one of the mechanic arts, and the improvements they have made in some old, and the

invention of many new instruments, are strong proofs of their skill and enterprise." In such a society the creation of a patent office (1790) inevitably precedes the creation of such an institution as the Smithsonian Institution (1846) for the "increase and diffusion of knowledge among men." American emphasis on applied science is seen in the fact that from 1790 to 1800 there were 276 patents granted, from 1840 to 1850, 6,480, and from 1890 to 1900, 221,500 (H. U. Faulkner, *American Economic History,* New York, 1924, p. 554). Important results from 1800 to 1870 include such matters as the electric telegraph, the cotton gin, the McCormick reaper, the rotary printing press, the sewing machine, the domestic furnace, the friction match, lighting by gas, the vulcanization of rubber, and so on indefinitely.

36. The means by which American geology progressed is a striking testimonial to the appeal of "practical" as opposed to "pure" science. Until about 1840 American geology had been mainly dependent upon European theory (*A Century of Science in America,* New Haven, 1918, chap. ii). The first state geological survey of real importance was Hitchcock's "Report on the Geology of Massachusetts" in 1830–1831, but the obvious commercial value of such a survey was such that, mainly in the thirties and forties, there was a general rush of the states to create similar surveys (Connecticut, 1835–1837; Delaware, 1837; Georgia, 1836–1840; Indiana, 1837–1838; Kentucky, 1838; Maine, 1836–1839; Maryland, 1833–1842; Michigan, 1837–1845; New Hampshire, 1839–1844; New Jersey, 1835–1837; New York, 1835–1936; North Carolina, 1824–1828, an early survey, apparently without much influence; Ohio, 1837–1839; Pennsylvania, 1836–1842; Rhode Island, 1839; South Carolina, 1843–1846; Tennessee, 1831–1850; Vermont, 1844–1856; Virginia, 1836). These surveys were naturally of varying merit, but the better ones undoubtedly increased geological knowledge (G. P. Merrill, *Contributions to a History of American State Geological and Natural History Surveys,* U. S. National Museum, Bulletin 109, Washington, 1920). In the meantime the national government authorized the first coastal survey in 1816, which was put in charge of the Swiss, Rudolf Hassler, who had practically to create everything, and whose work was constantly interrupted by political pressure because immediate and "useful" results were not forthcoming (F. Cajori, "Swiss Geodesy and the U. S. Coastal Survey," *Scientific Monthly,* XIII, 117–129, Aug., 1921). Government reconnaissances of the West, which by 1880 had accumulated sufficient data greatly to alter geological theory, were only incidentally scientific in their purpose, the geologist or the naturalist being merely "attached" to the party, as is the case with Major Long's expedition of 1819–1820,

Schoolcraft's journey of 1818 being, as it were, amateur. The first Federal appropriation for geological purposes of this sort did not come until 1834, when Congress set aside $5,000 for the Featherstonhaugh report of that year, but both this expedition and that associated with D. D. Owen in 1839 were motivated by a desire to utilize the public lands. The military expeditions to the West in 1850–1860 had their obvious economic and political purposes, the geologists (men of the rank of Hall and Hitchcock) being merely "attached." See G. O. Smith, "Governmental Geological Surveys" in *A Century of Science,* chap. v.

37. One or two examples must suffice. Thus J. W. Wilson wrote in the *Journal of Science* in 1821: "It is not the best theory of the earth, that the Creator, in the beginning, at least of the deluge, formed it with all its present grand characteristic features?" Exactly twenty years later Edward Hitchcock, who thought that the major valleys and mountain passes were structural in origin, wrote: "Is not this a beautiful example of prospective benevolence on the part of the Deity, thus, by means of a violent fracture of primary mountains, to provide for an easy intercommunication through alpine regions, countless ages afterwards?" (Quoted in the chapter on "Physiography" in *A Century of Science*). Agassiz thought: "All organized beings exhibit in themselves all those categories of structure and existence upon which a natural system may be founded, in such a manner that in tracing it, the human mind is only translating into human language the Divine thoughts expressed in nature in living realities" (E. R. Corson, "Agassiz's Essay on Classification Fifty Years After," *Scientific Monthly,* XI, 43–52, July, 1920).

38. Davy, for example, concluded his career with *Consolations in Travel* (1830), a series of dialogues on religious and moral problems, and all of his life opposed materialism and skepticism. The religious character of Faraday is well known. Sir David Brewster, William Whewell, Sir Charles Bell, and Sir John Herschel are other examples of "reverent" scientists.

39. The titles of the earlier scientific professorships are significant. Silliman was made professor of chemistry and natural philosophy at Yale; Denison Olmstead was professor of natural philosophy and astronomy (Yale); Gurdon Saltonstoll was professor of mathematics and natural philosophy at Alabama (1831–1833), a chair which became "mathematics, natural philosophy and astronomy" in 1837 when F. A. P. Barnard held it; at Amherst Hitchcock was professor of natural theology and geology; Renwick was professor of natural philosophy and chemistry at Columbia, etc., etc.

40. The intellectual development of Benjamin Silliman is a *locus*

classicus of this theistic interpretation. As a Yale student he sat under the sermons of President Dwight, and read Paley (I, 38–39); when he went abroad he associated with the serious-minded Edinburgh group, recording with pleasure the "perspicuous and highly philosophical views" of chemistry he received from Dr. John Murray, whose "mind was of a highly philosophical caste" (I, 167), as well as those of Hope, Gregory, and Black in chemistry; Dugald Stewart; and the Scotch geologists, then debating the Wernerian and the Huttonian theories. He resolved to form his professional character upon the Edinburgh model (I, 195), since "a kind Providence . . . as with an unseen hand" had guided him thither (I, 196). He participated prayerfully in the various religious revivals at Yale, writing his mother in 1802 that "Yale College is a little temple: prayer and praise seem to be the delight of the greater part of the students" (I, 83); and recording with deep delight in after years the religious experiences of his children. While he was debating the offer of a professorship in science at Yale, he thought that "everything in Nature is straightforward and consistent. There are no polluting influences; all the associations with these pursuits are elevated and virtuous, and point towards the infinite Creator" (I, 95). His attitude of mind, while giving the Lowell lectures on geology in 1839 characterizes his whole mental set; he approved highly of the design of the foundation: "The investigation and exhibition of physical laws, while they are to be applied, by his [Lowell's] direction, to the illustration of the attributes of the infinite God, are to be summoned also to prove the harmony of his revealed word with the visible creation, and of both with his holy character. . . . With feelings then in perfect harmony with the testamentary injunctions of our founder we turn to our more immediate duties" (I, 385). Newspaper comment on Silliman's lectures of 1843 is equally illuminating: "Admiring as we do the perfection of science exhibited continually by the lecturer in all that he has undertaken to explain, we have yet a higher love and reverence for that beautiful exhibition of divine truth to which Mr. Silliman constantly alludes, as seen in the wonderful works which he has successfully presented as designed by the Almighty power, and made known to man by human intelligence. This is the source of our respect for this accomplished Professor, in comparison with which our admiration for his scientific attainments sinks into insignificance" (George P. Fisher, *Life of Benjamin Silliman* . . ., 2 vols., New York, 1866, I, 398).

41. Silliman records with pleasure the honorable history of astronomy at Yale, noting that the discoveries of Newton and theological, ethical, and metaphysical subjects lay cheek by jowl in the eighteenth century,

that "The Rev. President Clap" was "an eminent mathematician and astronomer," and that President Stiles hoped that after death, "he would be permitted to visit the planets, and to examine the rings of Saturn and the belts and satellites of Jupiter" (Fisher, *op. cit.,* I, 88). The obvious influence of Chalmers's *Astronomical Discourses,* preached at Edinburgh, on the American attitude towards astronomy has never been pointed out. Contrast the horror felt at the black abyss of space in such a book as J. W. Krutch, *The Modern Temper.*

42. Even so eminent a man as James D. Dana had the greatest difficulty in adjusting himself to the Darwinian point of view, writing in *The American Journal of Science* in 1857 that "all organic species are divine appointments which cannot be obliterated, unless by annihilating the individuals representing the species." Though successive editions of his *Manual of Geology* mark his gradual acceptance of neo-Lamarckianism, as late as 1895 he was writing that nature "exists through the will and ever-acting power of the Divine Being" (Charles Schuchert, *A Century of Science in America,* chap. ii). The struggles of Silliman to discover whether his geological and other scientific friends were sound on the Bible are intensely interesting. He is grieved when James Woodhouse of the Medical School of Philadelphia failed to "make use of any of the facts revealed by chemistry, to illustrate the character of the Creator as seen in his works." Woodhouse "treated with levity and ridicule the idea" that the yellow fever might be God's punishment for sin, "forgetting that physical causes may be the moral agents of the Almighty" (I, 101). Dr. Wistar, who explained the "reasons that must have influenced the Creator in the adaptation of every part (of the human body) to every other," pleased him better (I, 106). Dr. Thomas Cooper of South Carolina, who "reviled the Scriptures" in a letter to Silliman, received no reply, that gentleman thinking it "a violation of gentlemanly courtesy" (I, 287). William Maclure, however, approved of one of Silliman's chemical lectures which explained "the moral relations of science and the exposition it gives of the mind and thoughts of the Creator," and is praised for his benevolence no less than for his science (I, 284 ff.). Silliman calmed the fears of the Rev. Mr. Taylor, the seamen's friend, as to the hostility of geology to Mosaic history (I, 357), and convinced Judge White of Boston "that after astronomy there was no branch of natural science which possessed such grandeur as geology" (I, 362). Fisher, *op. cit.*

43. The preface to the 50th volume (1847) retains the same point of view: ". . . science is only embodied and sympathized truth and in the beautiful conception of our noble Agassiz—'it tells the thought of

God.'" The editor anticipates death, but "we will continue to labor on, and strive to be found at our post of duty, until there is nothing more for us to do; trusting our hopes for a future life in the hands of Him who placed us in the midst of the splendid garniture of this lower world, and who has made not less ample provision for another and a better" (quoted in *A Century of Science,* chap. i).

44. *Ibid.*

45. Thus Jacob Bigelow, professor of medicine at Harvard, in an effort to put an end to the "heroic" treatment of disease (cupping, drugging, and so on) sought to avoid specialization and advance treatment by seeking the law of nature in disease. By this law certain diseases were limited either in time or final outcome. There are, according to Bigelow, three kinds of ailments: curable, self-limited, and incurable. The self-limited diseases are in turn subdivided into (a) the simple, which observe a continuous time and have a definite seat, *e.g.,* whooping-cough; (b) the paroxysmal, which return at intervals, *e.g.,* angina pectoris; (c) the metastatic, in which the disease undergoes transformation from one organ to another (acute rheumatism). The task of the physician is then to ascertain which category he is treating. So far, the movement is away from specialization. Bigelow, however, a disciple of the great French medical teacher, Louis, emphasizes the importance of correct diagnosis, admiring the French "numerical method" or statistical study of cases for diagnostic purposes. See *On Self-Limited Diseases* (1835).

46. Consider, for example, the implications of this passage from the lectures of Jameson, professor of natural history at Edinburgh—a lecture of 1808: "It is indeed surprising, that men possessed of any knowledge of the beautiful harmony that prevails in the structure of organic beings could for a moment believe it possible, that the great fabric of the globe itself,—that magnificent display of Omnipotence,—should be destitute of all regularity in its structure, and be nothing more than a heap of ruins."

47. I shall cite three European exemplars. (1) Schelling's early philosophical essay, the *Ideen zu einer Philosophie der Natur* (1797; 1803) reviews combustion, light, air, the behavior of gases, electricity, and magnetism, finding that in science the human spirit "strebt nach Einheit im System seiner Erkenntnisse, er erträgt es nicht, dasz man ihm für jede einzelne Erscheinung ein besondres Prinzip aufdringe, und er glaubt nur da Natur zu sehen, wo er in der grösten Mannigfaligkeit der Erscheinungen die gröszte Einfachheit der Gesetze und in der höchsten Versechwendung der Wirkungen zugleich die höchste Spar-

samkeit der Mittel entdeckt." (Note the dynamic turn given to the principle of parsimony.) He then argues (*Erste Entwurf eines Systems der Naturphilosophie,* 1799; *Einleitung zu dem Entwurf eines Systems der Naturphilosophie,* 1799) that "Absolute Tätigkeit ist das Wesen der Natur . . . Es gibt . . . in dem ideellen Subjekt der Nutur einen ursprünglichen Gegensatz van Kräften, eine nach auszen gehende, ins Unendliche vorwärts strebende und eine nach innen zurückgehende, hemmende Kraft. Über diesem Gegensatz der Tätigkeit aber schwebt das unendliche Bestreben des unbedingten Subjekts, der Natur, zur Einheit zurückzukehren." (The analogical arguments by which the principles of sciences are brought into a single unified dynamic view are curiously like those of Spencer's synthetic philosophy.) This view of science and of natural processes in turn forms the base of the *System des transzendentalen Idealismus* (written 1800), in which "die organische Natur ist die immanent teleologisch betrachtete Natur," and in which the creative activity of the artist is the highest product of, and the most accurate reflection of, the universal process. See R. Haym, *Die Romantische Schule,* 4th ed., Berlin, 1920, chap. iv, from which the quotations are taken.

(2) The same point of view is, of course, found in Goethe. Thus from the Goethe-Schiller *Xenia* (1797) I quote so representative an expression as this:

Menschliches Wissen

Weil du liesest in ihr, was du selber in sie geschrieben,
Weil du in Gruppen für's Aug' ihre Erscheinungen riehst,

Deine Schnüre gezogen auf ihrem unendlichen Felde,
Wähnst du, es fasse dein Geist ahnend die grosse Natur.

So beschreibt mit Figuren der Astronome den Himmel,
Dass in dem ewigen Raun leichter sich finde der Blick,

Knüpft entlegene Sonnen, durch Sirius fernen geschieden,
Aneinander im Schwan und in den Hörnern des Stiers.

Aber versteht er darum der Sphären mystische Tänze,
Weil ihm das Sternengewölb sein Planiglobium zeigt?
(*Goethe and Schiller's Xenions,* Chicago, 1915, p. 125.)

The *locus classicus,* however, is *Faust.* Dissatisfied with a partitive view of science (Part I, 11, 354–385), Faust summons up the Erdgeist, who thus addresses him:

Im Lebensfluthen, im Thatensturm
Wall' ich auf und ab,

> Wehe hin und her!
> Geburt und Grab,
> Ein ewiges Meer,
> Ein wechselnd Weben,
> Ein glühend Leben,
> So schaff' ich am sausenden Webstuhl der Zeit,
> Und wirke der Gottheit lebendiges Kleid (11, 501–509).

See also the symbolic episode of the Homunculus in Act 11 of Part II, and note the ideology of the debate between the Neptunists and the Vulcanists.

(3) Carlyle quotes the song of the Erdgeist in *Sartor Resartus,* chap. viii; and asks in that book: "Is there no God, then; but at best an absentee God, sitting idle, ever since the first Sabbath, at the outside of the Universe, and *seeing* it go?" (p. 147). He denies the claim of the "Foolish Word-monger and Motive-grinder" (*i.e.,* the rationalist) to truth (p. 147), finding Laplace and Herschel imperfect in their views, since nature is a volume "written in celestial hieroglyphs, in the true Sacred-writing; of which even Prophets are happy that they can read here a line and there a line" (pp. 233–234). Nature is held together by "organic filaments" and is a "vast Symbol of God" (*Sartor Resartus,* ed. MacMechan, Boston, 1886).

Lest these three men be dismissed as "mere" poets, it must be remembered that at Leipzig Schelling studied mathematics, physics, chemistry, and medicine; Goethe contributed importantly to science and to scientific theory; and Carlyle received good training at Edinburgh in mathematics and science.

48. Oskar Walzel (*German Romanticism,* 5th ed., trans. A. E. Lussky, New York, 1932, pp. 60–61) points out that Haller led the way in substituting a vitalistic-organic interpretation for a mechanistic one, and that the wealth of new discoveries at the close of the eighteenth century inevitably led to excited speculation. Progress in electricity and magnetism was especially favorable to the "scientific imagination." "Magic and mysticism put in their appearance, and, impatient, outstrip the results of research, which, though moving rapidly, is nevertheless too slow for the restlessness and overzealousness of scientific enthusiasts."

49. The most revealing document is the *Cosmos* of A. von Humboldt, which carried great authority because of Humboldt's prestige. I quote from the six-volume American translation of 1868. From the "Introduction": The noblest result of the study of physical phenomena is "a knowledge of the chain of connection, by which all natural forces are

linked together, and made mutually dependent upon each other; and it is the perception of these relations that exalts our views and ennobles our enjoyments" (p. 23). "Nature considered *rationally,* that is to say, submitted to the process of thought, is a unity in diversity of phenomena; a harmony, blending together all created things, however dissimilar in form and attributes; one great whole . . . animated by the breath of life. The most important result of a rational inquiry into nature is, therefore, to establish the unity and harmony of this stupendous mass of force and matter" (p. 24). The first sensation in contemplating nature is that "the mind is penetrated by the same sense of grandeur and vast expanse of nature, revealing to the soul, by a mysterious inspiration, the existence of laws that regulate the forces of the universe. . . . The earnest and solemn thoughts awakened by a communion with nature intuitively arise from a presentiment of the order and harmony pervading the whole universe, and from the contrast we draw between the narrow limits of our own existence and the image of infinity revealed on every side, whether we look upward to the starry vault of heaven, scan the far-stretching plain before us, or seek the dim horizon across the vast expanse of ocean" (p. 25). "We . . . readily perceive the affinity existing among all forms of organic life . . . the spontaneous impressions óf the untutored mind lead, like the laborious deductions of cultivated intellect, to the same intimate persuasion, that one sole and indissoluble chain binds together all nature" (p. 27). He pays tribute to Goethe as a scientist (p. 41) and holds that our knowledge of physical laws "increases our sense of the calm of nature" (p. 42). "The immeasurable diversity of phenomena which crowd into the picture of nature in no way detract [*sic*] from that harmonious impression of rest and unity which is the ultimate object of every literary or purely artistical composition" (p. 79). ". . . a sense of longing binds still faster the links which, in accordance with the supreme laws of our being, connect the material with the ideal world, and animates the mysterious relation existing between that which the mind receives from without, and that which it reflects from its own depths to the external world" (p. 80). This is probably the only great scientific work of the century which gives equal weight to the imagination as exhibited in poetic descriptions of nature, landscape painting, the cultivation of exotic plants in greenhouses, and what we should consider scientific method, as yielding insight into the universe. See vol. II. Note such a sentence as this: "In order to depict nature in its exalted sublimity, we must not dwell exclusively on its external manifestations, but we must trace its image, reflected in the mind of man, at one time filling the dreamy land of physical myths with forms of grace and beauty, and at another developing the noble germ of artistic creations" (II, 20). Humboldt finds Buffon "deficient in almost all that flows from the mysterious analogy existing between the mental emotions of the mind and the phenomena of the perceptive world," whereas Bernardin de St. Pierre (!) exhibits "marvelous truth" in his natural descriptions. If the *Cosmos* is anywhere incomplete, says Humboldt, it is in "that portion . . . which treats of spiritual life, that is, the image reflected by external nature on the inner world of thought and feeling" (III, 8). The word "God" does not, however, appear in the book.

50. "The great and solemn spirit that pervades the intellectual labor of which the limits are here defined, arises from the sublime consciousness of striving toward the infinite, and of grasping all that is revealed to us amid the boundless and inexhaustible fullness of creation, development and being" (pp. 10–11). ". . . the inquirer into nature, in his investigation of cosmical relations, feels himself penetrated by a profound consciousness that the fruits hitherto yielded by direct observation and by the careful analysis of phenomena are far from having exhausted the number of impelling, producing, and formative forces" (p. 25). "Deprived of a great, and, indeed, of the sublimest portion of his ideas of the Cosmos, man would have been left without all those incitements which, for thousands of years, have incessantly impelled him to the solution of important problems, and have exercised so beneficial an influence on the higher spheres of mathematical development of thought" (p. 104). "The first and predominating interest excited by the heavens is directed to the fixed stars . . . and it is by them that our highest feelings of admiration are called forth" (p. 117) *Cosmos,* vol. III. Humboldt also thinks that "the moving planets . . . agreeably enliven the aspect of the heavens" (IV, 107); and that the moon "animates and beautifies the aspect of the firmament under every zone" (IV, 158). In general, astronomy yields an "impression of the sublime" which "passes almost unconsciously to ourselves beyond the mysterious boundary which connects the metaphysical with the physical. . . . The image of the immeasurable, the boundless, and the eternal, is associated with a power which excites within us a more earnest and solemn tone of feeling, and which, like the impression of all that is spiritually great and morally exalted, is not devoid of emotion. A certain impression of peace and calmness blends with the impression of the incomprehensible in the universe. . . . It takes from the unfathomable depths of space and time those features of terror which an excited imagination is apt to ascribe to them" (V, 6–7).

51. The principal influences upon American transcendentalism seem to be: (a) Goethe, the German romantic school, and the transcendentalist philosophers, known either indirectly through Coleridge and the British group or through Madame de Staël, Cousin, and the French, or (imperfectly) known directly either in translation or the original; (b) Wordsworth, Coleridge, Carlyle; (c) the French eclectic school, especially Cousin and Jouffroy; (d) Plato and the neo-Platonists; (e) Hindu and Chinese "wisdom books" known, of course, mainly in translation. There is an extensive scholarly literature.

52. Note the attitude towards science and art in Poe's "Sonnet—To Science" and "Israfel," the latter concluding with the idea of an interchange between the earthly poet and the heavenly singer, in whom art causes the stars and the moon to stand still; and note, in "The Poetic Principle," his statement that the descriptive poet is inadequate, since, "inspired by an ecstatic prescience of the glories beyond the grave, we struggle, by multiform combinations among the things and thoughts of Time, to attain a portion of that Loveliness whose very elements, perhaps, appertain to eternity alone." For Emerson "the world proceeds from the same spirit as the body of man. It is a remoter and inferior incarnation of God, a projection of God in the unconscious. . . . Its serene order is inviolable by us. It is, therefore, to us, the present expositor of the divine mind" (*Nature,* section vii). In the essay entitled "The Poet" it is the Orphic quality or art which corresponds in the subjective world to this "serene order"; "The poets are thus liberating gods. . . . If a man is inflamed and carried away by his thought, to that degree that he forgets the authors and the public, and heeds only this one dream, which holds him like an insanity, let me read his paper, and you may have all the arguments, and histories, and criticism. All the value which attaches to Pythagoras, Paracelsus, Cornelius Agrippa, Cardan, Kepler, Swedenborg, Schelling, Oken, or any other who introduces questionable facts into his cosmogony, as angels, devils, magic, astrology, palmistry, mesmerism, and so on, is the certificate we have of departure from routine, and that here is a new witness." Hawthorne's "The Birthmark" rests for its plot on the assumption that analytical human science can never achieve perfection, but note, in contrast, that at the conclusion of "The Artist of the Beautiful," Warland looks placidly upon the ruin of the butterfly he has made because he has risen to an inner grasp of the nature of things. As the reader is expressly informed: "This so frequent abortion of man's dearest projects must be taken as a proof that the deeds of earth, however etherealized by piety or genius, are without value, *except as exercises and manifestations of*

the spirit." (My italics.) In the "Ode" of 1842 one finds Lowell setting forth the Orphic concept of the poet, a being more fearless and free than other men, from whose nature the "tree of wisdom grew with sturdy rind." He calls for the reappearance of such an artist:

> "Awake, then, thou! we pine for thy great presence
> To make us feel the soul once more sublime,
> We are of far too infinite an essence
> To rest contented with the lies of Time."

In contrast ("Credidimus Jovem Regnare," written 45 years later) note the highly dubious reception Lowell grants to Darwinism, Huxley cannot help the poet; and in comparison memories of his youthful attitude are more valuable. Science fails to offer the key to the "Great Mystery" which the poet of the "Ode" has in his possession. The likeness of much of this to the quotations already given from Humboldt is striking.

53. "The European Background," in *The Reinterpretation of American Literature* (New York, 1928). See also in the same volume "The Romantic Movement" by Paul Kaufman, and the suggestive introductory essay to Tremaine McDowell's *The Romantic Triumph* (New York, 1933).

54. The underlying philosophy of most of these cults is usually some form of vitalism, and therefore allied to the dynamic view of nature. Another element is intuitionalism, and another, the mistaking analogy for homology. Thus the vegetarian Lewis Hough held that "the purpose of nutrition is merely to replenish the waste, which takes place in the organs from the action of the soul through them, in its maturing for a future state," a fair sample of the "philosophy" underlying most of the movements (quoted in E. D. Branch, *The Sentimental Years,* New York, 1934, p. 261). The water-cure originated in Silesia; *The Water Cure Journal,* founded in 1845 by Joel Shew, is a characteristic production, intended "to lay broad, deep, and enduring foundations of the True Mental Philosophy, and to apply it to the harmonious and highest development of the *Human Being"* (*Herald of Health, N. S.* [the new name of the original paper], Jan., 1863, p. 6). The vogue of phrenology, that key to life in "all its multifarious aspects and interrelations" is too well known to require comment, though the amusing discussion in Branch, *op. cit.,* pp. 278 ff., should not be overlooked. Poe took the "science" seriously as a guide to character, and wove it into the tissue of his art, as did Whitman. See E. Hungerford's two articles, "Poe and Phrenology," *American Literature,* II, 209–231 (Nov., 1930) and

"Walt Whitman and His Chart of Bumps," *ibid.,* II, 350–384 (Jan., 1931). Poe also took mesmerism with some seriousness.

55. There is no American equivalent of Tieck's *Lucinde,* Gautier's *Madamoiselle de Maupin,* or Hazlitt's *Liber Amoris.* American Byronism is melancholy, adopts the theory of love as a fatal passion, and pretends to world-weariness, but omits the sensualism, the cynicism, and the Satanism. There is likewise no American equivalent until recent decades of that interest in the perverse, recorded by Mario Praz, *The Romantic Agony* (London, 1933), except in the case of Poe—and possibly Melville. As for the American repudiation of "immoral" romanticism, magazines of the period shake with denunciation. See, for example, my "American Comment on George Sand, 1837–1848," *American Literature,* III, 389–407 (Jan., 1932). Since French romanticism was better known than German, denunciation fell upon the French, who enjoyed, in addition, the heritage of dislike from Revolutionary times. The morals (or lack of them) of Hugo, Paul de Kock, Balzac, and Sue were especially reprobated, whereas the "ideality" of Chateaubriand and Lamartine was stressed.

56. See especially Meade Minnegerode, *The Fabulous Forties* (New York, 1924) and E. D. Branch, already cited. The American preference for Canova and his kind in sculpture prettified the work of Greenough and Powers; the influence of Düsseldorf on American landscape painting was in the same direction; the success of Etty, Frith, and the British genre painters encouraged the vogue of "conversation pieces" among American artists; the French and British annuals were the models of the American gift books; and in architecture, despite the vogue of the classical style, the British pseudo-Gothic (probably influenced by the taste for a sentimentalized version of things German) begins to appear in all its falsity before the Civil War. See T. E. Tallmadge, *The Story of Architecture in America* (New York, 1927), chap. iv; Fiske Kimball, *American Architecture* (Indianapolis, 1928), chap. ix. The popularity of Irving may have helped to make "Sunnyside" a model; and undoubtedly the English cottage style is connected with the new feeling for getting close to nature. Among the painters, at any rate, Ruskin was being talked about before the end of this period. Investigation will, I think, reveal that there was an immense circulation of Ruskin in the middle of the century, with interesting effects upon public taste.

57. The Newtonian universe may awaken a sense of majesty (as in Addison's hymn), but it offers small emotional basis for moral and aesthetic improvement. Contrast this passage from Sampson Reed's *Observations on the Growth of the Mind* (ed. James Reed, Boston,

1910), which strongly influenced Emerson: "When there shall be a religion which shall see God in everything, and at all times; and the natural sciences, not less than nature itself, shall be regarded in connection with Him; the fire of poetry will begin to be kindled in its immortal part, and will burn without consuming" (p. 54). "If it were desired to make a child thoroughly acquainted with the work of a genuine poet, I would not put the poem and lexicon in his hand, and bid him study and learn—I would rather . . . point him to that source from which the author himself had caught his inspiration, and, as I led him to the baptismal fount of nature, I would consecrate his powers to that Being from whom nature exists. I would cultivate a sense of the constant presence and agency of God . . ." (pp. 73-74). I do not suggest that Reed was merely a sentimentalist, but I am interested to show the basic differences in approach. I use "sentimentalism" throughout my text (as Branch does not) in the quasi-technical philosophic sense of the point of view often held in the eighteenth century, and inherited by the nineteenth.

58. M. E. Woolley, "The Development of the Love of Romantic Scenery in America," *American Historical Review,* III, 56–66 (Oct., 1897), traces the development through the eighteenth century. N. Foerster, *Nature in American Literature* (New York, 1923), is mainly confined to nine nineteenth-century authors.

59. Jefferson and Crèvecoeur were both touched by the feeling for the picturesque. See the description of the Natural Bridge in *Notes on Virginia.*

60. Woolley, *op. cit.,* notes some literary expressions of the picturesque and the romantic. John Trumbull records in his *Autobiography* (New York, 1841) how "My taste for the picturesque here (at Lake George) received a splendid gratification." Contrast Allston. The place of the picturesque in Thoreau has been noted by W. D. Templeman, "Thoreau, Moralist of the Picturesque," *PMLA,* XLVII, 864–889 (Sept., 1932).

61. Foerster, *op. cit.,* p. xiii. The volume is a *Tendenzschrift.*

62. Otherwise Europeans would not have recognized in American paintings and descriptions anything more than the presentation of novel items. The critic at the Paris Exposition of 1867 who wrote: "No one is likely to mistake an American landscape for the landscape of any other country. It bears its nationality upon its face smilingly" (H. T. Tuckerman, *Book of the Artists,* New York, 1867, p. 18), had in mind a felt qualitative difference, not a mere novelty of description or enumeration. Similarly, when Balzac writes of Cooper's prose: "You incar-

nate yourself in the country; it passes into you, or you into it, and you know not how this metamorphosis, the work of genius, has been accomplished; but you feel it impossible to separate the soil, the vegetation, the waters, their expanse, their configuration, from the interests that agitate you. The personages become what they really are, a small matter in this grand scene which your eye measures" (Foerster, *op. cit.,* p. 5), he has the same qualitative difference in mind.

63. Brockden Brown struggled to make Philadelphia "real" in his novels, but failed for lack of proper artistic insight. In Cooper, on the other hand, Balzac felt the vastness of a continent. In the years when English fiction was producing genre novels like those of Jane Austen, Susan Ferrier, Maria Edgeworth, John Galt, and other examples of regional fiction, the United States was developing little of the same sort. Similarly in poetry, the loving regionalism of Wordsworth has only a faint echo in Bryant, who is more characteristically the poet of panoramic distances. Bryant seems genuine, whereas the well-meant attempts of Drake and Halleck to endow the Hudson River with a local poetry are artificial. Irving is more to the point; yet, though it is undeniable that "The Legend of Sleepy Hollow" is "local," "Rip Van Winkle" broadens to include the majesty of the Catskills, and it is characteristic that Cole, who "with his palette and brushes retraversed the ground that Washington Irving made famous with his pen" (C. H. Caffin, *The Story of American Painting,* New York, 1907, p. 75), is one of the most grandiose of painters.

64. Thus Cole painted five immense canvases entitled "The Course of Empire," to illustrate the changes wrought in a landscape by the rise and fall of nations—an analogue to Volney's *Ruins of Empire.* Tuckerman (*Artist-Life,* New York, 1847) notes the affinity of Cole to Bryant (p. 118), an affinity which Bryant himself recognized when he said of his pictures that the spectators "delighted at the opportunity of contemplating pictures which carried the eye to a scene of wild grandeur peculiar to our country, over our aërial mountain tops, with their mighty growth of forests never touched by the axe, along the banks of streams never deformed by culture, and into the depths of skies bright with the hues of our own climate" (Tuckerman, *Book of the Artists,* p. 225). It is significant that in writing descriptions of the canvases of the Hudson River School Tuckerman, himself a product of the epoch, insists upon the vitality and grandeur of the landscape. Thus, describing a lake scene of Durand, he writes: "Whoever has sailed across one of our *immense* lakes—the inland seas of this *vast* continent—at the close of a day when summer was *verging* into autumn, and the keen

wind *swept over* the *broad* waters as they *glowed* with crimson or saffron in the *magnificent* sunset, cannot easily forget a scene *unequalled* in any part of the world . . . as twilight comes on, the view grows *sublime,* and when the *vivid* tints gradually vanish in darkness, a deep and almost sacred impression is left upon the mind." Durand's Lake Scene, it seems, is of this order, and "if we had encountered it in any gallery abroad, we should have instantly recognized one of the most characteristic phases of nature in America" (*Artist-Life,* p. 79. The italics are mine). Of a New England landscape by the same artist he says that the noblest elms in the world are in New England, that the maple in autumn has as brilliant a tint as the vegetable creation anywhere possesses; and speaks of majestic willows, a rich variety of magnificent forest trees whose "felicitous introduction constitutes one of the most effective points in American landscape" (p. 86).

65. One's memory of Bryant is conditioned by such pieces as "Thanatopsis," "The Prairies," "The Flood of Years," and the like rather than by "To the Fringed Gentian" and similar "smaller" pieces. In "To a Waterfowl" the bird is seen against an immense tract of empty sky.

66. Church was strongly influenced by Humboldt, his canvases illustrating the interest in tropical scenery which that scientist had aroused. In America he was attracted to Niagara, the immense lonely seas around Labrador, and the like. Moran and Bierstadt were at one time or another connected with scientific and exploratory expeditions to the West.

67. These landscape painters "accompanied the first explorers into the wilds of the Rockies and the Yellowstone. They thought that the size of the great lakes, the mighty rivers, and the boundless prairies must reflect itself in the greatness of the national art. They were patriotic, boasted themselves to be the first really native school (which was true), and spared an incredulous Europe not one jot of the blazing vermilion of the autumn foliage" (S. Isham, *The History of American Painting,* new ed., New York, 1927). The tendency to confuse bigness with greatness was ridiculed by Longfellow in a well-known passage in *Kavanagh,* but the aesthetic error is immaterial to the present argument.

68. G. Catlin, *North American Indians,* 2 vols. (Edinburgh, 1927), I, 7.

69. Philarète Chasles wrote in 1851: "A magic power transported us into the forests which for so many years this man of genius has trod. . . . Imagine a landscape wholly American, trees, flowers, grass, even the tints of the sky and the waters quickened with a life that is real, peculiar, trans-Atlantic. On twigs, branches, bits of shore, copied by the brush with the strictest fidelity, sport the feathered races of the New

World, in the size of life, each in its particular attitude, its individuality and peculiarities. Their plumage sparkles with nature's own tints; you see them in motion or at rest, in their plays and their combats, in their anger fits and their caresses, singing, running, asleep, just awakened, beating the air, skimming the waves, or rendering one another in their battles. It is a real and palpable vision of the New World, with its atmosphere, its imposing vegetation, and its tribes which know not the yoke of man. The sun shines athwart the clearing in the woods; the swan (!) floats suspended between a cloudless sky and a glittering wave; strange and majestic figures keep pace with the sun, which gleams from the mica sown broadcast on the shores of the Atlantic; and this realization of an entire hemisphere, this picture of a nature so lusty and strong, is due to the brush of a single man . . ." (quoted in F. H. Herrick, *Audubon the Naturalist,* 2 vols., New York, 1917, I, 359–360).

70. The school of interpretation which explains such matters by citing the influence of "Rousseauism" or of "French Romantic Philosophy" is especially at fault. Bryant and Cooper, two of the principal examples of the changed attitude toward landscape, were avowedly hostile to "Rousseauism"; and if, as is sometimes alleged, Wordsworth influenced Bryant decisively, shall we also argue that he influenced Cooper? Washington Allston admired Turner, and advised young painters to study the Liber Studiorum, but Allston's direct influence upon American landscape painting seems to have been negligible, though he may have helped to spread a transcendental philosophy of art, and by his exaltation of Michelangelo done something to inculcate a taste for grandeur (see J. B. Flagg, *The Life and Letters of Washington Allston,* London, 1893, especially pp. 199–206). The influence of Düsseldorf and Rome seems to have been technical rather than philosophical; as Isham observes, though the landscape painters went abroad, they were never overwhelmed by foreign academies (*op. cit.,* pp. 243–244).

71. Introduction to the Everyman's Library edition of Buchanan's (unsatisfactory) *Life and Adventures of Audubon the Naturalist,* p. x.

72. Herrick, *op. cit.,* I, 184. See also note 69.

73. In July, 1826, crossing the Atlantic, he read the poem for the third or fourth time, and enjoyed it more than ever (I, 93). In December, he recorded in his journal that he longed for Scott to visit America "that he might describe, as no one else ever can, the stream, the swamp, the river, the mountains, for the sake of future ages. A century hence they will not be here as I see them, Nature will have been robbed of many brilliant charms, the rivers will be tormented and turned astray from their primitive courses, the hills will be levelled with the swamps,

and perhaps the swamps will have become a mound surmounted by a fortress of a thousand guns ... *Without Sir Walter Scott these beauties must perish unknown to the world"* (I, 182. My italics). When he attended a session of the Académie Royale des Sciences in 1828, and heard Cuvier praise his work, he wrote: "Poor Audubon! here thou art, a simple woodsman among a crowd of talented men, yet kindly received by all—so are the works of God as shown in His birds loved by them" (I, 312). The quotations are from M. R. Audubon and Elliott Coues, *Audubon and His Journals,* 2 vols. (London, 1898).

74. Thus, in Labrador, he writes of migratory birds: "That the Creator should have commanded millions of delicate, diminutive, tender creatures to cross immense spaces of country to all appearance a thousand times more congenial to them than this, to cause them to people, as it were, this desolate land for a time, to enliven it by the songs of the sweet feathered musicians for two months at most, and by the same command induce them to abandon it almost suddenly, is as wonderful as it is beautiful" (*ibid.,* I, 424). Again, on the Missouri River (*1843*): 'On looking along the banks of the river, one cannot help observing the half-drowned young willows, and cotton trees of the same age, trembling and shaking sideways against the current; and methought, as I gazed upon them, of the danger they were in of being immersed over their very tops and thus dying, not through the influence of fire, the natural enemy of wood, but from the force of the mighty stream on the margin of which they grew, and which appeared as if in its wrath it was determined to overwhelm, and undo all that the Creator in His bountifulness had granted us to enjoy. The banks themselves, along with perhaps millions of trees, are ever tumbling, falling, and washing away from the spots where they may have stood and grown for centuries past. If this be not an awful exemplification of the real course of Nature's intention, that all should and must live and die, then, indeed, the philosophy of our learned men cannot be much relied upon!" (I, 460). He wondered at "the enormous mass of waters, collected from the vast central regions of our continent, booming along, turbid and swollen to overflowing, in the broad channels of the Mississippi and Ohio . . ." and thought Niagara "the most magnificent of the Creator's works" (*Delineations of American Scenery and Character,* ed. F. H. Herrick, New York, 1926, pp. 29; 78).

75. Audubon counted among his friends the Englishman, William Swainson, who advocated Quinarianism, or the doctrine of the esoteric significance of the recurrence of the number five in nature. Swainson, following W. S. MacLeay, taught that "all things that have life have

been created upon one plan, and this plan is founded on the principle of a series of affinities returning into themselves; which can only be represented by a circle." The unphilosophic Audubon did not adopt the theory, though the kind of thinking it represents was evidently not uncongenial to him. See F. H. Herrick, *Audubon the Naturalist,* II, 94; 116–117.

76. Agassiz writes in 1827: "I am often busy too with Oken. His 'Naturphilosophie' gives me the greatest pleasure" (I, 35). At Munich Oken's lectures, including "his famous views on the philosophy of nature" "made a strong impression" on Agassiz (I, 53). He called Oken "the most fascinating of our professors," exercising "an almost irresistible influence over his students. Constructing the universe out of his own brain, deducing from *a priori* conceptions all the relations of the three kingdoms into which he divided all living beings, classifying the animals as if by magic, in accordance with an analogy based on the dismembered body of man, it seemed to us who listened that the slow laborious process of accumulating precise detailed knowledge could only be the work of drones, while a generous commanding spirit might build the world out of its own powerful imagination." Agassiz pays tribute to the powerful influence of the Oken school in his criticism of this instruction. "With the school of the physio-philosophers began (at least in our day and generation) that overbearing confidence in the abstract conceptions of the human mind as applied to the study of nature, which still impairs the fairness of our classifications and prevents them from interpreting truly the natural relations binding together all living beings. And yet, the young naturalist of that day who did not share, in some degree, the intellectual stimulus given to scientific pursuits by physiophilosophy would have missed a part of his training . . ." (I, 151–154). He listened to Schelling lecture in three courses (I, 53). In 1833 Humboldt reproached him in a letter with clinging "to the idea of internal vital processes of the earth" and thinking of "the rocks as products of metamorphosis." Yet, though Humboldt denies that the term *life* can be applied to geologic change, he goes on in the same letter to announce that he believes "there are nervous storms (electric) like those which set fire to the atmosphere," and distinguishes between the "vital process" as a particular mode of action, and other forms of change (I, 228–229. The quoted passages are from E. C. Agassiz, *Louis Agassiz: His Life and Correspondence,* 2 vols., Boston, 1886).

77. *Ibid.,* I, 92–93; 245. "I speak of the relations of the creation with the creator. Phenomena closely allied in the order of their succession, and yet without sufficient cause in themselves for their appearance; an

infinite diversity of species without any common material bond, so grouping themselves as to present the most admirable progressive development to which our own species is linked,—are these not incontestable proofs of the existence of a superior intelligence whose power alone could have established such an order of things?" (I, 244). He thought of species as appearing and disappearing "at an appointed time" (I, 245).

78. *Ibid.,* I, 384–385; 389–392.

79. "The Silurian Beach" is characteristic. The scientist thinks creatively the thoughts of God after him (I, 30–31), and the life of the Silurian Beach is a life of "such profusion that it would seem as if God, in the joy of creation, had compensated Himself for a less variety of forms in the greater richness of the early types" (I, 37). "Harmonious relations underlie the whole creation in such a manner as to indicate a great central plan, of which all things are a part [and] at the same time a freedom, an arbitrary element in the mode of carrying it out, which seems to point to the exercise of an individual will" (I, 38). The quotations are from the first volume of the Boston edition of 1886.

80. Contrast, for example, the following extracts: Louis Agassiz and A. A. Gould, *Principles of Zoology,* rev. ed. (Boston, 1869, ten years after the *Origin of Species!*): The Animal kingdom "is the exhibition of the divine thought, as carried out in one department of that grand whole which we call Nature; and considered as such, it teaches us most important lessons. Man, in virtue of his twofold constitution, the spiritual and the material, is qualified to comprehend Nature. Being made in the spiritual image of God, he is competent to rise to the conception of His plan and purpose in the works of Creation" (pp. 25–26). ". . . in the study of Nature, we may be astonished at the infinite variety of her products; we may even study some portion of her works with enthusiasm, nevertheless remain strangers to the spirit of the whole, ignorant of the plan on which it is based, and fail to acquire a proper conception of the varied affinities which combine beings together, so as to make of them that vast picture in which each animal, each plant, each group, each class, has its place, and from which nothing could be removed without destroying the proper meaning of the whole" (p. 26). ". . . he who considers only the manifestations of intelligence and of creative will, without taking into account the means by which they are executed . . . will be very likely to confound the Creator with the creature" (p. 34). Now turn to Huxley's lecture "On the Advisableness of Improving Natural Knowledge," delivered in 1866: ". . . the physiologist finds life to be as dependent for its manifestation on particular molecu-

lar arrangements as any physical or chemical phenomenon; and, wherever he extends his researches, fixed order and unchanging causation reveal themselves, as plainly as in the rest of nature. Nor can I find that any other fate has awaited the germ of Religion. Arising, like all other kinds of knowledge, out of the action and interaction of man's mind, with that which is not man's mind, it has taken the intellectual coverings of Fetishism or Polytheism; of Theism or Atheism; of Superstition or Rationalism." ". . . every step . . . made in natural knowledge has tended to extend and rivet in their minds the conception of a definite order of the universe—which is embodied in what are called, by an unhappy metaphor, the laws of nature—and to narrow the range and loosen the force of men's belief in spontaneity, or changes other than such as arise out of that definite order itself" (*Lectures and Lay Sermons,* Everyman's Library ed., p. 52).

81. The principal European influences toward this change were (a) Coleridge, Maurice, and their followers (not excepting the Oxford movements and the Christian Socialism movement in certain phases); (b) Lessing (especially *The Education of the Human Race*), Kant, Schleiermacher, and the "Logos" school in Germany; (c) Spinoza; (d) Swedenborg, Böhme, and other mystics; (e) Hegel, and the British Hegelians. According to W. M. Horton, *Realistic Theology* (New York, 1934), the influence of the school of Ritschl in the middle of the century (which lays emphasis upon the humanitarian aspects of Christianity) tended to neutralize the influence of Schleiermacher and Hegel, but this, in the naive form in which it is put (p. 32) I cannot quite believe. See in this connection C. C. J. Webb, *Religious Thought in England from 1850.* Theodore Parker read German theology and philosophy; Bushnell was strongly influenced by Coleridge's *Aids to Reflection.* The influence of Egbert C. Smyth at Andover (he was tried for heresy in 1886) comes later than our period, but it is important to learn that he studied at Berlin and Halle in the sixties, revolutionizing theological instruction at Andover after his return.

82. The discussion of Parker in Parrington, *Main Currents in American Thought,* II, 414–425, is excellent.

83. "But this progressive development does not end with us; we have seen only the beginning; the future triumphs of the race must be vastly greater than all accomplished yet" (John Weiss, *Life and Correspondence of Theodore Parker,* New York, 1864, II, 471). Parker thought the Unitarians had made a profound mistake in failing to emphasize "the all-beautiful and altogether lovely God of the universe" (Parrington, II, 417).

84. From Bushnell's *Christ in Theology*, quoted in Buckham, *op. cit.*, pp. 16–17. Cf. the following from Bushnell's *Sermons on Living Subjects* (New York, 1872): "What tremendous powers of motion and commotion, what dissolving, recomposing forces come upon, or into a soul, when it suffers the love of God. For it is such kind of love as ought to create, and must, a deep, all revolutionizing ferment, in the moral nature" ("Letting God Love Us," p. 43). ". . . it is the whole endeavor of [God's] management to be known. He not only meets our understanding processes in the facts of his Bible, but he offers himself to be known without any process at all, just as the light is; nay, if he will have it so, to be a kind of second consciousness in us, and be known to us even as we know ourselves. He is even pressing himself into knowledge when our eyes are shut—in our self-will, our hate, our denial, our desolation" ("Knowledge of God," p. 125). Note the doctrine of immanence. ". . . the spiritually minded person spiritualizes temporal things and the temporal life, by nothing but by just seeing them in their most philosophic sense. He takes hold of the laws, finds his way into the inmost thoughts, follows after the spirit-force everywhere entempled, and puts the creation moving, at every turn, in the supreme order of Mind" ("In and By Things Temporal are Given Things Eternal," p. 284). ". . . all the wisdom and character there may be in the Uncreated, will of course be entered somehow into the advancement of the created. . . . Of course he has not put his infinite quantities into every or any finite creature, but all the wisdom he has, all the goodness, all the privilege of nature that he has in himslf, is just so far entered into his creature as it can be" ("Our Advantage in Being Finite," p. 331). "We, as being finite, have our best enjoyment in the sense of progress. We advance in thought, we accumulate force, we run with large volume and momentum, as rivers fed by new and larger tributaries on their way to the sea. It is very difficult for us to conceive the Infinite being as existing in a way of eternally stationary completeness, without associating some concern lest he be staled in the exactly full orbed perfectness of his knowledge and power" (*ibid.*, p. 333).

85. Thus even Bushnell preaches a sermon on "How to be a Christian in Trade" (*op. cit.*, 243 ff.), instancing a number of "Christian merchants," British and American, and declaring that "profits are as truly earnings, as any of the fruits of hand labor." The "supplies and comforts of the different regions must be gathered by the merchants, transported to the parts where they may be wanted, distributed into small parcels, and sold out to customers for use. . . . They do, in fact, a work very much like that of the rain, or the rain clouds, which in-

stead of leaving the world to be watered by waterspouts falling here and there once in a thousand years, take up the water that is wanted in parts remote from the sea, carrying it off thither by their wind sails, and there, making small the drops for a gentle and general distribution, let it fall on the ground, sprinkling it all over." Rainclouds, in fact, are "the merchants of the sky."

In the case of Beecher there is little question of direct European influence, but he was wonderfully adept at understanding the Zeitgeist. Phrenology apparently had some influence upon his younger years, helping to offset the Calvinism of Andover; at Lane Theological Seminary he proved to be an *advocatus diaboli;* he read Scott, Byron, Burns; published as his first influential work the famous *Lectures to Young Men* (1844), which advocated all the economic virtues in the spirit of Samuel Smiles; then, in Brooklyn, swung into that vague, golden optimism, that union of "art" and "theology" which made him so powerful an influence. In the first series of *Plymouth Pulpit: The Sermons of Henry Ward Beecher* . . . (New York, 1869), one finds such characteristic passages as these: "I call the New Testament the Book of Joy. There is not in the world a book which is pervaded with such a spirit of exhilaration. Nowhere does it pour forth a melancholy strain." "The fountain and unfailing source of this sober exhilaration was found in the divine nature, as it had been revealed to the apostles." God "penetrates and pervades the universe with his nature and with his disposition." "He penetrates and pervades the world with more saving mercies than does the sun with particles of light and heat. He declares that this nature in himself is boundless; that this heart of mercy is inexhaustible; that this work of comfort is endless." ". . . throughout the vast heaven, throughout time and the universe, the blood of the world comes from the heart of God. The mercies of the loving God throb everywhere—above and below, within and without, endless in circuits, vast in distribution, infinitely potential" (from "The God of Comfort," pp. 13–27, preached September 27, 1868). See also the sermon on "The Divine Influence on the Human Soul," especially the conclusion. In "The Love of Money," after castigating the usual vices of the money-mad, he concludes: "If God calls you to a way of making wealth, make it; but remember, do not *love money.* If God calls you to make wealth, do not *make haste to be rich;* be willing to wait. . . . Do not try to get rich quickly. There is no need of it." The clear implication that God is behind money-making of the right sort outweighs the italicized phrases.

86. See Ray Strachey's absorbing *Religious Fanaticism* (London,

1928), especially chap. iii, "An Account of the Foreign Religious Sects in America in the Early Nineteenth Century." The Mennonites, of course, date from the earlier period. George Rapp's followers (Germans) settled Economy, Ohio, Rapp dying in 1847, but not before another German named Müller had taken 250 Rappites from their allegiance. The Amana Society (Ebenezer, New York), dating from 1842–1846, was led by two Germans, Barbara Heinemann and Christian Metz. The Bishop Hill Commune (Swedes) came in 1846 under Eric Janson. The Russian Bruderhof Communities came in 1862. Ann Lee, an Englishwoman, founded the Shakers earlier, but they may fairly be counted among nineteenth-century phenomena. Of the Owenites and Fourierites I have already spoken. The Englishwoman, Frances Wright, who founded a community at Nashoba, Tennessee, cannot be overlooked, nor should the influence of Swedenborg on various spiritualistic movements.